imagined spaces

In memory of Eddie Small (1951-2020)
who brought so much joy to others.

IMAGINED SPACES

EDITED BY GAIL LOW
& KIRSTY GUNN

THE VOYAGE
OUT PRESS

First published in Great Britain in 2020 by The Voyage Out Press

Cover design and typesetting ©Sian MacFarlane 2020

Printed by Winter and Simpson Print
16 Dunsinane Avenue
Dunsinane Industrial Estate
Dundee DD2 3QT

ISBN: 978 0 9955123 4 4

The publisher gratefully acknowledges the support of the Royal Society of Edinburgh,
the Saltire Society and University of Dundee.

About the Author

William Wayne Farris received his doctorate in history from Harvard University. He is the author of numerous articles and five previous books dealing with the social and economic history of pre-1600 Japan: *Population, Disease, and Land in Early Japan, 645-900* (1985); *Heavenly Warriors: The Evolution of Japan's Military, 500-1300* (1992); *Sacred Texts and Buried Treasures: Issues in the Historical Archaeology of Ancient Japan* (1998); *Japan's Medieval Population: Famine, Fertility, and Warfare in a Transformative Age* (2006); and *Daily Life and Demographics in Ancient Japan* (2009). He is currently Sen Sōshitsu XV Distinguished Professor of Traditional Japanese History and Culture at the University of Hawai'i.

Contents

Tracing lines...
Essaying For Our Times

Gail Low & Kirsty Gunn

Here is a beginning…. A possible—barely delineated—way in to an imagined space:

'We had been sitting and talking all day about essays.'

Yes, that is a nice way to start. A sentence to set there at the top of the page, beyond which lies the introduction to the rest of the book you now hold in your hands. That begins—

We had been sitting and talking all day about essays. We had been talking. Not debating or arguing, we were just musing, thinking aloud, asking questions, enjoying the back and forth exchange, the gifting of ideas and hypotheses that is the stuff of conversation. Essays. We were discussing reading, writing and teaching essays and how we were to introduce this book, how to talk about the particular and distinctive collection of pieces that follows here. Who might these be for?, we asked. What sort are they, the essays gathered together in this book? And what's so interesting about an essay, anyhow, that they should comprise an entire collection? Essays are for schools or universities aren't they? Why might anyone want to read a whole book of them or find that an enabling and life-affirming thing to do?

To clear my head, I thought to walk across the river on the road bridge, opened more than fifty years ago, connecting Dundee to Newport-on-Tay in Fife. An engineering triumph that opened in 1966—a bridge that is roughly 1.4 miles in a straight line, made from 42 concrete 'spans' supporting a concrete slab on which two dual carriageway roads are laid. Situated in between the two roads is an elevated central walkway for pedestrians and cyclists, flanked by protective railings and lampposts on either side. The Tay bridge is necessary to the lives of daily commuters, to the cyclists or occasional walkers who pass each other with a friendly nod of acknowledgement.

Off I went, then, on this walk in the early evening light…

Making a journey, I suppose you might call it. Yes, that's it exactly. That I'm forming a kind of trajectory in my thinking as I walk my way across this wide connection, a bridge, with one piece of land behind me, another up ahead, writing as I go. Moving forward in ideas and words—an essay on foot, this—with the conversation from before, the things we were discussing earlier, turning over in my mind as I continue to walk a line with the surge and charge of the water of the Tay below, quieting now as the spring tide turns. Seeing, as I go, along with the title of this introduction, the opening line, and the one after that, and after that, all following me as I take one step and then another step. Nothing in writing is left behind.

The Tay Road Bridge is built as a straight line, the shortest distance between two coastal points, yet Fife, seeing it there in front of me, seems a long way away. Parallel lampposts on both sides of the walkway's strait recede to a vanishing point in the distance. It's funny, I think, that each lamppost is carefully labelled with a number; almost as if counting down is necessary on the long strait, and I find I am indeed counting them as I walk: 15, 16, 17, 18… To amuse myself, I read all the signs that I pass, however bland—'Communication Equipment', 'Cathodic Protection equipment', 'Lighting Dundee', 'Weather monitoring equipment'—or instructive—'Danger, Live Wires', 'All dogs must be kept on a lead'—or in bold letters, reminding cyclists and pedestrians that the space of the walkway is shared. 'Remember!' 'Remember!' I know these signs are functional, they're for my well-being.

'Remember!'

For isn't all language, whatever kind it is, wherever it is directed, necessary? Signs, words, syntax… Aren't these phrases, these sentences, vital—a sign of our being in this world, a kind of trail we leave behind us as we go… a note of presence? As though each word uttered, each line written, is an indication, no matter how trivial, of mark-making, a noting of where we've traversed, walked over, tracing a tentative line of our person, our self?

I continue walking as I think about this, and about our conversation… I am journeying—essaying, as we decided, during another discussion about this book, to call it. Walking and thinking as the words continue to stream out behind me and the land ahead, the 'Kingdom of Fife' it is called, is shown in all its large distance—those words I've just put down reminding me of the poet Peter Cole writing of a sentence being 'like a sill before a view…'

Half-way to the other side of the bridge I hear a 'Ha-Ha! Ha-Ha!' and look up. Two gulls, wings outstretched, effortlessly airborne… They hover a fraction of a second before swerving in a great swooping rush and gliding away. Dundee seagulls, despite what Jim Stewart—the poet and scholar, and our dear friend for whom essaying was a way of life—said, are real bruisers; yet here in the sky above me, they are endowed only with movement, an unbearable lightness of being. In Jim's poem, 'Gulls', they circle,

> Far away, under the glowering cloud
> Glint and teem in a storm of jewels.

It is only late afternoon now but dusk will fall early this evening. The river's flat-calm grey, rendered in a dull sheen by the low light, is like watered silk, and buildings in the distance, on both sides of the Tay, have already started to put on their lights. Cars on both sides flash by, a dream of steel and speed, to join or leave who knows what stories and lives as they exit from or come onto the bridge.

And—a 'span'… Remember that word from an early paragraph in this introduction? The concrete shape that would hold up a bridge? It's a length of time, too, I feel it now, underfoot, holding me up in a span of words that 'glint and teem' in a portion of published text, a length from here to there like a line of writing that starts from one side, as the cars motor onto the bridge, 'that reach and lead', and travels to another. From 'We had been sitting and talking all day about essays'—

To—

Where I am now. For now, approaching the end of the bridge, getting closer, I can see… What? A number of new signs but unlike those I read earlier. These seem less regimented, some smaller, some larger, typed on blue boards and secured to the railings. Still, they communicate. One says, 'Hi… you've just done the hardest part… It's not easy… to open up…' I read down, 'That's why there's Breathing Space', and, 'They try and make it easier for us to talk about what we're going through'. At lamppost number 75, I come to end of the bridge, exhausted and a little relieved. It's then, walking down the ramp, that I almost stumble into the mass of bouquets and tributes tied to the railings and two quiet floral wreaths spelling 'mummy' and 'friend'.

Between the seagulls, the river and the flowers, I think: this is what I want from essaying, to be surprised by and into life.

* * *

The writing and images gathered together here, across the span of this volume, have come about because of a belief that the essay itself is at a point of similar vital expression. That its very nature, its form, is on the turn, unloosed from its dry academic associations and jump-starting us into being. In these days as we are racked by the uncertainties of our lives, our futures, it has never seemed so necessary to have processes by which we can learn to think and feel as individuals and become aware of what is around us. And it has never seemed more useful to exercise a means of communication that lets us be who we are—disparate but sociable and connected. Less inclined to make declarations or pronouncements, to be restricted and roped into political zones of belonging and unbelonging, and tending more towards a representation of ourselves that reflects our human ebb and flow. To discover a way of writing and thinking that is expansive, that follows our minds' tracing, tracking up and down, and across and over, ideas and the world that have imprinted their images and dramas upon us… Yes, this is what I want from an essay now.

In 'Mr Bennett and Mrs Brown', her richly imaginative intervention signalling a change in the in the practice of fiction published in the early part of the twentieth century, Virginia Woolf asks readers to consider different and surprising ways of imagining and rendering character. Mrs Brown, an 'extremely small', 'threadbare' 'pinched' old lady, 'everything buttoned, fastened, tied together, mended and brushed up', shares for a time a railway carriage with another more aggressive burly man, 'dressed in good blue serge with a pocket-knife and a silk handkerchief, and a stout leather bag', who presses her for something. In Woolf's critique of how Georgian novelists might write that character, she observes that much might be made of Mrs Brown's background, her social economic class and society, her place of residence, the content and context of her circumstances. Even the very detail of her dress, 'accurately and minutely', might be sketched— 'tools' that lay 'an enormous stress upon the fabric of things'—in order to make the character come alive. But instead of such scaffolding, Woolf suggests a way of seeing that person in the very flow and quickness of life:

> For she is just as visible to you who remain silent as to us who tell stories about her. In the course of your daily life this past week you have had far stranger and more interesting experiences than the one I have tried to describe. You have overheard scraps of talk that filled you with amazement. You have gone to bed at night bewildered by the complexity of your feelings. In one day thousands of ideas have coursed through your brains; thousands

of emotions have met, collided, and disappeared in astonishing disorder. Nevertheless, you allow the writers to palm off upon you a version of all this, an image of Mrs. Brown, which has no likeness to that surprising apparition whatsoever.

At its close, Woolf reveals Mrs Brown to be, of course, 'the spirit we live by, life itself.' Reading this again, this writing about writing by the great modernist author and critical practitioner, our imagination leaps and somersaults. The writing changes us. We aren't who we were before we read it; our own life has taken flight.

Just as Woolf writes about fiction, that we might not be 'palmed off' with some 'version', so we may have arrived here, in this volume, at the beginning of a similar sea-change in thinking about how to write—or draw—a new and particular kind of prose and image that, yes, engages with Mrs Brown, dances with her, before she hops off—surprisingly agile—onto the railway platform. For in the work that follows, in lines and in texts that wonder aloud on the page, attend to and call up in words and marks an expression of human activity, signs that we have been here and thought for ourselves as we meet and collide in this world. Here you will find a kind of thinking and writing, an inscribing, that is curious, nakedly ruminative, artful yet genuinely open—outward facing, risk-taking, surprising—that seeks to topple that self-congratulatory 'I' , perched, hands-on-hips, with her single-minded 'I think', and brings to the fore instead two editors who write without demarcation, to introduce a group of voices speaking separately but joined in chorus to make a text that is composite and enjoined, porous and inclusive and generous… Essaying by writers, theorists, artists, educationalists, mental health practitioners, teachers, students, all of whom have created for themselves in the pages here a way of thinking on paper to make a context, a habitat, an environment, that might nourish our being.

So we have here, one editor, another editor, one writer, another writer, this drawing, that idea… Individual upon individual brought together in one first person voice envisaging a celebration of essaying as a new way of thinking that might wake up the reader too. From two of us here is a book that is all about multiplying 'I's, the all of us, the all of me; that *Imagined Spaces* might not just reside in one, or the other, or another, but is instead multiple, various, inclusive. I've written at length and excitedly on the 'sharing of my first person pronoun' elsewhere, in conversations, in the classroom, in seminars and conference, about how 'letting one "I" speak for another, interrupting and inserting and overwriting' enables the borders of self to 'dissolve', and that in so doing I may 'come to understand in the experience of writing', as writing itself. Less the marking out territory as ownership, this kind of activity—here my space, there's yours—or as understood by University research assessment regimes—what portion of this essay is yours, and which hers?—but mark-making where my 'I' becomes yours in the act inhabiting each other's sentence. No more narcissistic parades, then—life writing that is always me, me, me—but using instead personal experience to make another kind of communal story where both reader and writer might take up residence, and find a home in words.

The Humanities, that discipline of thinking about what it is to be human, seems slow to catch up, though, with such new forms of such critical expression. Writing in the Sciences, directed at imparting information, outlining a thesis to fill in, carefully charting the steps to an arrival, deducing reasoned conclusions, has dominated humanist education far too long. And for too long, in order to gain credibility, have the Humanities sought to mimic this goal-oriented, instrumentalised approach as vital to its disciplinary professionalism. This has led essays in Philosophy, History and above all Literature in the English language to bolt themselves onto some kind of unbending teleological, epistemologically-driven model, rigidly emploted in explanations and argument, punctuated with rivets of scholarly citations displaying critical ballast and prop. Not so much a conversation, this, but a monologue. And the petrification of thought in such exercises! The concrete-like fixings of such positions! The Research Excellence Framework (REF) aims 'to provide accountability for public investment in research and evidence of the benefits of this investment', and to institute 'benchmarking information'; the REF matches research funding to quantifiable grids of research significance, predicated on, precisely, rules and regulations that close down ideas of expansiveness and risk-taking in our thinking. Of course writing has to be rigorous—we would not be in universities reading it otherwise—but why be hostage to such institutional methods and, specifically, the economic and managerial lexicon that traps thinking within the constraints being applied? For how else but in the same kind of language can 'units' of 'assessment thresholds' be empirically ascertained and measured? How else but on a grid chart can 'aim' be set next to 'outcome'? All this so-called 'rationalisation' has flourished while ruminations, wanderings, attempts, tests, approaches, transgressive and speculative writings—Michel Montaigne's *essais, essayer*—have all but disappeared. It's as though doubt itself, that live, untethered question that hums in the centre of the thinking, might be an awkward, wayward cost to the outcome—best to be avoided. As if such musings, meetings of mind, conversations, exchange, must be relegated to a place off the published page. We all know where such doubt leads, the orthodoxy seems to warn us, and it's nowhere near an 'aim' or an 'outcome'.

How did we get this way? To be so in thrall to the straight line across the bridge that we don't get to stop, and gasp and be startled into being on the way? When did it become the norm to give ourselves no room—no imagined space—to be surprised by—or into—life? As critic and cultural theorist Stefan Collini writes, what we admire of work in the Humanities—should admire even—is vitality, illumination, dexterity, 'the flexibility of intelligence or responsiveness', 'understanding', 'the texture of expression', 'the specific touches by which a world, an episode, a figure, or a book is conjured up and given density or inwardness'. Not to mention those gifts of pleasure, affect and imaginative flight that have underwritten and enriched all writing and reading for centuries. Where has all that gone, in the studies of Philosophy and History and Literature? Where is being human, now that we've all been sky-jacked and remade as 'professionals'?

So then, this volume is also born out of frustration—that so much of our lives in education—as well as elsewhere—is mortgaged to what can be 'proven' and 'quantified': all those statistics that arise from polling questionnaires; teaching feedback tick sheets measuring 'knowledge or prescribed or recommended texts', 'organisation' or 'quality' of argument, 'bibliographic skills' and so on. All those algorithms that predict our tastes, predisposition to act, and the endless management studies to better transform us into units harnessed for productivity. This book has been put together as a wilful defiance of those codes and practices, to resist the world where such traits seem to be the only virtues there are. Donald Rumsfeld famously said, 'there are known knowns; they are things we know. We also know there are known unknowns; that is to say we know there are some things we do not know. But there are also unknown unknowns—the ones we don't know we don't know.' How his words speak, unintentionally powerfully in favour of the project here! For that which we don't know is exactly what we do need to reckon with, be challenged by! The pronouncements emanating from The White House, Westminster and Holyrood Parliaments—trumpeting well-worn paradigms and trafficking variously held prejudices in exchange for political gain—could not be further from the imagined space of ethical, philosophical and imaginative thinking that dares ask 'What if?' and 'How about?' that lets all our questions to go free.

This is what we hope for in these *Imagined Spaces*… Room to think and be. The philosopher poet Li-Young Lee once said in an interview, 'Thinking and thought are two different things. A thought is encapsulated and already dead. It's a noun. Thinking is a verb which means it's in action, and I wanted to capture the action of thinking.' So our word 'essaying'—less noun, more verb—has been with us from the start, offering the opportunity not to write or read simply *about* a subject or an idea, but rather to write and read *into* it, write *towards* it… Ascribing a place where reader and writer and artist are all thinking together. And what space there is, in such thinking! What imagined air! What possibility!

This excitement sounds, in many voices, throughout the pages of this book. For, as written earlier, and as you will come to see, there is no more a single 'I' making any of these pieces here, in a single-minded way, than there is a single 'I' who edits them and writes this introduction. Here is a project only of inclusions, where the intersections of gender, race and economies, all might meet, in a space that is expansive, in writing that breathes, is charged with hesitations, beauty, pleasure, that reads to think and to write some more. And just as *Imagined Spaces* celebrates this mutuality, all the various contributors to this volume enseamed together as though on one continual line of text, so 'I' who writes this introduction, a first person voice shared by two of us, here invites you, reader, to enter in—reading towards, in this process of gathering up a disparate body of texts and materials to enable an experience in which all kinds of 'I's, meet and exchange and share.

This means another kind of present tense writing—of 'bethinking', as one of our contributors Linda Chown calls it—can be enacted for the reader on every page, the beginning of a conversation between text and reader opening out in the space between two. That tendency we all have to summarise and finish? That 'what am I getting at here?', the 'what I mean is' or the 'to summarise let me say?' That relentless drive towards closure? All that is put on hold here when one writer meets another right beside them on the page. An 'imagined space', is a page in a book not policed by a 'brief' or an 'outline', nor by the destination-bound trudge of thought fixed tightly to its subject. Instead, the writers and artists, teachers and architects who've all contributed, who have something important to say, invite readers to share in the processes of their thinking, are encouraged to let their deliberations roam outwards, onwards. Across a bridge hanging in the air over the water, heading towards that space in the distance and who knows who they'll meet on the way? And who knows, too, how long it will take? There's a word length set in place, maybe, but it was always envisaged that this publication would give room for the mind's journeying, encouraging sentences that make up any one piece to point to any number of others, in a confluence of ideas that run off the edge of the page and spill into the water below.

So, here we are. Essaying on, essaying in, essaying towards…

And here we go…

In Tomiwa Folorunso and Hamzah Hussain's writing that circles centripetally and centrifugally around the idea of home, home is not only a physical place but also an imagined space of filiation and affiliation, populated with memories, practices and rituals, and artefacts of habitation. Home as plural, complex and sometimes contradictory. Home as creative, enacting, performative even—'what and where you make it'—settlement when and where we can. For Dai John, essaying means the clear and present danger of military life collides with a more ruminative reflection on the meaning of that life outside those conflict zones. Do the lines and worlds of war and civilian life overlap? How are they held and made real in the imagined spaces of a soldier's mind? Meaghan Delahunt, writing on death and dying, and on her work in a hospice, confronts fearful representations of death and our reticence to talk about what awaits all of us; quoting Toni Morrison she suggests that a writer's task is to imagine 'the unthinkable' as 'a way to liberate the imagination'. Susan Nickalls writes within this anthology of the marvellous spaces and gaps necessary to the Kengo Kuma's architectural thinking. In look-out apertures, separations between particles embedded in the concrete exterior of the building. Kuma's understanding of music, and of nature, which necessitates pauses, pulses and spaces between, provides him some of the structural inspiration for the V&A Dundee. Jane MacRae's decision to set up Bloom as contrapuntal learning practice to what has been instituted in educational curriculum becomes an essay here, as she describes a new way to learn from an imaginative idea about holistic teaching, and a concept of harmony in nature. She writes of the process of thinking and practising and rethinking as 'a little like essaying, a kind of ongoing process of thinking and writing'.

Our venture also has been, as suggested earlier, to move the conventional humanities' essay away from a sermon from the mount—where tablets from on high, from a place of high expertise or wisdom are dispensed—towards a place of conversation, collaboration, with one partner pushing the other on. A new kind of dialectic, this, a Socratic method without resolution. Accordingly essayists appear in pairs, most of these twosomes meet for the first time on the page. What would happen when strangers with overlapping interests wrote with one another? How would they manage the real processes of co-writing, fusing conversation and dialogue to the page? And we've been rewarded. No one-way directional thinking here. In addition to Folorunso and Hussain's writing on home, essaying pairs are imaginative and attentive to form, investigating the page as space where the line of thinking shapes as much as delivers the subject matter. In Emma Bolland and Elizabeth Chakrabarty's writing, the space of the essay is a ruse, a fiction that embeds the telling of an affective truth clocking the present ebb and flow of life—love, friendship, loss and dying—as well as an exchange of words as witnessing. 'To listen is to love' they write together in an exchange of intimacies that reveals also our shared humanity. For Stephen Carruthers and Fiona Stirling, the question of how to write depression as an all too commonplace, albeit invisible illness—how to be faithful to its highs and lows, to make its stops and starts, its clarity and fogginess material on the page—is tracked insistently. There is room 'for the unknown, the door into the dark' as one 'I' yields to another in a writing experiment that challenges, and builds something new. Lorens Holm and Paul Noble range over how capitalism with its voracious appetite to consume is made real in the spaces of our lives, how it registers in the spaces of the body or is resisted satirically in art and conversation; their email exchanges traverse the relationship between words and buildings, as well as more personal matters, and is also a living trace of an encounter, 'a line of footprints we leave as we walk and talk ourselves across this dusty earth.' In Duncan McLean and Kenny Taylor's 'The Flicker of North' two journeys converge, one writer reflecting his passage by foot across a great expanse of empty moorland in the Scottish North as a series of attempted communications with the other who is even further North, but located on an island, thinking about the meaning of setting off on an adventure as he stays at home, following his fellow traveller with his mind's eye.

Imagined Spaces also helps us with new metaphors to enable new thinking. Whether these be 'line drawings', 'tracings' that foreground media as the membrane between inner and outer worlds, or the intense inhabiting of a media—a 'being in the moment'—as a way to render present time and tense as transcendent or timeless, or attentively attuning to 'a niggling quiver in the gut, the lilt, rise, and quaver of the heart. The beginning of a vibration that one is compelled to follow… make manifest, sound out, realise.' These pieces by Graham Johnston and Chris Arthur, and Stephanie Bishop probe the kinship between art and writing, and music and writing, essaying on a bodily understanding of art, music and writing in a way that enables our mind to move laterally and associatively, instead of rationally pick-axing a way to a desired end. Bishop's sense of learning to play the cello turns into a metaphor for writing as listening and feeling one's way along some inner melody, 'Writing or playing, I attend to a bodily intuition of a prosody that is gradually cloaked in some more ornate, and increasingly dense aural experience, sometimes words.' Johnston writes… of art as 'tracing consciousness', how inhabiting different media defamiliarises to make new: an encounter between consciousness and the media one works in results in a creative 'cognitive disruption—something which does not fit within or be explained by what was previously known'.

Other essays such as that of Gabriel Josipovici's show reading also as a kind of making; no passive activity here but an inhabiting of all of the sonorous and metaphoric richness of language—tracing that line of sound and sense. In Linda Chown's essaying on reading, she writes of gaining intimacy with the text through a slow lingering attunement to language so that the time and world within a text meld with that which exists outside it—'depsychologicalization', she calls this state of being, where the self is not a means to an end but a opening out to other selves. Still other writers suggest a mentoring affiliation that is a reading and a writing of a life's work as in Graham Domke's personal, fragmentary, roundabout essaying on John Calcutt. In all these chapters, Chown's insights hold, 'I often find that by letting go purpose, I uncover or discover swirling forms slithering in and infiltrating my prose, nuggets of biography, summaries from a time in history, lines of poetry which perfectly deepen the subject, discovery of a haunting word which becomes unexpectedly and hypnotically necessary to write of at some length.'

Two writers in this volume are full-time essayists. America's Philip Lopate, with characteristic humour and self-deprecation, writes of his love of the form, reminding us that 'the essay by its very nature and word-derivation is an attempt, an experiment, a venture into the unknown' but is capacious, to include argument and sense too. Chris Arthur, his contemporary in the UK, talks of of revealing the extraordinary within the ordinary as a life's work; essaying as a mode of 'imaginative depth' that characteristically bears the hallmarks of 'openness… to discoveries and surprises, and the fact that as line-drawers/writers we don't know where our lines will take us.'

Finally, in her evocative word and image essaying, pushing the boundaries of both, Whitney McVeigh reminds us—aphoristically, in poetic lines—of transformations practised in essays and art; 'On paper, the emergence of movement and existential paths into memory—a discourse of mind and materials as the ink lays bare on the page.'

So does that ink spill and trail… A mark of being, a line that shows the trace of thought. Drawing thinking in writing, tracking across the page to create a space of consideration, a shared space of intellectual enquiry and deliberation… This is how this book was imagined from the outset, and we feel its urgency even more so now that it has come together in this final form.

For while I am writing this introductory 'tracing' in 2020, as the volume is being prepared, now, for publication—as I see these very words as they appear on my computer screen—a global illness sweeps across the world, devouring everything in its wake—lives, jobs, communities, culture… And we are to learn how to be together now, but physically isolated inside in our homes. The space in which we conduct our affairs, this has become small indeed. We are to be separate from others yet to operate as a group; protect ourselves and the lives of everyone around us, while the old forms of contact with each other are reduced and minimised. What can be imagined and discovered now? In this way? In this time?

Yet here I might call back the sentence hesitantly evoked at the start of this introduction, 'We had been sitting and talking about essays'. To consider again that particular space, that teaching room, of learning and speaking and listening and thinking, to put myself again in that place of being with students, to converse with them our young people, the generation who come after us in order that they make take their place ahead of us in line. For when I was with the students that day, I was talking about essaying as a means of harnessing their own experiences when they sit down to write about reading a text or piece of criticism; as a way, I suggested, of using the personal as an engine by which they may power their thinking, not to remain within themselves and their own worlds but to move outwards to others. In these uncertain times, when education itself has been stilled, classes gone online and teaching rooms are closed up and empty, it seems even more pressing, this idea of a 'towards' that could help all of us discover ways of engaging with life and texts that are, in Gayatri Spivak's phrase, 'outside *in the* teaching machine'. For there is, even in the beginnings of a powerful, imaginative impulse that comes from an individual response to the world, a kind of core experience—reaction!—that might in turn help shape and foster critical thinking in the institutional spaces we inhabit. 'This reaction can power all kinds of writing', I said, 'but in essays especially it might help you understand all kinds of ideas and concepts which can be put to work in powerful, life-affirming ways.'

Perhaps, I wonder, does this introduction written here now rest with those young people I was with that day? That for them I might offer a way of walking towards—of going out? That they might find a path to take them home to themselves, to whoever that self might become? That I might encourage them as they go: See this? Did you notice that? What is your thought here, and there? What then? I ask them. What now?

Even as my journey across the Tay is over, even so, I keep walking… Onwards, ahead… Across the 'sill' of this sentence to the next and the next, to where I can see an imagined space beyond and there are all kinds of people there. So many selves.

Imagination is what makes us human. This is something that we can remind each other of, show to each other and practise in our ongoing thinking and conversing, questioning and dreaming. Essaying for myself, for yourself… For ourselves, and for all those who come after, our children, and their children's children…

A beginning starting here.

Songs I Can't Play

Stephanie Bishop

This is where you are now, my teacher said, as she passed me a piece of paper. I give this to the children, she told me, to help them understand. But a better comparison for you might be the second stage of labour, when you think *I just can't go on.*

On the piece of paper was a picture of a boy pick-axing his way through an underground tunnel. The walls were made of rock—the boy was clearly exhausted, sweating, hunched over. He must have been digging for a long time and could not see what we see: that less than half a meter away is the open air. It was an image of endurance: only a few more heaves and the boy will break free. I told her that I couldn't actually remember the second stage of labour, that by that point I was too far gone. She acknowledged this as a challenge in itself—the thinking back—and told me that at the same point she decided she was just going to walk home, thank you very much, and someone pointed out to her that there was still the baby to come.

For three months I had been trying to play open D, then open A on the cello, but just open D would have done. I couldn't hold the bow properly. I couldn't find the weight. My palms sweated and my thumb muscle spasmed. You're so close, my teacher said. It might just be two more sessions, and then you'll have it. I felt myself near to tears, which seemed ridiculous. A three-year old could play this. If it was a matter of brute force, pick-axing my way to the sound, I might manage it. But this was a foible that my teacher had already spotted and cautioned me against. You hit a block and you just try to ram through it, she said some weeks back. We have to find a way of you not pushing and shoving against the problem.

I tried again, scooting over the strings. Where was the traction? The gravity? Where is your neutral? She asked me then, and I looked at her in complete confusion. Neutral? I said. I generally don't have a neutral. Or maybe my neutral is seasonal.

But nor do I drive, so I maybe I don't really know what you mean by neutral? She looked at me with some concern.

I am wary of horses and dogs and sometimes even cats because it always seems they can sense something deep inside me that is not admirable, that is perhaps hard and scrooge-like, that is too hurried, and that is therefore feeble, not soft enough, not malleable, too determined. While I play I feel my teacher's gaze similarly: how does she deduce this corner of my character simply from the way I failed to bow? Or, more precisely, from the way I did bow? Let's try again, she said, and I repositioned the instrument.

That morning we had started the lesson with me lying on the floor, on my back, with the cello on top of me. From this position I had played my open strings. Now she stood over me and repositioned the bow on the string whenever it was necessary. We play, she had said at one point, in the way that we live. Can you feel that now? she asked. For months we had been trying to find the sensation of weight in my shoulder blade and arm, a weight that would let the bow rest on the string, that would let the cello carry the bow, a feeling that would circumvent my instinct to hold the bow on behalf of the cello. Yes, I said, I can feel that—my shoulder blade working against the carpet, low pile and stained with black ink from where a child broke a pen. Then I stood up and played the cello as if it were a double bass, then sat down and tried again from a seated position. The feeling of weight was there for a moment, and then gone. Where did it go? There was sensation, and then just as suddenly, no sensation. Watch for this, she said. Sometimes I seemed to not be able to feel my arm in space at all. There was a flicker of feeling: a kind of muscular fluttering, a corner of my body felt pixilated, and then, at a certain point in the bow stroke, something hardened and all subtle sensation disappeared.

Ten years earlier I was playing Bach, maybe badly, maybe much worse than I thought, but the enthusiasm was vivid. Then I suffered an injury, and for years after this couldn't open a jar or turn a door handle, I could hardly use the breaks on my bike. Simply to pick up the cello bow caused a terrible shooting pain through my right arm. I had no choice but to lock the instrument up in its case. At a certain point my husband suggested we get rid of it. And while there was nothing to indicate I would ever be able to play again, I couldn't give the instrument away.

For Christmas some time later I was given a clarinet. I had reasoned to myself that another instrument would have to do, and that something in me needed music in a way I didn't need to understand but had to honour. I unwrapped the gift, put it all together, then huffed and puffed to make a tiny squeak of sound. It looked beautiful and shiny, but it felt entirely wrong: too small, too narrow, no strings attached. It went back in its box never to come out again. But what it made me realise was that there was only one instrument for me: this was not actually a general desire for music, but a specific one for a particular object, and a particular sound. I could not look back and think I had missed this. There must be a way, I decided.

A friend gave me the number of a Suzuki teacher. She wrote it down on a yellow post-it-note, and I stuck it to my fridge. I knew enough about my old way of playing to know that I had to subvert it, that I couldn't place any physical pressure on myself to work through repertoire, or think about scales and theory, that I didn't even want to play in that way but had no idea of what the alternative was. Still, every day, for a whole year, I glanced at the phone number and wondered if I would call. I had excuses: I couldn't really afford the lessons. I didn't really have the time, it was possible that I wouldn't be able to do it anyway. But when the following summer came around, a year after my one and only attempt on the clarinet, the faded post-it-note started to feel like an affront. I tapped in the numbers on my phone, palms sweating, and left a message.

It took more than four months before I could play *Twinkle Twinkle Little Star*. I proclaimed this achievement to other adults, and was crestfallen when they didn't grasp the significance, the joy. They looked at me askance, a little bewildered. Now, at last, two years later, I am muddling my way through a nearly grown-up piece. I call it a song, but technically it is perhaps not a song, more like a long exercise, but I like to think of it as a song. Although this thinking in itself, the assumption of a completed set of sounds, draws me into a thicket of new troubles: I aim for the endpoint and as a result the bowing comes undone: I play a down bow when I should do an up bow, lose the thread, skim over the crossings and stop halfway through, unsure of where I've come, what path I've taken, how the music ended me here. My hand hurts. My shoulder hurts. In the lesson we try to break this down. Where does this incomprehension start? In the limbs of the body? In the ear?

Before I arrive at this point where I can even come close to playing the piece, I have already been listening to it for years, months, weeks until it is memorized in a strangely deep way. I listen to it in a state of distraction, I listen to it closely, on repeat, and eventually I dream of it, or can't sleep because certain sections run endlessly through my head in the dark. Then, when I sit down to play I suddenly seem to have forgotten it. I can't find the exact sound or note with which to begin, but sense instead the pulse of the song, the rhythm or not even that but a dim sense of a rhythm, yet to crystalise or accumulate sound. There is always an element of here of near-improvisation, of winging it, of trusting that my ear will recollect the sound just in time for my body to catch it. It is less a song that is being played, than a journey made through a childhood landscape: once known so well, so intimately, many decades ago and now being revisited at night. I am struck by points of intense familiarity—the particular roll of stones under the soles of the shoe, the rise of the mountain; shadowy, unseen, sensed, out to the west. The rhythm, the shape of the landscape, is the last part of the song to remain as memory failures occurs: it is the bones, the residue, the pulse, underlying and invisible, undecorated. On the wave of this sounds reaccumulate.

The song is not a snake, you cannot learn it that way, my teacher reminds me. But you will hear it that way before you can break it down into playable parts, whereupon it becomes complete once again.
Put your bow in your mouth, she tells, me.
What? I ask. And she shows me.
Like this, she says through tightened lips, the bow between her teeth as a dog might hold a stick. I try but am laughing so much I can't keep my mouth closed around the bow. I try again, without laughing.
Now lift your hands above you head. And sway. Can you feel that?
Yes, I say.
We try again. And once more it breaks apart.

The piece, my teacher tells me, is like a landscape in fog for you right now. There are some trees, some mounds of grass, but you cannot see the details, you can't see the path. I tell her it feels comparable to the disorientation of starting out on a new book, where I move over the territory roughly, in some disoriented bewilderment, shading in, finding the obvious dynamics, before going over and over the marked-out ground, working into the details. Yes, she replies. I can see the comparison, but the difference is that this piece is here, and that book, when you are starting out, doesn't actually exist. Here, you don't need to work over the whole in order to find it, because it has already been made. The chipping away and chipping away comes as you break down the parts that have been composed, as you figure out how to play them.

I agree with her, then come away uncertain, because a book feels, at least to me, like it already exists, only in some region or realm slightly ahead of me, or slightly above me, just beyond reach. To reverse this idea: when I close my eyes, and play from ear, from memory, the music seems to arrive from the left and the right—as if it were hiding in the wings of a stage, in the dark corners just out of conscious thought and what I must do in playing is to find a way to articulate an intuited form, to interpret my sense of its form. To my body, the song seems not to exist until I have played it, or am playing it, as if it exists only in the playing and in the listening but really not as a preserved, material, pre-existing artefact. The challenge is to find the song in the air and run it though my body, or to find the aural memory of the song that lies in wait in my body, that has developed over time like sediment and give it shape, set it free.

But improvement is slow, and I chafe against this. You are trying to do too many things at once, she says. You are trying too hard. Have you been looking at the score? she asks, a note of disapproval in her voice. There is no point in not confessing, the fault is obvious. Don't, she tells me. The score is a guide only. And particularly unhelpful for you.

I must learn not to expect to 'learn' a piece: dot learning, my teacher calls this old method. Following the rules. Some of her students are 'good' students, she tells me, and they think they have to play what the score tells them. She does not need to explain the task of errancy because she already knows that trying to follow the rules only terrifies me, even if I think I should follow them when I'd be better off not.

Instead, I am asked to arrive at the song from the inside. It is a process that involves an uncanny practice of anticipatory listening—the body following the lead of the inner ear that recollects the song, the timing always double and just out, close to syncopated—as I enact a melody that has already occurred, a fraction earlier, in my head. If I do not anticipate the sound, if I do not listen outside of my own lived time, my body will not play, or rather the sound will be off, awkward, discontinuous, unfelt. This sensation of listening is almost identical, I come to realise, to the kind of attention experienced in the act of writing. The attunement to a vague internal melody, occurring still some bars away, in the distance—muted but discernable, felt. The attunement of the ear in playing—the matching up of inner to outer ear, this too feels like a refinement of the listening that precedes any putting down of words onto the page, as one moves from feeling to hearing, to sounding out. The moment that the melody is lost, the moment one is distracted, the moment the internal listening drops out—then the thread of musical thinking slackens, and the ear seems to lose all surface tension. Writing or playing, I attend to a bodily intuition of a prosody that is gradually cloaked in some more ornate, and increasingly dense aural experience, sometimes words.

Indirectly and by association, because the activities are often undertaken back to back, and because I have a habit of hearing things in my head, and because the unedited, incomplete version is always of more interest to me, for all of these reasons experiencing sound in this way compels me to radically rethink the feeling and therefore the act of fictional thinking—no longer as a development of any complex scaffolding in which characters live and move, but rather as something that acquires meaning only in the practicing of it, as a listening forwards into the dark. It is a musical thinking, or perhaps musical thinking is a fictional thinking. Increasingly they feel one and the same.

But if I had to say what the difference is between the two practices, between writing and playing, what would it be? Only that they occur at the far ends of the same spectrum: while one moves through vibration towards words, the other passes back in the opposite direction, away from words. They each pick up the vibration, run the texture of this through the body and shape it differently. There is no chronology, no hierarchy, just an affinity. It is the meeting points that interest me most, the co-dependence that I slip in and out of: the writing mind relies on a principle of musicality, of variation, of rhythm. The musical mind, or the musical body, relies on the emotive foundation of sounds that will often come together to form a narrative design, or else plunge us into the bewildering absence of this. The ear always listens for the sound of the story: the pitch of beginning, the silence before the start. The body waits, eager, to be drawn into the music of the tale. The writing self and the musical self each depend upon, and emerge from, or start with a state of deeper and very wordless feeling which, in its earliest form is that niggling quiver in the gut, the lilt, rise, and quaver of the heart. The beginning of a vibration that one is compelled to follow, or follow through on, enlarge, maximise, make manifest, sound out, realise.

Maybe there is, as someone pointed out, meaning here in the relationship between the cello and the voice. The range of the cello is akin to that of the human voice, to the human voice singing in particular. And although the cello can obviously surpass the reaches of the human voice there is a meeting point, where the human voice and the cello might stand in for one another. The writing voice, freed from the physical constraints of the speaking voice, can seek to match the sonorous dexterity of the cello, can be extended by the knowledge of what it is to embody those sounds. When I play, the underlying pulse of the writing—the emotional core that is felt as a vibration leading to rhythm before arriving at words—is strengthened, repeated, rehearsed, re-encountered from new angles. I once listened to a teacher of mine, a poet, read out a poem, many years ago. It was strangely moving although I couldn't say why and didn't understand what the poem was about, what it was saying. What did you hear then? he asked us. There was a long silence. Then he read a section again. Vowels, I said. Open vowels. The feeling is never just about the words.

Why don't you call these pieces you play tunes? a friend asked. Why songs? They are perhaps too simple to be called songs, too brief, my friend said. I call them songs because a song is given the privilege of belonging to the voice and the body, a song that emerges through and in relation to the body. A tune is what you whistle on your walk, a half-remembered ditty that you might hum before remembering the song proper—something deeply internalised, a somatic memory anticipated and which only belatedly emerges.

Have we talked about the different movements of the joints? My teacher asks. All your joints are trying to take the lead at the same time. What happens if you just let the shoulder own that movement. And at what point does the shoulder need to give way to the movement of the elbow? I close my eyes and bow slowly. Halfway into the bow stroke there is a flurry of confusion in my arm as if it isn't sure in what direction it should be heading. The bodily panic is very quiet but also very clear: like a flurry of dove wings in a small dark space. Dusty. Disoriented. That's the moment, my teacher says, when the exchange between occurs. Maybe you just need to sit in that for a while.

Meanwhile, my left arm is going rogue. A strange and sudden pain breaks across my shoulder blade. It is as if, in the process of attending to the residual habits and difficulties of my right shoulder and the bowing arm, my bodily quirks have simply migrated and transferred themselves to the other side. We start over, making no sound and just trampolining my fingers on the strings. My proprioception is all out. To regain this we map my body in relation to the instrument: with my left hand I touch my nose then the fingerboard, then my nose, then my left shoulder, then the fingerboard again, then my nose. Once more, we start over. The repetition of this—the endless recommencement—has become itself a source of comfort, a pleasure and a release from the vortex in which one is expected to claim more and yet more territory, to accumulate and display. Instead, we just go further in to the same place.

I think of a post that I saw on Instagram, one that shows a handwritten note which reads: 'Everyone has something they wish they could talk about with someone who is not in a hurry'. I realise that in the act of playing I must be that person for myself. To listen without haste or irritation, and to listen not just to the sounds, but also, and perhaps first, to my body, and then to play without feeling hurried because I know I am listening. The listening comes first: an attitude or bearing that precedes any sounded note, that is just ready, for whatever comes. I listen doubly: for what is there, for what arises—and for what lies just up ahead. Like any good friend, I am attentive to the developments of the story no matter how small or seemingly insignificant. Although in this act of listening I cannot treat the completed song as the aim or destination, the thing I am listening for. To do this would be to create a response in my body that is the experience of expectation—a tightening and straining around suspense, the demand to get it right and finish on time, and in the midst of this I forget to pay attention to the landscape that I am surrounded by, the resonant sound, the texture of this, even the fog. More especially, this is how I used to play, it is how we are generally taught to play, how we are taught to think, to argue, to live. I can reach the end of a piece in this manner, but know that my body will be broken by it. What is the alternative route? Check yourself, my teacher reminds me. Each note, each phrase, each bow, each transition, must feel to come from, and be, a movement of complete ease. Slow it down, and each time the body tenses, experiences strain or roughness, displeasure in the playing, then stop, and in that moment of stopping treat it just as a pause in the playing where you rest the tension, drop it back, settle, find your neutral, and make the transition you need to make—preparing the string crossing, shifting position—and then and only then do you listen in and carry on. The kind of listening required here is only one strand of a broader sensitivity in the body, one that I must cultivate in the process of re-learning how to play—a sensitivity that injury radically short-circuits. In a protective gesture, the body resists the stance of openness and fluid movement that leaves it susceptible to the repetition of pain. But if my teacher holds my bowing arm for me, or lifts my shoulder blade, creating on my behalf the movement my body needs to learn, then I feel the gesture anew, without effort. Ninety-nine percent of this is in the bowing, she tells me. I give her the whole weight of my arm. The sound that emerges could be coming from a different instrument, not mine.

What does that feel like? she asks. What can you attach to this in order to imprint it?

In E.M. Forster's *A Room with a View*, Mr. Beebe says to great effect that 'If Miss Honeychurch ever takes to live as she plays, it will be very exciting—both for us and for her.' It is a dare almost, a test of character regarding her potential for growth. The assumption is that she plays better than she lives, at least more passionately, with a greater sense of freedom and ease. The correlation between how one lives and how one plays is beautifully observed, as is the recognition of fruitful crossovers between habits of performance; the performance of self, the performance of music, the way art might release itself into life and vice versa. Miss Honeychurch does of course fulfil this promise of the novel, and learns to live as she plays. Now I too must take this question seriously. Or, to place a caveat, as I'm sure Miss Honeychurch would have also wished, I must learn to live as I play when I play well, to learn the habits of this, so that I do not, in a slightly different way, play as I too often live.

My teacher lets go my arm and I try once more. Seeking to un-think my own reliance on the concept of a socket, a joint, hand and fingers, to think of the whole movement rather than isolated parts, the feeling of ease, when it happens of its own accord, is like flight. The arm weightless, the gesture of the bowing akin to a wing beat. At the beginning, when I was trying to re-find the feeling of playing in my injured body, I watched videos of large winged wetland birds as they came into land or soared overhead—Brolga's and Sandhill Cranes. I watched them close-up, and in slow motion, attending, on repeat, to the movement of their wings. Some are flying to India for the winter. Others take off from the Platte River to feed in nearby cornfields. I kept a photograph of a crane standing on a rock at the water's edge, its mighty wings held out to dry, and when I sat down with the cello, I tried to think my way, or feel my way into the hypothetical of this sensation—the balance and flex of wings, the arm as an extension of the shoulder blade, the bow as an extension of the arm, the uninterrupted movement from spine to feather tip, just as the cranes' wings appear in the video when the flock takes flight. The weight of the wings, then the air against them and underneath them, because the song too must eventually be carried on the air.

Line Drawing

Chris Arthur & Graham Johnston

Graham Johnston, *Hospitalfield House*, South-East Elevation, Pen and graphite on paper, 1980.

Over a year ago I was in Arbroath attending a conference, 'The Essay: Taking Ideas for a walk',
organised by the editors of this book. The theme of the event was to explore the form and value of
the essay. I was attending partly as a curious fan—I have no vested interest in the medium other
than the comparatively recent realisation that essays have probably delivered most of the concepts
about the world that have truly changed my thinking, but the other undeniable reason I was there
was because the venue, Hospitalfield House—an eccentrically designed and lovingly constructed
Victorian country house—exerted a strong emotional pull.

Almost 40 years ago I had stayed there for a summer residency with painting students selected from the four Scottish Art Schools. Actually, it was my second art school visit to Hospitalfield and the building—with its brooding baronial faux-castle turrets and parapets and its potted-history approach to interior styling—made for a fascinating place to draw. The sketches from that first visit—absorbed in the technical aspects of representation—nonetheless trace something intimate, something of that moment. Ironically, while those drawings may have influenced my tutors' decision to choose me for the subsequent residency, by the time I arrived at Hospitalfield, I was experimenting with abstract painting and confined myself to the purpose-built 19th C. studio spaces on the estate; the buildings became a backdrop, not the subject. So, my presence at the conference was wrapped in both emotional and intellectual excitement. The ideas that were unpacked in the sessions have stayed with me and skewed much of my thinking since.

A few sketches I made on the last day capture the passage of a moment. The moment of their making, certainly—but also, a particular moment of reflection and swirling of ideas about where I've been since my first visit; the ideas generated by the conference; and why it should be that after all the media I've attempted to find some kind of mastery in, I always return to drawing. By the end of the conference, Hospitalfield had thrown open the possibility that the essay was a sibling medium to drawing in its directness, its simplicity and its flexibility. It also marked the beginning of a year-long dialogue with Chris Arthur—a passionate advocate and practitioner of the essay—exploring the connections between the two practices.

One of the things that was coming into focus from all those years ago and during that first visit to Hospitalfield as a student was the realisation that some kind of extraordinary experience is everywhere—and that with a medium in hand, you have an antenna to tune in to it. Forty years later I'm more convinced of this than ever and while I'm equally convinced that creative media have the capacity to trace this experience… successfully communicating it to others is much more elusive.

The title of the conference that led to this book—'The Essay: Taking Ideas for a walk'—recalls one of Joseph Epstein's essay collections, *A Line Out for a Walk*. Explaining his choice of title, Epstein recalls that a reviewer of one of his earlier books suggested that essays are best defined by a remark of Paul Klee's. Talking about how his own art takes shape, Klee said: 'I take a line out for a walk.' Although he's forgotten the name of the reviewer, and at one point misattributed Klee's remark to Kandinsky, what remained indelibly fixed in Epstein's mind was the saying, 'I take a line out for a walk.' This embedded itself in his memory like the motto on whatever coat of arms the essay bears. According to Epstein it describes 'exactly, precisely, absolutely' what he does.

It seems appropriate to start this chapter with reminders of the walk begun in Arbroath in June 2018, and to quote the intertwined words of an essayist and an artist talking about lines. Because this chapter has its roots in the idea that the creative DNA of essaying and drawing is sufficiently similar to suggest that the two activities share much common ground. In our own ways we are each preoccupied with line drawing—whether lines of text on a page or pencil marks or brush strokes on a canvas. The lines we make in our chosen mediums might be seen as lassos or contours or ropes or isobars—there's a rich spectrum of metaphorical possibility that might be mined to cast light on their nature—but however they're conceptualized, our lines are cast in an effort to catch whatever aspects of the world happen to spark our interest.

Epstein explains that the 'line' for him is the subject of his essay and that just as Klee didn't know in advance where his drawn line would take him, so the essayist is likewise unsure about where the written lines of an essay may lead. In fact it is 'the chanciness of the enterprise, the element of discovery and surprise in it' that is the appeal of writing in this genre. We've certainly been surprised by the directions and duration of our walk, and delighted by the discoveries we've made on it. Neither of us anticipated when we met at Hospitalfield House how long a journey it would be. Conferences often end when the final session finishes and delegates go home. The Arbroath conference was notable not only for gathering such a rich diversity of people, but for starting conversations that have continued long after they dispersed.

Our walking with ideas has resulted in the exchange of over 30,000 words of emails as we've pondered the nature of essay-writing and drawing. Obviously we can't share all these lines of correspondence in full. Instead, we've picked out four areas that cropped up repeatedly in the course of our exchanges. These areas could be seen as viewpoints that we came to along the way. They offer particularly good perspectives on what essays and drawing are attempting. Under each of the four headings—and the list is not intended as an exhaustive typology of similarities—we've offered some comments. These are followed by an afterword that looks forward to further conversational walking, and the hope that the lines we've drawn will encourage others to trace them out and explore the fascinating terrain they lead through.

Conveying the Extraordinary Nature of the Ordinary

What do essays try to do? I'm wary of making general pronouncements given the diversity of material this genre encompasses. Even just looking at my own work and trying to identify key characteristics is risky. Each essay starts anew and doesn't follow any pre-set pattern. Instead, it unfolds according to whatever fits the particularities of its composition as this addresses the ideas that brought it into being. The independence and unplanned nature of each piece notwithstanding, I think it's fair to say that, overall, my essays are variations on the theme of highlighting the extraordinary nature of the (apparently) ordinary. In writing them I'm trying to see beneath the skin of the quotidian, the language of routine naming and assumption—our everyday diction—which tends to settle on things like a veil, stopping us from seeing their real nature.

The nineteenth century Scottish essayist Alexander Smith said, 'The world is everywhere whispering essays and one need only be the world's amanuensis.' I agree with Smith that there are openings into essays all around us. But his use of the word 'amanuensis' makes it sound as if essay writing is just a simple process of taking down dictation. First, you've got to hear the world's whispering—and that's harder than it sounds. There's always plenty of distraction and of course it's easier to lapse into conventional labelling and description rather than portraying things with the kind of depth and detail that hints at the incredible cargoes they carry.

At the end of his magisterial pilgrimage to the dawn of life, *The Ancestor's Tale*, Richard Dawkins says something that I think can be applied to way the torque of my essays is geared to moving readers into positions from which the extraordinary nature of the ordinary becomes more evident. Dawkins talks about 'the sublime grandeur of the real world'. It's glimpses of that grandeur that my essays try to give. I share Dawkins' dislike for those outlooks—no matter whether they're religious or secular—that 'represent a narrowing-down from reality, an impoverishment of what the real world has to offer.' In writing essays, a large part of my motivation lies in a desire to try to scrape away the dust of impoverishment from my vision and to see the astonishing richness of our experience. You don't need to travel to exotic places or look for fantastical objects in order to appreciate this richness. All of the ordinary things around us are imbued with it. It's just (just!) a matter of being alert to it, of not letting routine dull our perception. An observation of Mary Oliver's sums up what I think of as my essayist's credo: 'To pay attention, this is our endless and proper work.' Unless that attention is properly in gear, the ordinary will just seem ordinary. Fellow essayist

Patrick Madden catches well the way in which essays mediate between the ordinary and the extraordinary:

> Essayists are keen observers of the overlooked, the ignored, the seemingly unimportant. They can make the mundane resplendent with their meditative insights… For me the magic of an essay is so often tied to its exploding of the commonplace, its deep investigation of something we tend to overlook or think entirely mundane and unworthy of our attention.

Why do we miss so much? We assume our technologies must gift us extraordinary experience and yet our attitude towards wonder seems to place it in the attention-seekingly-gigantic or somewhere outwith our sphere of everyday encounters. This is not because we are victims of an alienating, transactional society—although in the West we surely are—but because we are bound by one of the evolutionary adaptations that have made us so successful as a species—we ignore stuff. This is bundled in a paradox in which our survival and efficiency is tied up with a capacity to override sensory data when we don't need it, then to switch on our refined sensory perceptions and skills when we need to solve problems outside our previous experience.

Neurologist Daniel Wolpert, a self-described 'movement chauvinist', has asserted somewhat provocatively that we only have brains as large as we do 'in order to perform complex and adaptable movement.' The brain has the problem of processing vast amounts of sensory information every second; in order to be able to function efficiently and respond safely to new situations the brain performs a simple trick—it ignores the senses, generally. Wolpert argues that the brain, in order to keep itself unburdened by this storm of information and yet be able to anticipate required actions, makes predictions about what is about to happen based on what it knows has happened in the past. Unless sensory information contradicts the prediction, we carry on with our business blissfully ignoring our senses and acting in the world as we know it, or rather as we imagine it to be. We act in accordance with a 'forward model' of our own construction.

We must all have experienced this, of reaching an end point and not really remembering how we got there, of performing habituated tasks without thinking about doing them. That last cup of tea you made… were you conscious of getting the teabag out of its container and into the cup? What we do pay attention to, though, is when something pops into a scenario which was not in our prediction. Generally, our vast store of experiences will offer up something analogous and we can make new predictions to overcome the obstruction. But if something unpredicted becomes an impediment, and we have no predictions in the mental bank to draw on, then something else takes over. We engage, not our internal capacity to predict, but our external sensory capacity to probe for an understanding of the material obstructing us and the environment that it, and we, are a part of.

Cognisance begins in the senses. But, this sensory attention is expensive—energy and resources intensive—and so we cycle, according to circumstances, between speedy, energy-efficient-predictions-and-ignoring to slow, energy-intensive-senses-and-attention engagement.

Of course, for this to be successful, the senses need to be in good condition. The problem is that our senses wither in a habitual environment, become untested. This is especially so in an environment where delight and wonder are offered up on a screen, or served, pre-packed, on a shelf or delivered to our door. Certainly, there is a small neural reward for effortlessly acquiring what we want but such experiences are often unsatisfying. Far bigger dopamine hits come from overcoming more complex problems and successfully deploying the full resources of our senses and skills. For example, to cook a meal from fresh ingredients presents a succession of small challenges: the variations in the quality of materials; their response to heat or being combined with other ingredients. Success in this simple, and yet rather remarkable, task brings a range of sensory and emotional rewards. Yet, we have been weaned off this process by diminishing circles of habit and convenience. Instead, the extraordinary becomes the mini-miracle of an instant meal. The focus becomes the end point and not the walk to get there; the neural reward in the journey is displaced by more abstract satisfaction. The everyday-extraordinary of using dexterity and a knowledge of processes to cook, withers.

What we lose is an immersion in experience, an engagement with the moment.
What we think we gain is time, but what we are doing is losing our presence in the passage of time—of being in-the-moment. We are less and less engaged with our senses, with alertness, but are instead 'free' to ignore, to arrive at perceived fulfilment without obstruction.

Being in-the-Moment

How, then, do we return to the moment?

John Berger has written often about animals and their importance to humans. In one essay he describes how dogs have been taken on by humans not merely as pets, but rather, because of their different sensory range: dogs can pick up on sounds and smells before humans. Having them as companions has utility; it extends our sensory resources. Anyone who has been for a walk with a dog will recognise this—our engagement with our environment is extended through the dog's 'different' awareness. The dog is an in-betweener, a medium between us and our environment. Dogs, of course, live much more than humans 'in-the-moment' (maybe entirely so) and one of the gifts that they innocently bestow on us is a capacity, through this extended engagement, to be more in-the-moment ourselves.

And almost every circumstance of being in-the-moment I can think of—of having a deeper alertness—involves a key element: exposure and engagement to the experience and through a medium.

At a basic level, the most immediate and important medium we have is our own body. It is between our inner life, our consciousness, and the environment and phenomena we interact with. But we have extended this consciousness through various 'companion' skills, processes and tools so that we can now sample and manipulate the phenomena around us to a greater degree than our naked selves. This array of media can give us little gateways to fulfilment; they provide the tools to overcome the obstructions we encounter.

But more than this, a medium, like a dog accompanying us on a walk, introduces us to things we hadn't predicted, are out-with our previous experience, or are even beyond our naked sensory range—stuff we might habitually have ignored. And by waving these little flags, by winking at us, the medium seems to alert us to the different, the extra-ordinary. It primes action and, because it sits between the two, triggers the movement from habit to engagement.

Many practical and productive activities deploy the use of a medium—cooking for instance, though few outside the circle of artist chefs would probably think of it as such. And yet, it is in-between us and our interaction with material. Certainly, to extract value from a medium requires a degree of acquired skill—we are nothing if not a skills-based species—and it's telling that in this age of obstruction-free consumption and gratification, there is a palpable yearning for the expression of skills in the popularity of a range of competitive, craft-based programmes on television. From baking and sewing to masterchefs and potters, ballroom dancing and pop-singing, are these shows a kind of skills-voyeurism? Are they, as it were, dog-watching? Do they express a yearning for the presence of a companion medium?

Week after week, viewers tune in to competition hopefuls all engaged in a basic human narrative of overcoming obstructions through the deployment and development of a skill. This absorption in a task—where hours may slip by in a process sometimes known as 'flow'—is a common feature of being in-the-moment. In this state, time becomes a qualitative experience—not a quantitative one.

Most of the individual essays I write are in the range of 5000–8000 words. Occasionally I opt for something outside this, though I rarely go for less than 1500 words or more than 12000. Books, where a clutch of essays is shepherded together to make a collection, are usually around 80,000 words. Given these parameters, it may seem odd that I'm drawn to haiku poetry, but most of my books make substantial reference to this verse form. My third collection even incorporates haiku into its title. As a writer of lengthy prose pieces, why am I so attracted to these poetic slivers? Despite their obvious disparity in length there are striking similarities between what haiku and essays are attempting—just as there are between drawing and essays.

Haiku are slivers of verse traditionally arranged in three lines of five, seven and five syllables each. Heavily influenced by Zen Buddhism, their emphasis is on that most difficult of tasks—being aware of what's here, right now, in front of us. Haiku cut like scalpels to the heart of perception. They put us in touch with things in a way that seems electrified. Their few words come charged with a voltage that often eludes longer compositions. Deft, economical, startling, exact, haiku seem to possess the kind of super-density you sometimes read about in science fiction stories when a tiny fragment of alien rock, no more than a dust-speck, turns out to weigh more than an elephant. Haiku catch moments that have touched their writers deeply, skewering the experience on their tiny tridents of verse and offering them up so raw and freshly cut that it feels we can live them again.

Unlike so much prose—the sort that pins, imprisons and dissects—haiku seem able to cup their hands around the delicacy of a moment without crushing it. You can feel the tickle of its wings fluttering against your palms, like a butterfly held there safely until the hands are opened again and it's allowed to fly free as the reading eye finds the words on the page. That's something I attempt in my essays. In fact the first essay in the collection I'm currently working on, a piece entitled 'Pulse', is quite explicitly an attempt to chart/catch/picture/describe a moment in words, trying to show the density of connections that are built into it. Of course I can't cast the lines of an essay so that they completely enfold a moment and present it in perfect verisimilitude. But the recognized impossibility of the goal doesn't stop me from aiming for it repeatedly.

According to Graham Good: 'Anyone who can look attentively, think freely, and write clearly can be an essayist.' That prescription is easier to state than to put into practice. Looking attentively demands an alertness to the moment as it lays its presence upon us. This kind of looking occupies the same cognitive bandwidth as Mary Oliver's paying attention. It's a fundamental prerequisite for both essay writing and drawing.

Tracing Consciousness

What is the difference between an art and a craft? Ken Robinson described creativity as being 'the process of having original ideas that have value.' The defining characteristics of an artwork surely lie in this territory. All arts require craft just as all crafts have the capacity to produce art. Some craftspeople may be more skilful than artists using the same medium yet may never produce something regarded as an expressive work of art.

Whereas both arts and crafts must overcome technical and cognitive obstructions, a crafted work becomes art because of the value it expresses. While a craft requires awareness of material as well as self-awareness and a knowledge of the limits of both, its primary concern is to complete something correctly to a given standard, or to propose incremental improvements which may then be acceptable as a new standard or orthodoxy. In craft the medium has a summative role; it embodies achievement, both of the individual's practice to a particular level and also that of the culture or genre of the activity.

Art is more, by intent, a formative process and in it, the medium is the messenger: it delivers insights and questions by tuning in to covert phenomena in the world; it facilitates cognitive disruptions. In the instant of its use by the artist it both enables the identification of the unpredicted, the unseen, and at the same time offers a pathway to new cognitive propositions. Simultaneously, it records this process and presents, externally embodied in the medium, a kind of archaeology of the consciousness.

This is the remarkable, symbiotic feature of any medium: it is the 'in-between' from the inner life of an artist and their consciousness extended out into the world. At the same time, the product of that medium is also in-between the source experience of the maker and the inner life of the receiver: the viewer, listener, reader. The medium transfers… an echo of a process I used to enjoy as a schoolboy—to me, an everyday-extraordinary—tracing.

There was always something exotic and a little precious about the ritual of distributing tracing paper at primary school. Laid flat on a page the translucent film becomes almost transparent allowing a pencil to map the perceived points of interest or importance in the image below. When lifted off, the tracing reveals not only a summary of the source image but also a graph of the key subjective points of interest. Tracing is a technique I still use now from time to time as an aid to filtering or skewing objectivity; what I still find remarkable in this process is not so much the physics at work—the responses of graphite and paper materials to action—as what it reveals about what and how one is actually engaging with the material: the process of investigating value.

Something like this, for me, is at the heart of making art. The medium provokes a dialogue between the internal and external, and leaves behind a tracing of this process. It traces the consciousness of the maker while she or he discovers and engages with a cognitive disruption. That cognitive disruption—something which is neither explained by nor fits within what was previously known—and which is revealed by whichever dog-medium we have taken for a walk, is the key provocation to move from habit to engagement.

From ignoring, to being in-the-moment.

I've always liked the advice given by Japan's great master of haiku poetry, Matsuo Basho (1644–1694): 'Let not a hair's breadth separate your mind from what you write.' Essays attempt a close contouring between words on the page and what's in the writer's mind. Indeed Patrick Madden goes so far as to suggest that an essay 'mimics the activity of a mind at work.' That means that when an essay turns descriptive, it's probably not just giving a straightforward account of what the essayist is focusing on. Mark Doty puts the matter well in *The Art of Description*:

> What descriptions—or good ones anyway—actually describe is consciousness, the mind playing over the world of matter, finding there a glass various and lustrous enough to reflect back the complexities of the self that's doing the looking.

From Montaigne to the present-day, essayists have been fascinated by consciousness and have variously tried to give accounts of what it contains as the mind engages with whatever aspect of the world has given rise to a particular essay.

I agree with O.B. Hardison that 'Of all literary forms the essay most successfully resists attempts to pin it down'—which is why when I came to offering an indication of its nature in my 2018 collection, *Hummingbirds Between the Pages*, I gave 'Thirty-Six Ways of Looking at an Essay' instead of a single one. Several of those ways stress how tracing consciousness is an integral part of essaying. For example, I suggest that an essay is:

> A report from the crow's nest of the self; it tells us about the view and the viewer…

> A short prose track that simultaneously leads into the mind of the essayist and whatever aspect of the world that mind is engaged with…

Poetic prose tuned to follow the gradients of the essayist's experience, close-shadowing the twists and turns of thought and feeling…

A listening device that allows us to hear extracts from the music playing in another person's head…

In short, essays construct contour maps of consciousness in words; they eavesdrop on the essayist's mind.

Sometimes when I'm looking for a visual image of what I'm trying to do when I write essays I think of Magritte's painting 'Attempting the Impossible'. It shows an artist painting a life-size nude female figure into the space in front of him. The canvas pictures what looks like the creation of another person who's being brought into being just an arm's length from the artist. She's almost complete, but lacks most of her left arm. The artist is reaching out his brush to complete it. The picture provides a vivid reminder of how far any portrayal is from the reality it depicts, even if it's highly convincing visually. As Magritte famously put it: 'Ceci n'est pas une pipe.' However much an essay may seem to close Basho's hair's breadth, what's on the page is never going to be identical with what's in the mind or heart. But again—as with the difficulty of catching a moment—although consciousness won't submit to words, that doesn't stop essayists engaging in repeated efforts to catch it.

Heretical/Peripheral

The journey from efficiently predicting to being engaged in the moment is inhibited by the energy-conserving 'executive' centre in our brain. We are powerfully organised to go with what we know. The neuroscientist Beau Lotto points out that our eyes contribute only about 10% of what we 'see' and that 'the brain never sees the world as it actually is, only the world that is useful to see.' We ignore what doesn't fit our predictions—our default is to ignore. Research at the University of New Mexico has observed that the executive functions of the brain—judgement, autobiographical memory and decision-making—become temporarily dormant during creative activity. This indicates that when we enter a state of flow with a creative medium, we are connecting to our environment without the prejudice (or, at least, with a reduced level of it) from our preconceptions. We become free to trace what is salient to our individually tuned senses rather than impose what we believe, or want to believe, is there. In this, we are engaging the timeless apparatus we share as a species and transmit this experience, not in a private personal code of the executive centre, but the lingua franca of the senses.

This simple process, which has a vast polarity, operating on multiple levels, is loaded with the possibilities of discovery and transference of value. The consciousness that is traced may be about a lived experience, or about an interaction with a chosen medium, or the history of lived experience or the history of the medium itself—or even, an imagined example of any of the above. When it has value, it cuts through the personal preconceptions and reveals an aspect of experience, through the senses, in a medium. This tracing implies a certain degree of conflict: our dog may take us to places we didn't plan or want to go to, or even knew or believed could be there. It presents us with a spectrum of heresies and the medium is the vehicle for messages conveying these, first to the artist and then to the viewer through whatever 'tracing' the medium produces. It reaches forward from the artist to engrain the valuable complexities of an experienced moment—in flow—to leave behind for the viewer/reader a provocation, pleasing or otherwise, to retrace the steps—to flow back—to the inciting 'heresy'.

Heresy is what lies between past and future orthodoxy.

Some creatives may have strayed so far with their particular dog that they never experience a goldilocks moment with their heresies—that's to say, where the heresy is enough to attract interest but not too much that it repels. Other heresies may be too easily accepted as norms and the transformations involved, minimal or even reactionary. That job, of using a medium to reveal and hone aspects of our sensory apparatus and even shift or extend our consciousness became, from the late 19thC, the modus operandi of the avant-garde. But what starts as a radical denial of the norm soon becomes the norm. We are nudged, by the transfer of settings in Impressionism, for example (but substitute almost any 'ism' until the late twentieth century), to adjust the dial of our consciousness. After Impressionism we see the world differently. But that new heretical pattern of understanding quickly became a norm, especially when the value of the transfer is diluted through the second-hand experience of reproduction and mass-media—the inciting heresy is thus far removed. Impressionism, biscuit-tin-unfashionable though it may now be for those of an avant-garde leaning, nonetheless offers up a tracing of a sensitised consciousness.

Impressionism, if I may, was a dog.

Once, years ago, when I was an academic and the ethos in UK universities was changing from the old model of thinking-teaching-learning to the new one of productivity-profit-accountability, one of my colleagues tried to organize us all into 'research centres'—to conform to the expectations of a funding body. Of course I didn't fit into any of them. I remember a meeting at which I proposed an alternative framework. Those who wanted to could locate themselves in the new centres, whilst I and anyone like-minded would occupy 'research peripheries.' To some extent this was tongue-in-cheek—but there was a serious point too. I think it's in the peripheries, margins, borderlands that interesting ideas tend to germinate—far from the dead centre. Unsurprisingly, my academic career didn't last long after that.

It was Adorno who identified heresy as 'the law of the innermost form' of the essay. I applaud that characterization. The essay isn't obedient to the kind of orthodoxies that have become so deeply entrenched in the educational system, which means that essays (as opposed to articles) have become persona non grata in the world of academe. This is a non-centrist, non-conforming genre and the price paid for going its own way is a certain isolation and lack of 'official' standing. As Susan Sontag says, 'The culture administered by the universities has always regarded the essay with suspicion.' Understandably, academics are wary of a mode of writing that's independent, accessible to non-specialists, liable to digression, dismissive of authority. Sontag suggests that 'The good health of essay writing depends on writers continuing to address eccentric subjects.' Whereas eccentricity may once have been welcomed (or at least tolerated) in universities, increasingly it's been replaced by the conformity of team-players who are obedient to the institution's targets and mission statements.

According to Robert Atwan, who has done so much to promote interest in the form, not least through his editorship of the influential annual series *The Best American Essays*, the essay in the 21st century 'stays alive because it dares to be unique and because it strenuously resists the encroachments of standardization, whether social, cultural or academic.' Such resistance to prevailing norms has meant a certain degree of marginalization. As Rebecca Solnit puts it, the essay is widely dismissed as:

> A literary birdcage capable of containing only small chirping subjects,
> as distinct from the lion's den of the novel and the open range of the poem.

Solnit's writing constitutes a potent argument against such a view. She's a brilliant essayist; her nonfiction work takes readers into territory every bit as exciting as that explored by poets and novelists. Yet despite writers of Solnit's calibre, the essay tends to be viewed in the negative terms of her characterization. Whether the quality of work being done in the genre today will change this remains to be seen. Perhaps publications like *Imagined Spaces* will help redeem the essay from the misperceptions that dog it.

Afterword/Non-Conclusion

Since I was a boy, I've been aware of dogs in my life. Not real dogs, but companions in a medium. I had no idea about this at the time of course, but looking back, I can see how practising through a medium offered up little disruptions, asked questions and facilitated answers which in turn led to more questions, and so led to cognitive repositioning. It's a process which has never ended, for me as both maker and receiver. Similar to any dog-handler, it has required the development of skills along the way and a constant checking of the practices and breeds of other dog-handlers.

What is your dog? You will be able to identify several, I'm sure.

Hospitalfield, through hosting an exploration of the essay and as the place which had been so formatively important to me, has revealed fresh value in two long-standing companion dogs: drawing and essaying. Crudely, each has served a role for me, as maker and receiver, by crystalising value as individual forms and also as part of a wider culture.

Art and culture seem sometimes to teeter on the brink. Their role of conveying the new is now almost an end in itself, a craft of, oxymoronically, maintaining a standard of disruption. Value becomes an insider's pursuit in which new heresies seem to be extruded directly from old heresies and lie between each other rather than as those 'in-between' messages for artist and viewer. Cognitive disruption—so vital in galvanising movement from ignoring to engaging—feels more often manufactured for closed or preconceived ends. Disruption has become a byword for economic renewal, something old and energy-inefficient must be smashed and replaced by the energised new. Disruption becomes the goal—the value—because it leads to material benefits.

Drawing and essaying seem to resist this because for both, disruptions—cognitive disruptions—are the means not the end. It's tempting now to look at the thought process above—and in this year of correspondence—to try to pull threads together and identify the nature of the common DNA between drawing and essays. The mistake would be to look at the content produced by each media and then to contrast and compare. The beauty of both forms, and their similarities, lie in the degree to which they lightly lead us, like curious dogs, close to the ground, as makers and receivers, away from habit. The executive centre is shed and something more universal, something inherited in our DNA rather than derived from our preconceptions, is engaged.

A common quality is in their likenesses to tracing paper—visible from both sides—a medium between inner and external lives: our consciousness and the unpredicted. Both mediums, in their simplicity of means, facilitate an uncluttered, simultaneous and symbiotic process of identifying and recording cognitive disruptions. They each are a dog, singular—not a complicated pack of ideas like a painting or a novel—and the clarity of their responsiveness, a key part of the value they ferry, lies in this simplicity. Walk on a short lead with a drawing or an essay and you have very little to shed (such little luggage) that you are there, unencumbered, in-the-moment, in no time.

We started the chapter with Paul Klee's 'I take a line out for a walk.' It seems appropriate to draw things to a close with another of his comments. This one likewise applies as much to essays as to art. Klee says that 'art does not reproduce the visible; it *makes* visible.' The lines of an essay or a drawing don't simply close-shadow their subjects' visible contours with slavish obedience to their shape and size and colour so that replica models can be produced. Replication isn't the point. The essayist or the artist isn't simply trying to lay down their lines such that they create a kind of visual simulacrum, a doppelganger laid out on the page. There may be an element of plain representational writing/drawing—and the skill needed to do this well shouldn't be underestimated—but that is never the main concern. Making things visible isn't just a matter of reproducing the visual world. It has more to do with waking us up to the nature of the moments we experience and offering a means of sharing our insight into them with others.

Ariel Levy points out that 'Whatever its narrative style, an essay must have an idea at its beating heart.' That means that essays can't simply be written to order because 'the problem with ideas is that you can't decide to have them.' Levy is surely right that certain sorts of nonfiction 'can be made to happen' but the essays/art that we're engaged with don't belong to this kind of formulaic production. It's not just a question of focusing on something and recording its lineaments in the manner of an eye-witness report. It's more a case of recording the collision between a subject, whatever it might be, and the essayist/artist, chronicling how a particular individual consciousness reads particular pieces of the world's shrapnel that have made a special impact on the web of their interest.

The spaces we've imagined here for essays and drawing may not fit the way in which other writers and artists think of them. The territory we see them occupying is certainly very different from that in which they're contained (constrained) in most formal academic settings. The viewpoints we've explored are not intended as prompts for some kind of normative recipe laying down what every essay or drawing 'ought' to do. We've simply tried to identify what it is about these modes of expression that appeals to us and makes us want to continue working with them.

For the purposes of a chapter we need to bring our lines of inquiry to a close. But rather than ending with a full stop, with all its connotations of conclusion and closure, an ellipsis seems more in tune with the nature of our musings, or perhaps an ellipsis followed by a question mark. This emphasizes the openness of both genres to discoveries and surprises, and the fact that as line-drawers/writers we don't know where our lines will take us. Wherever they lead, we believe that in their explorations of the everyday things around us drawing and essaying can create an imaginative depth to counter the superficialities we so easily get used to. In their estranging of the familiar by the close looking they both foster, drawing and essaying highlight the otherness that's implicit in experience but often obscured by the conformities foisted on us by custom, convenience, and commerce. We like to think that essays and drawing have enormous freeing potential; that they can extend/enhance our sensory/cognitive range. However this might be, a dotted line rather than a solid one, and a question mark rather than a full stop seem more in keeping with the continuing nature of the journey. Ideally, of course, the dots would not be arranged in a predictable serial sequence. One of the hallmarks of the essay is that it rarely follows a straightforwardly linear route. But given the limits of typography it must be left to the reader's imagination to creatively disrupt the neatness of our terminal ellipsis. Can you think of a more appropriate ending…?

On Being Hit on the Head by a Poem

Gabriel Josipovici

With poetry and music as with love, every adolescent thinks he has experienced the real thing until the real thing surprises him. For my fourteenth birthday a much older friend had given me a volume of Shelley's poetry and as I read it I said to myself: 'This is poetry! How I love it!' And then, two years later, I came across Michael Roberts' *Faber Book of Modern Poetry* and found myself reading *The Waste Land*; the hairs on the back of my neck stood on end and I knew that something truly important was happening to me. This wasn't beautiful 'poetry'. It was something else. But what?

I didn't know then and I don't know now. I only knew that it was important and wonderful and I wanted more of it. I had no idea what Eliot's poem was about—and yet in a way I did, only I knew it with my body and not with my mind. And that is still how it seems to be whenever I re-read that poem, or any of the poems and novels that do that to me.

In the interest of 'relevance' school syllabuses are reformed by well-meaning educationists and poems like *The Waste Land* are taught in class. This inevitably means that students are taught what the poem is 'about'. So the first thing I had to do as a University teacher if I was teaching Eliot was to tell students to forget what they had been taught at school and try to return to the moment when they first encountered the poem. I am not there to slay the dragon difficulty, I told them, only to help you see that your sense of confusion on encountering this poem may be part of what it is about.

As a student at Oxford I was exhilarated to find an academic book that recognised and dared articulate what I instinctively felt. That book was Hugh Kenner's *T.S. Eliot: The Invisible Poet* (when Eliot was asked what he thought of the book he replied, I like the title.) Do not simply read the title of a poem of Eliot's, such as 'The Love Song of J. Alfred Prufrock,' and pass on, Kenner said, but ask yourself what that strange title is *doing to you* as you read it. Do not simply cast your eye over the epigraph to 'Sweeney Among the Nightingales'. See it is in a strange language with a strange alphabet (Greek in this instance); perhaps (if you are a diligent pupil) search for a translation and then pass onto the poem proper, but ask yourself why Eliot would have put this obstacle in your way at the start. (The less diligent will fish the word 'elitist' out of their word-hoard, but this does not solve anything, merely pushes the problem away.)

Eliot has chosen his epigraph with care. 'Alas, I am struck down, a deep and deadly blow!' is what the Greek says, and it is the cry of Agamemnon in Aeschylus's *Agamemnon* as Klytemnestra strikes him down in his bath, out of sight of the audience. Learning this we have to ask what relation it bears to the poem that follows. Are we meant to think that Sweeney meets a similar fate in the seedy bar which is the setting of the poem? The last two stanzas give us hints but no more:

> The host with someone indistinct
> Converses at the door apart,
> The nightingales are singing near
> The convent of the Sacred Heart

> And sang within the bloody wood
> When Agamemnon cried aloud,
> And let their liquid siftings fall
> To stain the stiff dishonoured shroud.

Are we meant to feel that history is endless repetition? Or that while the Greek tragedy drives towards its remorseless climax, in the modern world there is no place for tragedy, nothing seems to begin properly or to end definitively, all is half-light, glimpses and hints, no more, and there is therefore no place for a cry like that of Agamemnon, for we may be struck by multiple blows without even being aware that that is the case. In Eliot's poem something terrible or nothing at all may be about to happen. All the poem tells us is that in the nearby convent garden the birds sing as they have always sung and defecate as they have always defecated. For them nothing changes.

The poem would be nothing without its language. *Nightingales* was a Victorian name for prostitutes, so the implication is that Sweeney is in a low dive with a bunch of thugs and prostitutes. But, again, too quick a substitution of the metaphorical for the lyrical distorts the *effect* on us of those last two stanzas. We may start with that meaning as we take in

> The host with someone indistinct
> Converses at the door apart

but the last six lines take us in a very different direction: the Convent of the Sacred Heart, a bloody wood, Agamemnon's heartfelt cry. And what of the last two lines,

> And let their liquid siftings fall
> To stain the stiff dishonoured shroud?

Is it the stains of the birds' droppings that dishonour the shroud, or the fact that it is the shroud of a great general murdered in his bath by his wife? Or is it both, the birds merely adding insult to injury? And while the birds' droppings stain the shroud and dishonour it, they are also the manure from which new life may spring. What the words say and what they (and the measured beat of the line, invoking a funeral procession) *do to us* remains in ever fruitful tension. And, finally, think how different, how much weaker and less resonant the poem would be if Eliot had not found just those words 'liquid siftings' and 'stiff dishonoured shroud', and if the quatrain form, used with such extraordinary resourcefulness (think of the predictable quatrains of his Georgian contemporaries, including Housman), so that what had been weird and grotesque at the start ('laugh' and 'giraffe', 'seas' and 'knees') modulates into the funny in the middle ('coffee-cup' and 'draws her stocking up'), to end here with the solemn drumbeat of 'cried aloud' and 'shroud'.

The great works of the past are endlessly rewarding. And that does not just mean the great works you are told about by teachers and books but can, as with Eliot's discovery, recovery, of John Donne, be those you stumble upon by chance and find to be greater, richer, more consistently satisfying than your teachers imagined. But as Proust said in what is probably the greatest essay on reading ever written, 'Journées de lecture', we must not idolise them, must not fetishise them. They lead us to a threshold. The house we have to enter for ourselves.

Politics of Small Places

A conversation between Lorens Holm & Paul Noble

Dear Paul,

I thought I would kick with off with a couple of images to introduce myself. They say something about cities and habitation. I hope this dialogue will be a way to frame your forthcoming exhibition and our seminar on the social and civic ideas of Patrick Geddes.

I took some pictures in Wuhan China. They show what social life is like in the city. A narrow street with 4 to 6 story buildings almost touching across it, no more than two metres wide, perhaps less at the balconies; an outdoor sink. Building services jury-rigged up the corner of a building. Wuhan has a form of urban fabric which is unknown to me in European and American cities. It consists of huge city blocks defined by broad avenues, six or eight lanes across, central meridian, difficult to cross, and almost what we would call a dual carriageway. The blocks are maybe half a kilometre on one side. Big. Within the block is a smaller scale world of streets and housing, with shops and hustle and bustle. That's where this street is. I've turned off the big boulevard, and entered this tight labyrinth of family living rooms and shops spilling into the street. It is not always clear which was built first, but I assume that the boulevards were imposed later on this dense fabric. It occurred to me that maybe this is similar to the big-grid-small-grid morphology—but not the density—of UK new towns like Milton Keynes or Livingston (which were built at the same time).

Anyway, this is not meant to be a lecture on Wuhan, I simply wanted to give you an insight into where I have been recently, which was so amazingly different from any form of settlement that I have known or experienced. About twenty years ago, the architect Rem Koolhaas began talking about how different the size, scale, and density of Asia cities were from our safely proportioned mature Western cities, with their formation alongside the development of industry and labour relations—what

Lorens Holm, *View of residential street in working class neighbourhood of Wuhan*, 2018.

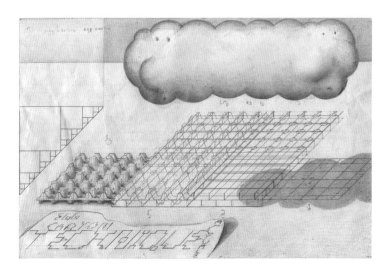

Paul Noble, *Egg Carton Technique Actuale*, 2003.

Patrick Geddes called the 'evolution', not the development, of cities. Forty years ago, Koolhaas coined the term 'the culture of congestion' in his book *Delirious New York* to celebrate the way the Manhattan grid allowed so many things to happen side by side. He reckoned that congestion was one of the key social conditions of cities but had no idea at the time how much more congested Asian cities would be.

I think the Chinese may have a higher tolerance for proximities than Westerners, where everything must be neatly separated by walls and regulatory barriers. Families living in their shops, domestic life blending into commercial life. I think this is going to be one of my themes at the seminar: proximity. You must have something to say about that in your work, which seems to focus, among other things, on the anality of small town life, the anality of 'eggheads' and 'eggfaces' and 'eggcrates' and eggy Nobson Newtowners.

All the best,
Lorens

***

Dear Lorens,

Thanks for the report on Wuhan. Possibly the occupants refused to live as neatly as the planners planned!

This reminds me of a situation in East London a million years ago. I was living in Limehouse. Work was just beginning on Canary Wharf. Yuppies drove Golf GTI's. New glassy apartments were being constructed for new glassy workers. Infrastructure plans included construction of the Limehouse Link. Tunneling work caused unforeseen vibrations weakening the foundations of existing council blocks which then necessitated the speedy decanting of their occupants. The only available residences were the newly built glassy apartments with their concierges, central communal garden and piazzas, running water over *zen* stones and giant bamboo. The unwashed were rapidly moved in with all their clutter which was for all to see as the new apartments had floor to ceiling glass walls, and no one had curtains that big. The views in the piazza showed not the crisp contemplation of some Mies van der Rohe-ish inside/outside thing but the comfort of slowly decomposing stacks of old soft furnishings and carpets. A bit like a worm farm or an unintentional dirty protest.

Great photos, I should have said that first!

Two more things regarding your descriptions of compacted living (small spaces). I was in San Francisco and walked past the head office of LinkedIn. Maybe you know this but the ground floor entrance via a massive glass wall takes you into a vast almost empty space, housing, at the time of my visit, two insanely large Frank Stella pieces. The presentation of such vastness and emptiness confused me until I remembered that San Francisco has insanely high rents and that what LinkedIn was presenting was a new Mecca. At the other end of the spectrum I was wondering what the smallest space might be—I think it's a name.

Very best,
Paul

***

Dear Paul,

Thanks for the quick reply. This is, I am afraid, a lengthy one.

The image of the soggy Limehouse underclass in the Miesian worm farm is extraordinary. I was not aware of that, and would like to know more—like how long they stayed and if they liked it. Wonderful if there were pictures too. A glass tower slowly filling up with nappies, sagging sofas, and those people who populate the *Modern Toss* cartoons. Slipping sideways here, I enjoyed the kerfuffle a few years ago between Tate Modern and the neighbouring glass-towered residents about privacy. The residents live in a glass tower next to a major museum, benefiting from its prestige and yet they complain about museum goers looking at them. Anyway, it is hard to joke about towers anymore, especially towers that local councils put their citizens in.

Geddes the activist, was trying to irrigate the slums of Edinburgh but never by replacing them with glass towers. Geddes the activist, who was not exactly the same person as Geddes the sociological thinker of cities, was involved in improving communities in the slums of Edinburgh and, subsequently, of Mumbai. He was not for moving people out and wholesale redevelopment, which almost always leads to gentrification, but for selectively opening out the most congested areas to let more light and air in. He called this approach 'constructive surgery'. If I remember correctly a lot of the backs of the slums of Edinburgh were filled in over the years with sheds of all sorts, and Geddes was involved in clearing them to recreate the small places that make life bearable—drying greens, private courtyards, and the like.

The idea of 'constructive surgery' is interesting in the context of modern *tabula rasa* planning where development begins by clearing a huge area, and then building something all new. Geddes was ideologically dead set against that. He was one of a long line of architectural thinkers (Giovanni Piranesi, Lewis Mumford, Aldo Rossi) that regarded the city as the single greatest artifact of civilization, a repository of knowledge about ourselves: about how we live with each other, about our wellbeing, our social and economic relations. To destroy that wholesale and without remainder was tantamount to the catastrophic loss of world knowledge represented by the legendary destruction of the library at Alexandria.

About the LinkedIn headquarters… I have always had an allergic reaction to LinkedIn. In fact, until about a year ago, I had never been able to read the name properly. I thought it was Linekin, pronounced line-e-kin, like the kin of a line, whatever that is. I pronounced it that way to a friend who said 'uh?' and who then corrected me. Sometimes, a big empty space is a symptom of overreaching yourself. You want more and more and more, but when you get it, you don't know what to do with it. (Solution? A couple of Stellas!) We have a space like that in the University, the huge lobby of one of our buildings. I'll take you if you come up again. I think, it had been designed originally with a grand stair going up to the main lecture theatre on the first floor, but as a cost saving measure—it's known as 'value engineering' in the building industry—the stair was removed and the design of the lobby was not otherwise adjusted to accommodate its absence. They now fill it with art.

I wanted to tell you that I saw your screen, *Nest*, when it arrived at the gallery the other day. I was amazed at the exquisite level of craftsmanship. I simply had no idea that it was so precisely put together (frame, fabric, marquetry, etc.), nor that it was actually embroidered like a tapestry. Really nice work. *Chapeau*, as they say. For the exhibition, this means that there are at least two scales to the work: a room scale where you see the overall image, and a really intimate scale where you get up close and you see the stitching and the beadwork and the different grades of yarn, and the perfectly flush joints of the marquetry. Peeking obliquely under the wrapping at the beadwork reminded me of an abstract landscape (rather like Man Ray's photo of Duchamps' *Large Glass* lying down, *Dust Breeding*, I think it was called).

Paul Noble, *Nest* detail, Cooper Gallery, Politics of Small Places, 2018.

Paul Noble, *Nest* with drawings by Geddes, Cooper Gallery, Politics of Small Places, 2018.

Speaking of landscape, it seemed that Nest was influenced by Chinese landscape painting, the way depth of field goes vertically up the screen. So if you are putting this work forward as part of an 'exploration' of Geddes, then there are at least two strands here, landscape (China) and Geddes (the inhabitation of small places).

I think I better stop here, Paul, but I was thinking … at some point, certainly before we enjoy this conversation too much, maybe we should impose some limits on it, like maybe word limits on our entries, and maybe agree some aims. Something to aim for … in this ethery email space that is so denatured from the heather space of the Scottish landscape. I'll think on that.

All the best,
Lorens

***

Dear Lorens,

I am back on a train, caffeinated and ready to go.

No, sadly, the yuppie slums were never documented and neither was much else I was involved in at that time. I (and my friends) were either a shy bunch or we never thought to step back and take a picture. This would be anathema today where it seems that life is justified only if it results in a photo opportunity.

Coincidentally, I was in the Tate Modern cafe with the penthouse views earlier this week. I'm not sure what the complaints are about. 'People in glass houses' as they say. The view goes both ways. Two days ago I waved at a man on a boat and he waved back! People in glass houses also makes me think of Ruth Benedict's Pueblo Americans who punished people curious enough to look through other's windows.

My Italian friends say Lin-Ka-Din, possibly a relative of Gunga! My Italian friends also say Al-Burr-Owney for AllBarOne. Having said all of this about my 'Italian friends' I would hate to hear what they would say about my pronunciation.

You are very right about the Chinese screen. There is too much to say about this here. Your description of Geddes is very interesting. Was he an Anarchist?

I'm glad he wasn't a Utopian. Is this right? Quite often Utopic is a metaphor for Megalomaniac. I once heard a fascinating presentation about le Corbusier's plans for Algeria. Do you know about these? The best of intentions but so very wrong on almost everything and every level.

Very best,
Paul

* * *

Dear Paul,

About Geddes' politics—to my knowledge—he was not a Utopian, although his politics is not clear, or at least he was not clearly aligned with any single political grouping. He was well read and references Marx in his most important text, *Cities in Evolution*, and was critical of capitalist development—not from a particularly ideological position, but simply from the practical point of view of what it was doing to communities, even in the early years of the 20th Century. I think it is important to remember that he was an activist and drew on ideas strategically, not necessarily consistently.

I want to go out on a limb here, if I may, and say a few things directly about your work. First of all, I had a question: what pencil lead do you use, or what range of pencils? I really like that freehand sketch that features in the videos of *Nobson Newtown*, it's almost like a key drawing or locator drawing, and I wonder how big it is.

Anyway, I did not realise how orificial, and how anal your work was. In fact, until I saw the videos, I did not make the connection between 'Nobson' and 'nob', and hence the reference to male genitals. The son of a prick. The new town of the son of a prick (I would like to see what sort of a den Nobson Oldtown is). Like 'bell end', a phrase which I just heard for the first time recently in an article about Scottish rock climbing and mountaineering—someone calling someone 'a bit of a bell end'. I mention this because your work and its fascination with the orificial reminds me of the work of one of the most extraordinary architects, the French Enlightenment architect Jean-Jacques LeQueu (1757-1826). LeQueu built very little but he published these incredible volumes of portmanteau buildings and careful architectural drawings of faces and genitals. Detailed hardline construction drawings of vaginas. Also he keeps cropping up in drawings of his own buildings in drag, wearing phallus necklaces. The work is exquisite but not beautiful. Too orificial and too anal to be beautiful. One of the ways

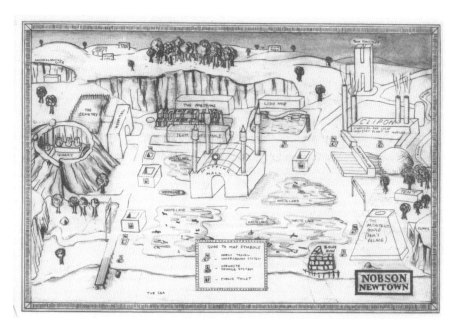

Paul Noble, *Nobson Newtown key map*, 1995.

Paul Noble, *Egg* with drawings by Geddes, Cooper Gallery, Politics of Small Places, 2018.

that my anality expresses itself is that I never feel I have completed something unless I can either staple the pages together or put the dates in. In science, the anal manifests as the forensic, and we pretend it isn't anal because it is objective and has a purpose. I guess the big question is what sort of community is *Nobson Newtown*, and what sort of vision of the world it represents.

I hope these comments are not too intrusive. To my mind, your *Nobson Newtown* and Geddes' so-called 'thinking machines' (volume 2 of *The City is a Thinking Machine*) endeavour to look at or address collective life, each in its own way. Your work seems to catalogue collective life. Geddes categorises it: the catalogical and the categorical.

All the best for now,
Lorens

***

Dear Lorens,

Names are amazing. There is a great essay by Neil Macgregor about The Master of St Bartholomew, a truly spectacular painter, there are a few of his paintings at the National Gallery. Because of his namelessness, an accident of the Reformation, he is much less regarded than Van Weyden or Altdorfer or almost anyone with a name. The curse of anonymity! What's this to do with… ? Is it something to do with cultural Darwinism? Not having a name is like not having kids, not furthering the tribe, wasting the seed.

The etymology of *Nobson Newtown*. It was very accidental, hastily conceived, took on meanings, lost meanings, became sounds. The 'project' (*Nobson Newtown*) began as a text for which I built a font using the software programme, Fontographer 4.1. The programme asked me to name my font. I was only allowed six characters and quickly tapped in NOBSON. This was meant to express my name, reduced, (NOB for Noble) as a place, NOBSON. I am Nobson. The place that is me. A very complicated tombstone perhaps. *Nobson Newtown*. NEWTOWN because I found myself anew in this new description.

But you are right. NOBSON says more. Are we not all sons (and daughters) of the NOB, an essential truth. We are animals first, humans second. But we are human animal deniers. We have problems with waste because we are animals when we shit.

LeQueu is great. I was given a tome dedicated to him by a fan who said 'you must know LeQueu'! The book, I think, makes the wild claim that the name AND complete works of LeQueu are in fact the work of Marcel Duchamp who fabricated and then placed said works into the National Library… A fantastic conceit.

I look forward to reading your work on Geddes. He does sound to me like a natural anarchist.

Very best, Paul

* * *

Dear Paul,

You say in one of your videos 'I don't think in words, I think out of words.' That's fantastic.

To me, that is either: I live outside of the world that is formed and shaped by words. I live in a non-linguistic world, perhaps a guttural, gestural world, like the world that a weight lifter must live in at the moment when they are yanking their personal best off the gym floor. Or: I make thoughts out of words, the way we make the walls of Venice out of stones. The words are building blocks and thoughts become concretised. The thoughts may or may not be meaningful, they may or may not be inhabited by a meaning the way a ghost haunts a house—that's Hegel's haunted house theory of meaning—but they are concrete.

Alternatively, my words escape me. They leap outside the boundaries that we normally set for words, like the proverbial herding of cats: I always think I am saying this and instead I am saying that. This email exchange will be like a line of footprints we leave as we walk and talk ourselves across this dusty earth.

And does having to undertake a shared project in an email exchange bind us more closely together than the conversation? Language is also a form of construction that binds us together, only we tend not to recognise it as such because we live in a linguistic environment, it is our air, it is all around us, as opposed to a jointly crafted object that we place before our eyes and hands.

Our speech disappears like labour. It is gone without remainder as soon as it does its job. Writing unlike speech, preserves a trace, but, as an artefact it is pretty slim, pretty degree zero. So we have an opportunity; do we make something more of this conversation than writing or do we leave it as writing. Of course speech and writing put ideas into the world which are every much as constructional and artefactual as a building, an ecology perhaps that preserves non-corporeal beings like ideas as well as living beings. People congregate around ideas as much as they congregate around buildings and camp fires. Although speech disappears without a trace, the ideas born of speech do not.

All the best,
Lorens

***

Dear Lorens,

I know that I didn't respond to your idea of towns, I was going to sidestep that and present an idea of 'place', less about a building but more to do with belonging through narrative projection. I'm back on my phone, this is my excuse for incomplete sentences (and thoughts)…

You are away and at last I am writing to you via a keyboard so perhaps I can catch up, fill in some gaps…

I had some more to say about the embroidered screen. It was conceived first as a companion to *Egg Face*, the other work in the show at The Cooper Gallery. *Egg Face* presents a face with a nose that is an egg that repeatedly births itself. It is a godly face that perhaps shouldn't be looked at, an Old Testament apparition, or a Medusa, a thing that shouldn't be seen.

Like things that shouldn't be seen I approached this image in reverse. The 'face' was made by filming a black model in a black room. The model was filmed from behind crouched over her knees, elbows tucked in. I had a black silicone egg made. The model held the black egg in her anus and a camera person filmed her releasing the egg. It was shot in black and white on 16mm film using a high speed camera. The footage was reversed from black to white and thus, miraculously, a face was revealed. The role of the screen was to hide the 'modesty' of the face, a mis-spelt rood screen and to protect the viewers eyes from seeing the unseeable.

Paul Noble, *Egg, One Wind Chime, and Negative Positive*, Museum Boijmans, 2014.

Paul Noble, *Egg Face and Black Egg*, Cooper Gallery, Politics of Small Places, 2018.

Screens have a dual function. They have a function to break space, prevent seeing beyond, while at the same time offering a metaphysical view. You know this. I'm just spelling out *NEST*'s relationship to *Egg Face*. The imagery of *NEST* is of an abject landscape with an egg, and an egg's home depleted of its mythic power, the egg carton, the SMALL PLACE provided for … How to say this? When we can't conceive of another species' special requirements we can treat them like shit (sorry I was struggling to find a polite way round this). Chickens and other food stuff animals are often only granted better living conditions because, it is said, stressed animals make bad meat that might negatively affect the meat consumer.

Paul

***

Hi Lorens,

Back on the train!

The traveling I've been doing is to visit my Dad who has been very ill for sometime and is now in a hospice.

I'm letting a lot of things slip at the moment and I can't really concentrate on what is supposed to be our conversation for the purposes of the exhibition. The only small place I can imagine is the one at the end of Gerrit Achterberg's poem 'Ballad of a Gasfitter', especially apt as my Dad was a Heating and Ventilating engineer and the family car was full of plumber's tools because everyone we visited always had a leaky pipe to repair. All this is making me sensitive to loss, why I was sad to see the THE go from the title. It is the Small Places that need the most attention, likewise the small words. I know this doesn't really matter. Would I die to save this THE? No.

Apologies and best wishes
Paul

***

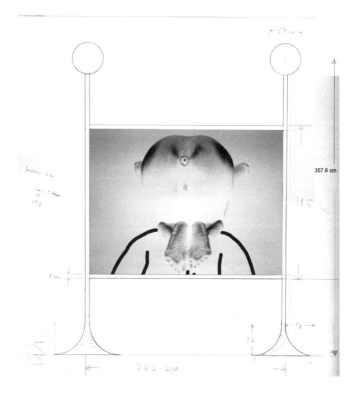

Paul Noble, *Egg Face*, installation drawing, 2013.

Paul Noble, *Nest*, Museum Boijmans, 2014.

61

Dear Paul

I am so so sorry to hear about your Dad the gas fitter. I don't know what to add except bits and pieces of my own experience, none of which are consolatory. It sounds from what you say (hospice) that this may be the end of the road. My own father died without an end. He died quite suddenly in 1987, 20 September 1987, at St. Luke's Hospital in New York City. The Upper West Side (Manhattan) is home sweet home for me. No small places there. Or rather, plenty of small places but all of them connected to Bigness. Dad had been admitted the day before because he lost consciousness. It turns out that he had an aneurism. As a kid, I remember looking at his face. He was a slight man with a narrow face with a broad forehead looming out of the shadows. Kind of triangular. I remember that the veins stood out on his forehead. I don't know if that is at all related to his fate.

After my dad died, I felt that my life had completely fallen into pieces and there was nothing to fix them into any order anymore. The pieces were the same pieces they had always been: teaching, girlfriend, architecture, art projects, rock climbing and mountaineering, but there was no order to give them sense and significance. When my mother died I felt terrible loss. When my father died I felt terrible chaos. My relation with my father had always been strained. He was very domineering of me, and I suppose I spent a lot of my life trying to be emancipated from him, and our relation was not always happy. I regret it now with all my heart and I find that—although it is a long time ago now and many things about him are distant memories and not vivid complex ones, more like a single faded image than a narrative—I return to those images all the time.

Enough about me, stick in there. Hang in there. Be a good son. Be a good brother. Be a good artist. Patrick Geddes' son was killed in the first world war and his wife died at about the same time (I think she and Patrick G were in Mumbai at the time). Not sure who died first but his son was killed before news of his mom's death reached him at the front, and she died before news from the front reached the Geddes family. So Patrick G was left to deal with two deaths alone. Neither mother or son were able to die knowing the fate of the other, which to me is the real tragedy in this story. It is about knowledge and the loss or lack of it. In this world, the most important things in the world are knowledge. And they died deprived of what is probably the most important knowledge of all.

All the best,
Lorens

***

Dear Paul

I am conscious of your family commitments and do not want to intrude upon them but I thought I would inch things forward from my side of things, I think of it as treading water…

In the *Charting of Life* diagram Geddes is trying to define how societies develop and how that development fits with, or is adequate to the develop of settlements from peasant communities to mature industrial cities like London, Paris, Berlin, Barcelona, New York, Chicago. Contemporary Chinese cities probably do not fit this pattern of long-gestation development. If Geddes' *Valley Section* diagram is geographical— aligning vocations and hence social groups with typologies of landscape—this diagram is temporal. It seems that he wants to say that the material forms of settlement are synonymous with or equal to the social forms which inhabit them.

Social forms—relations, laws, taboos, inhibitions, family entanglements, friendships, dreams, aspirations—these all have the tangibility of words not things. Words are tangible but it is a different kind of tangibility than the tangibility of things. I wonder if your work demonstrates this. You make an alphabet out of buildings. The closer words and buildings get to each other, the more the word is obscured. The more tangible the word becomes, the more difficult it is to read.

One of the things that is interesting about Geddes' *Notation of Life* is that there is no stage for the individual. Society comes preformed as a grouping of individuals. We can assume that there are individuals but they are always already grouped, socialised, as it were. Thanks. Me for now,

Lorens

***

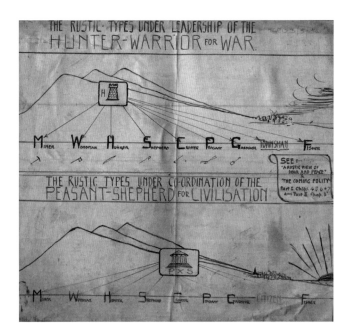

Patrick Geddes, *Valley Section* 'T_GED_3_5_54' University of Strathclyde Archives

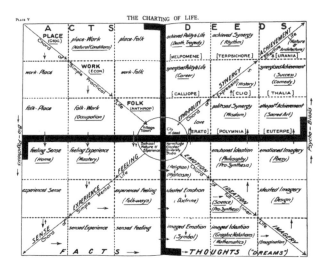

Patrick Geddes, 'Charting of Life' diagram from Patrick Geddes, *Cities in Evolution: an introduction to the town planning movement and to the study of civics* (London: Williams & Norgate, 1968/first published by Williams and Norgate, 1915).

Dear Paul,

This is probably our last note before we meet later this week, Wednesday I think. If I don't push this out now, I may as well hand it to you when I see you.

You wrote something a while back. 'I make drawings that sometimes look like buildings but really the buildings are words pictorialiscd or illuminated in pencil. The words are written in a font I designed called *nobson*. The letter shapes of *nobson* look like buildings. I write a word in *nobson* and it becomes a place. I write *TENT* and it is a tent.'

'I write *TENT* and it is a tent.'

There is something profound in that thought, it resonates, but it also eludes me. So I will simply cast a few lines of thought. It goes to the existential heart of what language does. Writing is associated with absence, that to which the word refers is never present to the word, but in *Nobson Newton* the word and the thing are the same because the word is made concrete. In the beginning was the word. It is an extreme form of nominalism, in which the word generates the world, it does not simply summon select bits of it for our contemplation.

'I write *TENT* and it is a tent.'

It collapses the distance and the delay between writing and the world. Normally we write *TENT* because we don't have one. Here you write *TENT* and it is a tent. Jacques Derrida argues that there is always a delay between the word and its meaning, the presence of meaning is always deferred, meaning is always present as an absence, we never actually arrive at meaning with our words, or with anything for that matter.

If *nobson* is a font, then *Nobson Newtown* is a text disguised as a town, which makes the text almost unintelligible, and inhabitation tenuous. We need to distinguish concrete text from inscription, even inscription on concrete. At *Nobson Newtown* meaning seems to be almost erased by a concrete form of writing, which seems to me to be a form of death. Not meaning inscribed on stone as text, but meaning made stone, like the human subject (passion, ideas, drive) made into a body (meat, spittle). As if meaning were what was living about the material world.

In the context of *Politics…*, I want to put your writing next to one of Geddes' quotes. *In Cities in Evolution*, Geddes writes, 'Town plans are thus no mere diagrams, they are a

Paul Noble, *Nobson Newtown* font, 1995.

Patrick Geddes, *Five drawings*, Cooper Gallery, Politics of Small Places, 2018.

system of hieroglyphics in which man has written the history of civilisation, and the more tangled their apparent confusion, the more we may be rewarded in deciphering it.'

For Geddes, the city was the single greatest artefact of civilisation. If we could read our city plans, we would find written in them the whole history of civilisation. It was why Geddes raged against large scale urban renew, what became known as modernist *tabula rasa* planning.

I also think that Geddes' quote suggests something creepy, the Freudian uncanny, the strangely familiar: something mysterious is encountered—the hieroglyph—out of which a meaning may emerge, a meaning which is a truth about ourselves and our civilisation. (Stories about mummies, the body preserved, and not alive but animated, seem to tap into the creepiness of hieroglyphs.)

In my own work on cities, we read city plans by performing acts of montage and acts of iterative drawing and modelling upon them. Cities, and city plans in particular, can be read, and we generate new cities and new visions of the social life of cities by reading old ones. We read cities closely—I borrow the concept of close reading from philosophy, you mention deep listening—and reading is generative.

Your *TENT* seems to go towards the end of reading and hence the end of life (reading generalised is almost synonymous with life). I realise that this is cryptic as a hieroglyph. I guess I am wondering out loud if meaning is a living thing that animates a text, and without it a text turns to stone. When we write in *nobson*, meaning is cast in concrete and dies. Either that or if meaning persists, it erupts like something ineffable, destroying the text, like the clarion call of the apocalypse. The world and all its past living beings are resurrected to meet their end. Everything becomes present. By contrast, Geddes' city seems to be the beginning of reading, reading or interpreting the city as a journey to an enlightenment that may be always already deferred. It is the difference between revelation and interpretation. There is an ambiguity in Geddes. Is he talking about the city plan or the city itself? We don't know, but the intention is the same because he seems to regard the city as a form of writing that can be read, an inscription in stone, tarmac, walls, windows, doorways, whatever, as if they were hieroglyphs.

I better stop before I scatter things further.
All the best, and I look forward to meeting at last,

Lorens

***

Dear Lorens

Funnily (?) I am reading an excellent book of Beckett criticism called *Samuel Beckett's Dying Words*—the end of everything—the end of words—cliché—words dead and almost dead, and sadly (?) words fail most at death when we happily embrace the vagueness of cliché.

There is a phrase in George Herbert's 'The Flower' where he writes, 'Dead to the world'—a fantastic two-way thing—is it the living world or merely the waking world? Dead to the world alive to dreams! Before words were pictures, diagrams, hieroglyphs, only 'uncanny' because not quite knowable, living with doubt, wild animals (sorry, Mum and I watched a cheesy nature documentary about tigers in the wild last night). Last minute notes to claim the smallest and biggest space for my work, the imaginative…

Very best

Paul

***

Dear Paul,

Still savouring last Thursday.

How do two people encounter each other and how does the exploratory nature of that encounter add layers of mythology to the world?

I have attached the transcripts of our conversation. I would like them to be published… They need to be edited a bit, and there is a question of whether we include images… But I hope that editing might be minimal.

I will be at a meeting in Brighton on Friday, and could see you on Friday night to discuss if that helps.

Lorens

***

Hi Lorens,

Great, let's meet Friday. Looking forward to it.

Best
Paul

* * *

A coda…

How to look back and find a way forward. How to bring this conversation to an end in a way that propels it into something else, something more.

One of the realisations that has marked my maturation is that a life does not conclude. We work like the dickens as if we were going somewhere, and then we fade away. We peter out. I used to think that public life concluded. That the architects and authors whose work I followed would end their public lives with a coda that made it all make sense. Instead, one day you notice that they have stopped publishing and wonder what they have got up to. The coda would be what validated the work as work, and its reception in the world as reception, in the way that we all want our parents to recognise us as who we want to be as we launch into the world. It would be the self-recognition that would say to the world, my work is all here, the offer and the offer accepted. If you go now to the website of the architecture practice Scott Brown & Venturi, you will see that in the past few years, that ground-breaking pop-culture practice who used irony so masterfully to resist the financial market world has simply faded silently into a series of A4 PDF project tear sheets. You google them and they are not there. And the practice has moved on, a different one, without them. The world did not stage a retirement bash or funeral bash. That recognition has to wait for the obituary, by which time it is too late.

How to look back and find a way forward. How to bring this conversation to an end in a way that propels it into something else, something more. A conversation does not have a beginning-middle-end, which structure, I have always thought, is the most fictional aspect of fiction. Conversations rarely come to conclusions that validate them. Conversations end by silent agreement, a nod, a gesture, palms down pushing off getting up from the dinner table. I will not speak for Paul Noble here, because we were not able to put our heads together on this ending, with him in London and me in Dundee, and although I feel comfortable speaking on keyboard, I do not feel comfortable speaking on phone. I think we discovered that we really like each other, or at least that we really like conversing with each other, and although we have not been able to find a way—yet—to convert conversation into a project, I think we would enjoy another encounter, an encounter that would give us the chance to share another (bigger? more purposive?) project. The conversation project ended by simply ending. There was a last click on the keyboard and then we met at the opening of his exhibition, *Politics of Small Places*.

Rigth: Paul Noble, *Black Declining Figures*, 2020.

Mind the Gap

Susan Nickalls

Thirty spokes meet in the hub,
though the space between them is the essence of the wheel.
Pots are formed from clay,
though the space inside them is the essence of the pot.
Walls with windows and doors form the house,
though the space within them is the essence of the house.
  Lao-Tzu, 6th century Chinese poet and philosopher

As the train I'm on clatters across the Tay Rail Bridge, I scan the rain-soaked foreshore for my first glimpse of Scotland's new £80 million design museum, V&A Dundee. Peering through the mud-splattered window, I can see the masts of *RSS Discovery*, the Dundee-built ship which took Scott and Shackleton to Antarctica. Next to it, smaller than I had imagined, V&A Dundee is snuggled into the former Earl Grey Docks as if it had always been part of the waterfront skyline. The stratified prow of the building juts into the Firth of Tay like the dramatic high sea cliffs that inspired the building's designer Kengo Kuma.

This unusual location between the land and the sea is what the Japanese architect says first piqued his interest in the competition to design V&A Dundee.

> When I saw the brief, I was so excited because it said you could have the building, or some part of it, in the water. That is very unique. As we started thinking about the project one of my colleagues showed me a picture of the cliffs of north-eastern Scotland—it's as if the earth and water had a long conversation and finally created this stunning shape. But this site was also a challenge because the wind and the flow of water is so strong. There were many high hurdles to solve as we needed a much stronger than normal building. It was a very challenging project but after eight years finally, I am very happy.

On the September day in 2018 when I meet with Kuma in Dundee, the wild and gusty weather appears on cue to illustrate his point. Emerging from the station, I join a crowd of wet, wind-bent people crossing the threshold of the design museum as its doors open to the public for the first time. Everyone I speak to, from the security guards to the locals in for 'a nosey', is captivated by the building. The inverted pyramid-shapes make the spaces inside seem larger than they are and more welcoming, as if the building is stretching out its arms to embrace the public. Kuma calls this area 'a living room for the city'.

> The floor area is not so huge, but people feel it's a big space because of the angles and the way the walls open out, so the total space can be very big. Most conventional box buildings of the 20th century are not human at all. They define themselves by vertical walls and horizontal floors and are not playful. The building looks like a landscape from the outside, and there is also a freer landscape on the inside so it contains much playfulness because of this loose geometry.

A lot of this playfulness is in the tiny details, especially the references to nature which are everywhere. Underfoot, I tread on the inky black Carlow Blue limestone sprinkled with white constellations of ancient fossilized sea creatures and plants. It makes me feel as if I'm stepping on the roof of the night sky itself. This reversal of the usual order of things is a hallmark of many of Kuma's projects. The addition of mussel shells to the concrete gives texture to the white walls around the café, shop and upstairs restaurant. The carefully spaced wooden panels that line the stairs, and part every now and then to give picture-postcard views of the river, echo the horizontal striations of the exterior walls.

Outside, as I skirt the perimeter, these stepped concrete panels are being lashed with rain while water sloshes noisily in the shallow pools in, around and through the middle of the building. This gap, where the two parts of the upturned triangles meet, frame the spectacular views of the Tay. Walking through this is like stepping through a tunnel. It's a nod to the Royal Arch built nearby to mark Queen Victoria and Prince Albert's visit to Dundee in 1844. Another example of how Kuma tightly intertwines the footprints of the past with his modernist present. When he first imagined the building for V&A Dundee, he saw this meeting point between the water and the land as a gateway connecting people to nature.

> In some of my other buildings, for instance in my Hiroshige museum in Japan, there is a simple cut in the centre which draws people to the mountain

like a magnet. For V&A Dundee I wanted to make the building as a land form so my first rough image is that of an organic shape like a sea-cliff with a hole in the centre. The building acts as a connector between the river and the city; creating a frame through which to see the river from the city and the city from the river. We tried to produce a design that reflects the two main axes of the city—Union Street and Discovery Point—and then connects them in a spiraling motion. The form is inherently dynamic as it grows from the street up.

Although Kuma says that his building is 'hard on the outside, soft on the inside', I'm fascinated to find that up close the angular sides of the building, especially its underbelly, are gently curved. Kuma has created this effect by varying the length, width and spaces between the 2,500 rough pre-cast concrete panels. And it is these spaces, gaps or apertures that lie at the heart of Kuma's architectural philosophy. Indeed he says that his design for Tokyo's Bato Hiroshige Museum, completed in 2000 to house Japanese wood block prints by the 18th century Ukiyo-ei artist Ando Hiroshige, marked a turning point in his career.

I first discovered the effectiveness of public apertures in the Hiroshige museum. However, they are unlike architecture gaps that are complete in themselves. The public apertures I am thinking of are capable of connecting to the surrounding environment. Once I began to elaborate in other competitions what I had discovered in the Hiroshige museum, I became successful.

So what are these spaces, gaps or apertures? Kuma says that these descriptors are the nearest English word equivalents to describe the Japanese aesthetic concept of 'ma', a space between particles. And in music, it also means the silence between the notes.

In Japanese culture, ma is more important than the particles. I try to be sensitive to the size of the particles and the gap. I'm inspired by music and feel a strong empathy with musicians because I'm interested in the rhythm of particles. I like the word rhythm. In music, rhythm is the most important thing, so if we find a good rhythm, naturally the music is comfortable. It is the same with architecture. Rhythm is the basis of my architectural designs, I try to compose something, to be a musician with the material.

At its most literal translation, ma means negative space or the space between two structural parts. But ma is much more than this. The Japanese and Chinese ideogram for ma, 間, is made up of the signs for 'moon' and 'gate', showing how moonlight can stream through a gap in an entrance. It is the emptiness of these voids or spaces that are full of promise and therefore just as important, if not more so, than the more solid things that frame them. When we speak, a pause for breath can add significance to the surrounding words that are spoken; a silence in music can inform the notes played before and after it and in Japanese calligraphy (Shodo) and other aspects of design and architecture, ma offers a space for things to grow.

This concept of emptiness and fullness dates back to Lao Tzu, the 6th century Chinese poet and philosopher said to be the father of Taoism. It is like Yin and Yang. One can't exist without the other according to François Cheng in his book about the language of Chinese painting, *Empty and Full*. 'Emptiness is not merely a neutral space serving to defuse the shock without changing the nature of the opposition. It is the nodal point where potentiality and becoming interweave, in which deficiency and plentitude, self-sameness and otherness, meet.' Cheng adds that without gaps, or what he calls a 'median emptiness', Yin and Yang would be 'in a relationship of frozen opposition'.

A term Kuma might apply to the work of some of his competitors given that his attitude towards gaps is not shared by most Japanese architects. 'At international competitions, it is often pointed out that the overall silhouette of my scheme has many gaps, even though most Japanese architects abhor them. The larger, organizational design offices in Japan in particular tend to fill in all gaps meticulously. Their schemes are indeed frozen.'

For Kuma, it is in these gaps between the materials, or what he also calls particles, that he says the truth, or essence, of his buildings lie.

> For me, we try to avoid the solid heavy wall as a canvas as this rejects the relationship we try to create between the particles. The wooden panels are not straight, they are a little bit waving and shaking. It is not so easy to create this natural undulation, but the secret is the particles. The particles have a gap which makes this building look more natural. It is the same with impressionist painting. There's always a gap between the particles and people feel that those impressionist paintings look very natural.

It's similar to the difference between analogue sound and digital sound, where the brain fills in the gaps. Seeing these gaps, apertures or gateways through the lens of nature and its connection to human beings is integral to Kuma's designs. When he wrote

Death of Architectural Desire, he referred to public buildings as 'repulsive' and 'useless monuments'. Instead, he blurs the lines between the private and the public, tending to use the characteristics of the latter more as textures in his work. So in V&A Dundee, he chose louvered oak planks to line the interior space, rather than solid walls, to give it the warm intimacy of a private house rather than a public museum. And there are variations in the wood, not just in the gaps between each plank, but in the knots and grains which in turn contrast with the rough texture of the concrete exterior.

Kuma believes that the comfort and security of this living room, or womb-like space, resonates with our deepest most primal feelings as human beings.

> Apertures, gaps and roofs are devices that entice and connect. They invite people in and create shadows. The shadows are important as they make a building more humble. The straight wall without shadows is shiny and rejecting. I think the shadow makes us calm. Maybe it's related to the history of humans. When we were living in the forest, we were living with the shadow of the forest. We had been living with shadows for a long, long time so the gap between the particles is the most comfortable element for architecture. V&A Dundee is not a small building, but if you look at it from the Tay bridge, it is marching into the townscape because of the option of shadows.

There are indeed many shadows cast from the stratified exterior of the building, especially in the surrounding water, both in daylight and at night when V&A Dundee is lit up. And what Kuma calls sun pipes, the many small windows in the roof that allow light into the space, also hark back to early human interaction with nature. They're inspired by the filtered fingers of light reaching through the leaves and branches in the forest. The Japanese word to describe this is 'komorebi' and although Kuma translates this into English as 'dappled', he insists that this word doesn't quite capture the full meaning. For him 'komorebi' is more akin to light being interrupted, rather than light flooding in all at once.

Whether a fragile forest canopy or a more substantial element, the roof or shelter is important to human beings. As in traditional Japanese architecture, Kuma often extends the eaves of his buildings to a lower point than the gables. He did this at the Hiroshige museum, as a way of 'abusing walls' in what he calls 'an epic drama between roofs and walls.' This is part of the way he constantly challenges and deconstructs the traditional elements that make up a building. So the idea of a wall, a floor or a roof is interrogated, rethought and transformed. Take his design for the

Granada Performing Arts Centre. Its honeycomb-shaped outer shell looks like a collection of three-sided rooms or 'folded multiple roofs' as Kuma calls them.

> I am interested in the roof, not as a matter of style, but as a method. Naturally I must at the same time be conscious of the connection between the ground and the roof, and the ground as a roof. I believe the idea of the roof as a method transcends the meaning the Japanese have traditionally invested in roofs and has greater universality. And, as long as we have bodies, human beings will be ruled by gravity. The question of how we relate ourselves to the ground will have to be confronted, no matter what sort of architecture we design. When we consider architecture as shelter, there are no elements more archetypal than the roof and the ground.

Keeping the scale of a building human, no matter how small or large, is also why Kuma prefers to build horizontality rather than vertically. Although an admirer of Le Corbusier, Kuma believes that the Swiss/French architect's 'vertical streets', or high rises, were 'not so alive, not so human' even though he accepts that a certain amount of 'roughness and noise' is necessary for street life. At V&A Dundee the space is vibrant and alive due to a certain amount of natural noise.

Even Kuma's design for the National Stadium for the Tokyo 2021 Olympic Games has a low silhouette, just under 50m in height. Echoing the welcoming aspect of historic Japanese buildings with their long eaves and semi-outdoor space, the three-tiered wooden latticed stadium with rings of trees on the exposed terraces, is also designed to draw people into the building. The Olympic stadium is significant in a number of ways, quite apart from the controversy over Kuma's design replacing the one originally commissioned from Zaha Hadid on grounds of cost. Kuma's daily commute takes him past the site of the new stadium, around a mile from Kenzo Tange's Yoyogi National Gymnasium built for Tokyo's 1964 Summer Olympics. This monument to Japanese modernism is the building that ignited the 10-year-old Kuma's architectural ambitions.

Although he was born in 1954 in Yokohama, his family is from Nagasaki where the Scottish industrialist Thomas Glover lived and worked for some time during the late 18th and early 19th centuries. After graduating from Tokyo University in 1979, Kuma was a visiting researcher at New York's Columbia University between 1985 and 1986 before launching his Spatial Design Studio the following year. This evolved into Kengo Kuma Associates in 1990 where he now has a staff of 150 in his Tokyo and Paris offfices. In 2009, he set up his own research facility, Kuma Lab, an incubator for exploring his architectural ideas such as those around particles or materials.

For Kuma, these elements are there to be challenged, weakened and in some instances made to 'disappear'. A prolific writer on his approach to design, Kuma once declared, 'My ultimate aim is to "erase" architecture, because I believe that a building should become one with its surroundings.' The nearest approximation he came to this was with his 1994 Kiro-San Observatory in Japan. Built largely underground it is practically invisible apart from two slits for the entrances in the hillside and an outdoor viewing platform. But after not winning a number of competitions—for instance the Nam June Paik Museum in Korea (2003) and Warsaw's Museum of the History of Polish Jews (2005)—Kuma came to realise that organisations commissioning new buildings want to make a statement, and that rendering a building all but invisible after much time, effort and money was not what they wanted.

Although his initial desire hasn't changed, Kuma realised it was an impossible goal to make buildings 'disappear'. So he is now more aware of having to balance what people want with his own ideas about architecture. In grappling with these contradictions, Kuma looked to American architect Frank Lloyd Wright and his philosophy of organic architecture. When Wright was asked to design Tokyo's Imperial Hotel (his 1920s building was demolished in 1968) he made the unusual choice of using Oya stone, a weak stone full of defects. It's a type of tuff, formed from the solidified ash of a volcanic eruption, and most often used to build local storehouses in Japan. Furthermore, there were soft brown bits in the stone from ash that hadn't solidified. Kuma saw a beauty in the weakness of the stone, and Wright's 'struggle to confront the overwhelming presence of material' showed him a way forward.

> Materials only show their true nature when you challenge them at the limits of their capabilities. Even if this fight is as foolish and reckless as that of Don Quixote, the resulting scars will remain as a memento. The fight is a serious one because of its audacity. Now I recognize that architecture can also become an icon, when, in the process of trying to erase it from its environment, the architect undertakes the cold task of challenging the overwhelming presence of materials. This is why architecture can become a presence to be remembered.

Wright's architectural designs drew on the techniques used by Japanese Ukiyo-e artists, like Hiroshige, who created three-dimensional space by using multiple layers of images in contrast to the perspective tradition favoured by most western artists. When Kuma first visited Scotland over 30 years ago as a student, he was intrigued to discover that Japanese art and design had also had an impact on the Scottish architect and designer

Charles Rennie Mackintosh. In particular Kuma was impressed with the avant-garde design of Mackintosh's 1904 Hill House in Helensburgh, as well as the Japanese influences on his use of materials.

> I am a big fan of Charles Rennie Mackintosh and when I was a student in the 1970s there was a revival of his work. I was so surprised to see in his book similarities with Japanese design, especially his watercolours. He tries to create the same sort of layering of space which is the most important method used in Japanese painting and wood block prints. It is very impressive. I myself was influenced by Charles Rennie McIntosh. In my architecture, I use particles to create layers and he does something similar with his furniture.

Kuma believes that a common love of nature unites the cultures of Scotland and Japan, but there are many other links between the two countries which Kuma has taken in. In interviews he's said that he believes the early days of economics when Adam Smith was expounding his laissez-faire principals in his 1776 *Wealth of Nations* are similar to the circumstances 20th century architects such as Le Corbusier found themselves in especially in relation to Keynesian economics.

> Today's society premised on capitalism is divided into two camps: a camp that believes a free market is the solution to everything and a camp that believes in regulating the market. Under Keynesian policy, which was premised on investment in public construction, the latter camp had the upper hand. The problem was that in controlling the market, it depended too heavily on the visual effect of new artifacts or objects.

And Kuma's solution for our 21st century heavily built up cities is an appropriate manipulation of the size or elements of the gaps used in buildings. Words like 'gap', 'aperture', 'particle', 'element' and 'material' occur frequently, and often interchangeably, in the language Kuma uses to talk about architecture. But much like his designs themselves, they continually shapeshift, evolving and changing over time. The meaning also changes depending on the nature of the project Kuma and his team are working on. But there is one constant in Kuma's process of conceiving and creating buildings, especially for competitions, and that is the use of the model. While computer design is part and parcel of modern architectural offices, few practices use models to the same extent as Kuma does with his team after the initial design concept.

The next step is for all the teams, not just the competition teams, to prepare the model, that is our method. If I draw a sketch, I cannot go beyond that. This method of design is also creative. We think together and work together to create something new, that is my approach. The models work our imagination, a drawing is not evoking the imagination. Rendering is maybe a good way to persuade a client, but for internal discussions, the physical model is very, very helpful and still the best way to go. We can check the view from every angle, compare the model on the same scale and check the impact on the building's neighbours easily.

Using the model also makes it easier to create and see the gaps. Just as the concepts of empty and full co-exist in the same space, Kuma also sees his architectural gaps as a place where the apparent polar opposites of freedom and ethics approach each other and converge as understanding deepens. 'My stance in every field has been to be skeptical of any logic that does not have gaps. My ideal is an architecture in which truth resides in the gaps.'

Ultimately, visitors to V&A Dundee, Kuma's first public building in the UK, will decide for themselves whether he has succeeded in his desire to create a building which has not only changed the city, but become its centre of gravity and a place for ideas and creativity to grow.

Graham Johnston, *V&A Dundee*, Exterior Study, Compressed charcoal on primed paper, 2020.

Life in the Bardo: Dying, Death and the Imagination

Meaghan Delahunt

I touch the pulse-point at my mother's elbow. The pulse runs fast. The skin there is fragile and purple-black and I marvel at this frantic thrum of blood. This is death running through her, I realise, her heart pumping hard—to keep up, to escape, to outrun—to what?—what is her heart doing, exactly? What is this marathon of body and spirit? In her final days, my mother still tries to push the blankets away. She tries to lift herself up, out of the bed. In *The Mara Crossing*, Ruth Padel observes a similar 'zugenruhe'—an unease or restlessness—in migratory birds prior to a long journey. She sees it 'in the to-and-fro twitchery… in swallows before they go, as their bodies are first preparing and then impelling them to fly.' My mother exhibits this same restlessness. It fires through her veins and elevates her pulse. If a migratory bird is restrained during its normal hours of flight, it flutters and agitates for as long as the journey would last. I see this in my mother. Her eyes are shut and her mouth is set. She is determined. She is readying herself for flight.

Where is she flying to? That is the question. And what is she thinking, what does she imagine at this point? I long to ask, but hold back. Am I more fearful of the question or the answer? At one stage, she opens her eyes and says, 'This is not how I thought it would go.' I think I understand what she means. After nearly two months of struggle, this final phase of dying—how did she think it would go? How do any of us, if we can at all imagine the end of our own story, *think it will go?*

I continue to feel my mother's pulse. I watch the way her fingers occasionally flutter up from the bedsheet, extending to the far reaches of the room to something I can't see. The way her eyelids flutter as if dreaming. When I start work five years later as a writer in a hospice, I recognise these signs in the patients on the ward. I wonder if the 'zugenruhe' of the dying person relates somehow to the time taken by the migratory 'self': the consciousness, soul, energy, light—call it what you will—after death? That the fluttering and unease relate to the time taken to wherever this energy is headed? That this is, indeed, part of the preparation in the space-time before death.

...

When my father was dying over a three-day-period, I stayed close to his hospital bed. In the middle of one particular night, as I meditated, I synchronised my breathing with his. I drew up the blinds in the hospital room and looked down to the empty street, illuminated by an orange street lamp. Suddenly, a scene unspooled below, in sepia, like old photographs come to life. There were young boys in shorts and school caps on heavy bicycles, a Ferris wheel, a horse and cart on a cobbled street... children skipping, playing jacks, playing hopscotch... an old Holden car... a football match.... I was in the slipstream of my father's mind. Somehow I knew this as it was happening. It was all very clear and vivid and we'd travelled back to the time of his childhood together. We were joined in the mind-roam of the dying, a telepathic space where—as in dreams—there is no actual past or future; it is all *the present*... simply the rush and tumble of time. Waves of past and present reared up from the street below. This was something I'd read about but now was experiencing... and then these scenes slowly dissolved and I moved back, away from the window to the hospital bed and placed my hand on his. I'd watched his life-episodes flare up and dissolve, flare up and dissolve. And I stood there, after this experience had played out, trying to imagine the dissolution of my own life and wondering when it came, whether I would have the courage to face it with the equanimity and grace of my parents.

...

In the Buddhist tradition the idea of 'the bardo' is important. A bardo is best defined as a transition state. The idea of impermanence and change is central to this concept and to Buddhism in general. Arguably, each minute of living, each day on earth, is a bardo state. Every breath, as Pema Chodron says, is a small birth and death. Major life events and relationships are bardo states. So too are the shifts of circumstance throughout a life—beginnings and endings, accidents, and lucky breaks. According to Tibetan Buddhist teachings, bardo states continue after death, as consciousness moves to its next incarnation or a different plane of existence altogether. In life, though, we tend to see everything as permanent; our mind clings to the illusion of stability. We also cling to a notion of ourselves that is fixed. We cling on, even as everything changes around us. Even as our clocks and calendars, our external and internal weather tell a different story. Nothing stays fixed, even though we struggle to maintain the illusion of fixity, even as we struggle to stay upright on ever-shifting ground.

* * *

Death always happens to someone else—until one day, it doesn't. I know that death will prise me away from everything which seems to define *me*—all the judgements that comprise my world and my seemingly immutable, singular self. And so I must try to accustom myself better to uncertainty and loss while I'm still alive. To practise living in the bardo. I try to let go. I start small. If I lose a piece of jewellery, say, or if I break a treasured cup. Small is relatively easy, I know. But if we don't start small, how can we accustom ourselves to the big? *Everyone I love: gone. Myself: no longer here.* As Jung said, the second half of life should be in preparation for death. Toni Morrison notes, 'Writers imagine the unthinkable as a way to liberate the imagination.' Just because the idea of our own death seems beyond words, beyond representation, beyond the beyond—the outer reaches of imagined space—means that we never stop trying to find the words and the means to evoke it.

* * *

This year, I tried to practise such letting-go at the end of summer at the end of a holiday in Greece. On Naxos, I watched tourists at sunset up near the Portara, (the remains of a temple to Apollo) the symbol of the island. Mobile phones held aloft, trying to capture and upload simultaneously. The scene felt urgent and slightly hysterical: *I was there.* A man rode past on a moped, almost knocking me down. He jumped off, turned his back to the view, took a picture of himself with the sunset and roared off again before the sun sank into the water. My judging mind judged him, judged everyone. I caught myself doing that and stopped, just in time. I thought, 'I'm separate and slightly better because I'm *experiencing* the sunset (a story I told myself) not furiously uploading to Instagram.' But was I? *I was here. I was once alive.*

I'm not separate or different from those tourists; we're actually all in the same boat. A sunset is transient and beautiful and we are too—why the hell not take a selfie? Life stand still here—that Virginia Woolf line—if I can let go my judging mind, step back from it, I enter the space which shows me that we are all constantly enacting this desire in our own way.

* * *

One day, there will come a day without me in it.

* * *

When I sit down to meditate I confront the insistent *self*. Often a repeating mantra disturbs the peace: *I am a writer. I am a writer. I am a writer*. But what does this mean? This hard-won identity? Then another persistent hum of thought: *I am an active person. Movement is important to me*. These key aspects of what I *believe* to be my identity fracture and fall into the blue of meditation in my yoga practice. Occasionally, when my mind can be still and I allow these thoughts to fall, the sensation, the sound, is like a glacier calving.

***

In recent years, these twin pillars of my identity—*I am a writer, I am an active person*—have come under challenge. In the Western religious and psychological traditions we speak of 'finding ourselves.' But this, more accurately, was a situation in which I lost my self, and what I clung to were tested and found wanting. I was forced to find the space beyond these fixed views. It was like a death, or a precursor of death and I mourned these aspects of self for a long time after.

The situation was this: my mobility declined over a few years as I waited for a hip operation. After a while, it became too difficult to walk anywhere without pain. In the end, I could no longer walk or practise or teach yoga. I was no longer an active person. Around this time, I also finished a novel which both my UK and Australian agents were unable to sell. My world became more and more circumscribed and I couldn't get over feelings of rejection. Because I was no longer mobile, I had to give up the job I loved in a Glasgow hospice. I kept writing, but in terms of the outside world, I was no longer a writer. I wondered if I would ever have another novel published. I felt the sting of rejection and failure, and physical vulnerability. I felt (and looked) much older than I was. And the 'I' in which I'd so heavily invested over so many decades no longer seemed to be the 'I' that was inhabiting this difficult present.

This was a period of daily physical, psychological, and creative struggle. It was the culmination of events following the death of my mother—illness, accidents, change—the somatisation of grief. The bardo of mourning. But, then, over time, a period of years, something started to change. Gradually, *within* my circumscribed physical and creative life, I found there was much to be grateful for. I couldn't walk, but I could swim. I couldn't sit at my desk, but I could lie in bed, read and dream, and doze. I watched a lot of Netflix. I couldn't get published, but I could keep writing, regardless. I could persevere. I could keep going. The Zen adage, 'to always be a beginner' had always guided my writing life, but did so now with added force. Here I was, once more, back where I started, without a publisher. I had to start over. I felt like a complete beginner. Sometimes, I felt happy, proud even, that I could cope with this much diminished version of myself. But I had to go beyond that, too. My ego, still clinging to what it could feel happy or proud about, even in diminishment.

There's a story of a forest monk whose only possessions were a set of robes and a bowl for eating. He became very attached to the bowl, felt that his superior maintenance of the bowl over many years differentiated himself from the other monks. But when, despite his care, the bowl eventually broke, he broke too. Or, rather, the idea of himself broke. And he broke through to a different awareness of what he had put store by, that fixed view of himself shattered. He was not who he thought he was. I was exactly like that monk. I kept writing, even though no one wanted what I had written. After the much longed-for hip operation there were even more difficulties. More obstacles. I needed blood transfusions and I had no energy after that. I could move my toes but not get out of bed. I was confined to the house for over three months. The healing of the leg and hip was delayed; my usual meditation routine collapsed. In hospital, after the operation, I downloaded a meditation app—something which I never thought I needed. It turns out I was wrong. Yet again.

During this long period, these years in the bardo of waiting, both pre-operative and post-operative—everything I thought I was or wasn't—fell away. Occasionally I glimpsed that place I'd like to have inhabited more fully, that place which the dead and dying know all about: the place where worldly cares and worries and ambitions drop; the space in which only love and a full understanding of beauty and loss reside.

***

Some time before my operation, I worked in a Glasgow hospice. I was a creative writing tutor there. I worked with families and bereaved children, men and women living with chronic illness and often facing death. I learnt how the imagination plays with the idea of death, sidles up to it, bargains with it, and finally comes to an acceptance or at least an accommodation of it. The range of end-of- life projects was astonishing: one woman wrote brilliant short stories as conversations with people, with emotions, with cancer; an older man translated short poems from the Latin into Glaswegian; a woman with lung disease embarked on a memoir through song lyrics; a man in his eighties created a handmade children's book, typing the text onto his mobile phone initially. Bereaved children created vibrant, ragged, graffiti art. People wrote cards of gratitude, and notes for their children and grandchildren—birthdays and weddings that they would never live to see. People took great risks, creatively and emotionally, and their view of themselves and their capabilities expanded. Things I thought I knew about death and dying—and I thought I knew quite a bit being an adept of death from a young age—were challenged and deepened. Neuroscientists now speak of the plasticity of the brain. When we attempt new things, this builds new synapses and new paths for learning. This opens up a space for us. For the notion of self. This means that, with support and encouragement, we are capable of change and growth and creative expression right up until the end.

***

How do we imagine death in the developed West? I close my eyes, and what comes to mind is a shark in a blue vitrine, jaws open: *The physical impossibility of death in the mind of someone living* is Damian Hirst's famous artwork—'More Steven Spielberg than Barnett Newman', as critic Luke White once noted. The shark as a threat is familiar to me from my Australian childhood. Every summer: the shark nets at the beach; the shark sirens and helicopters; the dark sightings of dark fins. The shark in Damian Hirst's blue tank was once sinuous, alive: a big fish in blue waters. Is the best part of this artwork its title? I think so. Even then, the title could do with an edit. The shark sculpture I saw at the Tate in 2012 looked terrifying, as if it was still moving, as if it could swim right through the glass, barrelling through the blue water and smashing the tank, threatening a flood across the gallery floor. But other things about this sculpture also bothered me then. They bother me still.

Hirst's shark sculpture seems dangerous because the contemplation of death by the living, especially in the contemporary West, is dangerous. Yet only a few generations ago, we were more closely acquainted with death. As Dr Kathryn Mannix notes, 'That rich wisdom was lost in the second half of the twentieth century.' She cites improved medical care and breakthrough treatments which have altered our experience of illness and life expectancy. Yet, as she says, these wonderful advances 'can only remediate us up to a point… the death rate remains 100 percent, and the pattern of final days and the way we actually die, are unchanged.… . What is different is that we have lost the familiarity we once had with that process, and we have lost the vocabulary and etiquette that served us so well in past times, when death was acknowledged to be inevitable.'

If we truly contemplated death as *part* of living, instead of something separate, we would all live differently. But our current social system leaves no time for contemplation of death and increasingly, no time for contemplation of the life we're actually living.

We are, quite literally, distracted unto death. We embrace cradle-to-grave distractions. We're exhorted to consume, to busy ourselves, to never stop, to constantly improve ourselves and everything around us. To strive, aim, post, like, and update.

Hirst's vitrine offers us a very Western view of death as something other and primal, something animal, something which takes us in its teeth and will not let us go. This is not the only conception of death in the world, but it dominates the Western Judeo-Christian tradition—resurrection and an afterlife notwithstanding. There is both a fear and a denial of death prevalent in 21st century Western culture. This generalisation comes with caveats. In Ireland, in Mediterranean Europe, in Latin America, there is more of an acceptance of 'death in life', outlets for grieving and mourning that anyone who has ever sat through Irish wakes and vigils for the dead, Mexican Day of the Dead celebrations, grief rituals in Greece or Italy can attest.

***

The shark as an image of death. In ancient times, in the writings of Pliny the Elder, and up until late medieval period, for example, the shark was known as *canis marinus* or *the dog of the sea*. The shark in medieval Europe was not a creature of horror. But the term 'shark' as we know it became current from the 16th century onwards as sailors on slave ships brought back new words and new objects from colonial raids and conflicts. In 1569, when a shark specimen was displayed in London, the term 'sharke' was first used to describe it. The term bears a relation to the Mayan 'xoc'(pronounced 'shok') which the sailors may have encountered in Spanish-ruled Mexico; certainly the British had little knowledge of the larger sharks of the Tropics before colonisation. Thus, the more domestic image of the 'dog of the sea' was replaced by the horror of the savage 'other' usually found at the ends of Empire.   To me, placing it in a vitrine and labelling it 'death' says more about the end days of that particular phase of the British Empire, and this particular time we're living through, than about the shark, or indeed, about death, itself.

***

That shark. I keep worrying at the image. I keep wanting to break it out of the vitrine. Hirst's first shark sculpture, after only two years, had begun to disintegrate in its tank in London's Saatchi Gallery. The Gallery in 1993 decided to gut the shark and stretch it over a frame which made the shark seem less real and more cartoonish. Hirst wasn't happy. Charles Saatchi then decided that he wanted to sell the sculpture to a hedge fund manager and Hirst offered to replace the shark for this new owner. And so a new shark was caught off the coast of Australia (a female tiger shark, in her middle years) and shipped in formaldehyde to Hirst on a two-month journey by sea.

Yet there is something 'off' here which I keep circling around. Female-sharking around—the inability to let 'nature be', to turn everything that is not white, male, profitable, wealthy, into 'the other'. Something about the pursuit of this second female shark from my part of the world and in her prime—the shark I saw in the Tate—gets to me. That she was female, and hunted to death to order, trafficked for rich men's pleasure, and then put on display. Such acts can only be considered abuse, a perfect metaphor for death then. But I reject the shark as a Western metaphor for the unimaginable—for death. For such an association seems to close down an imaginative space rather than opening one up. The tiger shark herself is now identified as a species 'near threatened'. The female shark, hunted and then shunted to the West is an image of ecocide and femicide, not death, as such. It is, rather, a very specific image conjured up at a very specific time by a certain white male artist, himself a product of late patriarchal capitalism.

Might death be imagined in another way? As a release into the next stage of life—another bardo state—rather than as a terrifying 'other'?

We must imagine differently.

***

Hirst locates his sculptures in a certain tradition of Western Art practice, specifically the tradition of medieval *memento mori* artwork which first arose in the period following the Black Death—cadavers and demons at the deathbed, *danse macabre* images, skeletons making music, entreating us to join hands with death, urging Christian contemplation, repentance and redemption. The artwork of the 17th century, in particular, the *Vanitas* paintings of the Netherlands show displays of wealth—luxe fabrics, gold, silver, kings and the aristocracy—juxtaposed with skulls, rotting fruit, decomposing nature. The message was stark: death spares no one, neither rank nor class will save you.

Work inspired by, or embodying non-Western traditions often takes different routes that are neither about evoking fear or repentance nor inciting guilt. I search for examples. I'm entranced by the work of Japanese artist Motoi Yamamoto. At the age of 27, he lost his sister to a brain tumour. As a young artist, he searched for a way to channel this loss and experimented with different materials. Eventually, he focused on salt as the medium for his sculptures and installations. In Japan, salt has a ritual function in many aspects of life, particularly beginnings and endings. Salt is offered at shrines, and at the opening of new buildings. It is thrown after funerals. Salt's oceanic origins—the origins of all life—mean that we cannot live without it. Each grain of salt contains memories of the sea. For all these reasons, Yamamoto began pouring salt into intricate shapes—lattices and labyrinths and spirals and swirls across gallery floors and walls. Each salt installation is different, beautiful and transcendent. In recent years, at the end of these exhibitions or 'saltworks', he invites members of the public to collect up the salt in containers to return to the sea.

This practice has much in common with the sand mandalas made by Tibetan monks. A mandala is a sacred circle inside which whole universes are depicted. It is a colourful object of meditation. As with Yamamotos's work, monks labour for days and weeks, months sometimes, to complete intricate mandalas in coloured chalk or in sand. Upon completion of a mandala, it is ceremonially wiped away, or washed away. The beauty is in the process of making and then the letting-go. This approach to art, to temporality, to death, is very different to how these life-events are depicted conventionally in Western art traditions. And it is this gentle, open, approach to death which most resonates for me.

***

In her 1993 Nobel Lecture Toni Morrison said, 'We die. That may be the meaning of life. But we do language. That may be the measure of our lives.'

***

In the hospice, I work with S. She is 37 years old; swimming in the middle of her life and death. She wants to write something for her children. She wants us, in the Art Room, to help her construct a memory box for them. She has three children and the youngest one, a 12-year-old girl with learning difficulties is sitting on her mother's bed when I enter her room. I take out the storytelling dice, sheets of paper, crayons, journal books and coloured pencils I've brought with me and ask the little girl to shake the dice and tell me what she sees—each dice has pictures of a person engaged in an activity. What does it remind her of? What stories, dreams? Could she draw what she sees? She loves this game; she rolls the dice, and starts immediately drawing a house with herself and her mother in it. She keeps drawing after each roll of the dice, a new frame of the story on a new sheet of paper. From these pictures, she starts to create a narrative of life with her mother, of things they have shared. She speaks out loud as she draws. I ask her if she wants to write these stories. Shyly, she shakes her head, No—but could I write them down for her? I become the scribe. I write everything down as she speaks. We spend nearly two hours doing this. These stories of a life together and of a life to be without her mother. Their daily routines. The things they enjoyed. Her mother lies on the bed in pain, offering up her own memories in a soft voice. I write these down too. They range over everyday favourite things and activities—foods, places they like to visit—the museum, the park, the pool—to cartoons, television shows—things that give them pleasure. A nurse quietly enters the room and gives S. a shot of morphine to the stomach. S drifts in and out of consciousness. She has a smile on her face. Her right hand flutters as she tries to speak. The stories keep coming and I continue to scribe. When the little girl has exhausted herself, I read the stories back as she silently arranges the pictures around her mother's bed. In that moment, S is not dying and leaving this child and her older children behind. In that moment, we are all deep in the bardo of life and creating something beautiful and transient, something which has meaning.

We are creating something and at the same time, letting it go.

You by Me: Writing Depression

Stephen Carruthers & Fiona Stirling

I have agreed to write an essay about mental illness with a stranger—with you.

We email back and forth. Our conversation fires up, hesitates, falters. We circle the soft ground between us, stepping into the centre a little more each day (when we can bear it). We want so badly to get this writing right.

I say: 'when I go for a walk, sometimes, all I can do is put one foot in front of the other.' You smile and say: 'one word in front of the other. But where do we go?'

We say: 'we want to wander through the subject of mental illness, setting no beginning, middle and end. Wander into those dark woods and see where we find ourselves.'

See where I find myself with you.

...

What I want:

I want to question the definitions—in dictionaries, in medical textbooks—that petrify and fix these bloody awful things. I want to scream at the world that this is complicated and messy and inconsistent and difficult. So often I think one way about it and then I think another and that is what inconsistent means. But that word doesn't convey what it is to find out that I disagree with myself. I want the reassurance that you feel some of these things too. I want to learn from what you might write and find some common ground. I want to learn from what I might write, discover what I feel and what I felt. I want to learn from being made to write, from being responsible to someone for staying on this journey together. I want a sense that all of this might *mean* something. No easy fix, but I guess I want hope.

***

That is why we need to work hard to write about this…

… work hard… share understanding… share hidden stories… work harder

Maybe if I am not alone in the struggle to find the words that never come easy…
None of this is easy. Maybe the world needs this. Maybe I need this.

***

We agree to wander out—out of our minds, out of our comfort, out of our individual
experience. Unguided, we will walk through whatever might be formed in this in-
between. Invite chaos into order. Confront that which has swallowed us before.

We agree to sink and drift, with purpose, into our past. Into now.

***

The first thing you asked me: 'so what is your diagnosis?'

Diagnosis (noun):

> the identification of the nature of an illness or problem
> synonyms: identification, recognition, discovery, whatthefuck?

Depression (noun):

> the act of depressing.
> the state of being depressed.
> sadness; gloom; dejection;
> shit you've got a problem.

***

For years we believed that there is something fundamentally wrong with us. Everyone has their struggles, but what if we *are* more awful, more pathetic, more useless. We talk about those memories and yet we *know* that there was happiness too. How can you be wrong in the head when you remember smiling, laughing, dancing? How can you be darkness when you know you were not like this all the time?

you were like this all the time

In the beginning, the cruelest trick depression plays on you is that you don't know that you are suffering from it. You just think that this is what life is like. The darkness.

you deserve to feel like this

* * *

Already, this writing feels too risky. Laying out these words—my thoughts—with you. It's like undressing. An emotional thoracotomy; cracking open my chest to judgement, disappointment, shame. I hear a whispering that my insides are rotten.

you're rotten

I don't even want to tell *you* my diagnosis. And *you* are my… what?
Co-writer?
Companion?
We're digging deeper into this subject, into each other. So let's be… canaries. Keep singing underground until the air becomes too toxic.

* * *

You change direction. Ask me about the first person I reached out to. My English teacher. She had the exuberance of a humming bird, flitting around the classroom chirping lines of poetry and encouragement, always smiling. She took her pupils seriously. She had a lightness of being.

I hoped if I sat down in front of her she would help me find the words.

Rehearsal:

'There's something I'm a bit worried about.'
'Miss, I think I need to tell you something.'

She pulled over a chair. She smiled, and listened.

What I didn't say:

'I've been feeling quite low for some time now.'
'I've been cutting myself and I don't really know why.'
'I've begun to have thoughts about killing myself.'

What I didn't say:

'I'm worried I will never stop feeling like this.'
'The thing is I'm faulty. It is pretty clear to me that I'm faulty.'

      you're fucked

She tried to respond but her words slipped and stalled. Her words had never done that before. I wanted to be saved. It was only much later that I understood that she couldn't do that.

She passed me on to someone else, just as she was meant to.
I never spoke to her about my mental health again.

* * *

'The trouble with trying to redefine depression,' you say, 'is that defining and defining is just thoroughly depressing'.

I laugh and tell you about a Sam Kriss essay I read years ago. He reviewed the *Diagnostic and Statistical Manual of Mental Disorders*, one of the guides used by doctors and health professionals for clinical diagnosis, as if it was a piece of fiction:

'As you read, you slowly grow aware that the book's real object of fascination isn't the various sicknesses described in its pages, but the sickness inherent in their arrangement.'

Nearly 1000 pages desperately defining boxes for humans to exist within. He asks: 'Who, after all, would want to compile an exhaustive list of mental illnesses?' You say: People want doctors and psychiatrists to have power, to provide an answer, but they don't fucking know either.

* * *

About 6 or 7 years ago my problems were getting too much to bear.

there is something very wrong with you

I'm not really sure what shifted.

you've always known that there is something very wrong with you

When I spoke to my GP it was actually a relief. I sat in her office and she was patient, reassuring. I sobbed in her office, that time, other times too. It was awful and a relief. She listened about the stresses of my job, the pain of dark winters, about my Dad, about my breakup…

She listened and she asked, 'so do you feel depressed?'

so do you?

She got me to fill in a form.

Over the last week:

I have felt terribly alone and isolated.
      ☑ sometimes.

I have felt totally lacking in energy and enthusiasm.
      ☑ most or all of the time.

I have felt like crying.
    ☑ often.

(There is a moment when it feels like I could be filling in just any form…)

Talking to people has felt too much for me.
    ☑ most or all of the time.

Tension and anxiety have prevented me doing important things.
    ☑ often.

I have felt despairing and hopeless. I have felt panic or terror.
    ☑ most or all of the time.
    ☑ most or all of the time.

I have thought about hurting myself.
    ☑ most or all of the time.

I have made plans to end my life…

    you're in a real fucking mess now, aren't you?

* * *

My diagnosis was depression. To be honest I have been given a bunch of labels over the years. Depression, anxiety, yadda yadda. I'm sure there are plenty more in my medical notes I am not aware of, theories about who I am according to various checklists. For many years, it seemed really important to 'know'. Like that could steer me to the right treatment, steer me to well-being. Steer a broken ship to shore. I wanted to learn everything I could about these words. If I knew what was wrong with me, then I could beat it; if I knew what was wrong with me, maybe I could be fixed.

A threshold concept: something that once learned cannot be unlearned.

    you *are* broken and you'll never be fixed

* * *

So what is depression to you?

A one-sentence story:

A tired, sick wee kid, who can't understand what it is that is making them feel bad, who doesn't know when, or even if they are ever going to get better, so they try to go on holiday from themself by sleeping in the spare room.

Another:

tired tired tired can't cope can't ever cope

Another:

Goblins hopping, trashing my mind, making sure the only memories I can hold onto are the ones about how I have failed/been failed; how I'm terrible/had terrible done to me.

It all comes down to storytelling—what story have we told ourselves about our lives? What story will we tell ourselves about who we are?

* * *

We've been telling each other our stories for months now. Listening. Reflecting. Questioning. Provoking. We have taken comfort in our similarities, and our differences. We have discovered rambling in a dark wood is easier when you have someone meeting you in there. So many times you would say, I would say: 'I'm sorry, I'm so sorry, I'm just rambling here.' And you would say, I would say: 'No, no, keep on keeping on— you're taking us somewhere really interesting.'

* * *

This essay would be formed, we imagined, from telling our stories in turn. We would maintain our separate selves, fastidiously mark out you and me. Once we began it was clear something was lost in translation. The ebb and flow of us together. The moments we most wanted to represent stubbornly refused to emerge on the page.

In *A field guide to getting lost*, Rebecca Solnit asks, 'Leave the door open for the unknown, the door into the dark… how do you go about finding these things that are in some ways about extending the boundaries of the self into unknown territory, about becoming someone else?'

'We' made the decision to become 'I'. We offered up our individual stories, so well-defined in our personal landscapes, and began to bend and blend, breaking the boundaries between me and you—building something new. A space where unknowns might creep forth.

It was uncomfortable, frightening. At first I was distant and careful with my words, feeling a need to maintain control. If you are told over and over that your thinking is faulty, how do you begin to trust it? How do you trust yourself to contribute to a writing experiment? To contribute to anything?

I was talking about the worst things in my life.

And I had to start by trusting you.

***

Crisis (noun):

>A time of intense difficulty or danger.
>>A time when a difficult or important decision must be made.

>like you can even make a decision. Fuck.

***

Rock bottom. Beneath it all, being reformed like the rock itself: erupting, crumbling, shifting.

I erupt from the flat which has become a place of despair, where I have begun to contemplate things I have never contemplated before. Like old biscuit crumbs in a corner I wait to be swept away. I know if I stop moving my life will take leave of me, right here and now. I wander and pace Waverley station as I wait for my connection, clutching a Cornish pastie far too tightly, unable to eat it. Cold pastry flakes off my fingers and onto the platform like brown, greasy flakes of snow.

you're broken, you know that don't you? nothing that can fix you, nothing left to be fixed…

where do you think you're running to?

It takes an hour-and-a-half to get home. To my parents' home. I feel some sort of relief at being back, even if it is a home I haven't lived in since I was 17. My old bed. Rolling the duvet round my fully clothed, shoed body, trying to feel nothing but the blanket.

And then things get worse. And worse.

***

Irrationally, relentlessly, painfully, I sob, giving in to the despair. I begin to stop: washing my body, changing my clothes, making sense. Mum is worried. She wants to know what I want.

I say: 'I want Help. Don't I? Help?'

I say: 'Just nobody touch me, I'll only sink. I can't breathe.'

I say: 'What do I want? A lifeboat, a rescue copter, a parachute. A blade.'

 I say: 'Fuckfuckfuck.'

She wants to know what she can do. (She'll do anything.) But she's out of her depth here. She's never had to deal with something like this before; the closest she's got is the great aunt who lost her mind that we all joke about at the holidays, but we only laugh because we're all so fucking scared that losing minds might be in our blood.

She says: 'I'm calling a doctor'.

***

Mum doesn't drive, but she could see I wasn't going to manage to walk myself to the GP. She called a neighbour because his car was in his driveway. Byron is the kind of guy who gives her a lift to the cattery when she goes on her holidays. Byron comes into the house and sees me sitting there and I can tell by his expression that he is shocked at how dreadful I look. (Zombie. That was the word he tells me later—zombie.)

***

I take some pills. Too many pills.

* * *

I'm in the back of a cab, a nurse either side of me. They bring me to a waiting room for clinical assessment and I'm ok with that, I think, because I have always been good at assessments. I pass the Generalised Anxiety Disorder and Patient Health Questionnaires with flying colours. My madness is exceptional.

'What symptoms have you been experiencing?'

'SadnessSadnesSadneSadnsSadnSadSaS. Myfingersaredulltheydon'tgraspthingsanymore. IfItrytosmilethereisarippingsoundinmychest.Breathingfeelslikethelastofmerushingout.'

'How long have you been feeling like this?'

'Onemillionyears.'

'Have you been admitted to a psychiatric ward before?'

* * *

Festive orange and black streamers hang low in the doorways. Halloween. The nurses are adorned with devil horns and halos. A patient, interpreting the nurses as demons, is losing her shit. She bangs on the metal grating of the windows and flips over a chair:

'I WILL BURN THIS FUCKING PLACE TO THE GROUND!'

* * *

What I want to tell myself:

You're a good person. You have a family and friends that love you. Being here is just a blip, you're going to get better.

What I actually tell myself:

'You're nothing. Nothing.
You're a blackholedressedasaperson
and when everyone finds out you've been here
they'll know how much you're broken.
Beyondrepair.'

things will be better if you just cease to exist

* * *

I accept a cigarette. Smoking gives my breath meaning and something to burn myself with.

* * *

Patients surprise me with their kindness.

I am reminded of an idea I had for a book to write while living in Siberia. Tough, lonely days of being the only foreigner in small-town provincial Russia far far away from anything. I was lonely. People seemed suspicious and unfriendly, but once you broke past that initial reserve, they would do absolutely anything for you. I wanted to write 'The Book of Kindnesses', a sort of record of the everyday nice things that people did. The cashier who stopped me buying horse salami by neighing. The internet café girl who smiled every time I went in there. The isolation made me aware of how important these acts of kindnesses were.

I will write that book one day.

* * *

We all watch Bargain Hunt. Both nurses and patients, united in spotting treasure. It's actually… nice, which is more than I deserve for not getting better faster. The woman from the bed next to mine throws a blanket across my shoulders. I think of it as a shield, huddle further into the couch. For the first time in, well, longer than I care to remember before this moment, I feel safe. But I will never really be safe until I stop trying to destroy myself. The television is knocked to the side by nursing staff wrestling a man with a sharp to the floor. This place is chaos.

just like you

Just like me.

* * *

~~I try to hang myself~~

* * *

The psychiatrist asks how I'm feeling. I want to reach over and pull her into the woods to wander through this essay with us; take her by the hand so she can follow every, single, step.

What do I want to do when I write about mental illness with you?

I want to be able to answer that question.

* * *

In this Anthology Stephanie Bishop writes about (re)learning how to play the cello, having to position her body in a new way to get where she wanted to be. I try an experiment to help me wander out, positioning my body in a way it had never been before. I climb under my desk at work. Get down on my hands and knees to inch under, a little animal seeking hibernation between computer cables and carpet tiles. I curl my legs by my side, balance my laptop on my chest, and stuff a coat beneath my head for support. My hip aches against the hard floor. I think, 'Let it hold the unpleasantness of this work so I don't have to support it anywhere else.' When I am finished I crawl back into the world with a stiff spine and two dead legs to shake back to life. I take a breath, acknowledge I am free from that little space, even though it still exists. I know I am able to wander out, and wander back again. There are many spaces for me to dwell.

The trick is remembering the way.

Can you remember the way?

Healing (noun):

the process of becoming sound or healthy again.

* * *

At the end of his book on depression, *Lost Connections*, Johann Hari writes, 'I am really wary of ending this book with a simple cry of "I did it, and you can too."'

He says: 'That wouldn't be honest.'
He says: 'I was able to make these changes because I am really fortunate.'

He knows.

Because when I am reading his book and finding much to think on in a calm and thoughtful way, much that makes sense, much that is in its own way *hopeful*, I also find myself thinking—but I just want to be better.

I just want to be better.

you're never going to

you're nev—

The seduction of the story—the book, the narrative—is its form: a beginning, middle and end. There will be an end to this. There must be an end. *I did it and you can too.* Of course you did Johann. There is honesty in saying that.

* * *

Question:

How on earth do I write about healing when at the moment things are this bad?

There is a part of me that can't face returning to our discussions about coping. Because I am not. I am falling off a precipice in my own home.

* * *

My therapist is at pains to remind me that I am coping. Sometimes I need reminding what coping is. Getting up. Going to work. I have been worse. Maybe this is exactly the right time to be writing about healing. To be reminded what it is.

you're scared for fuck's sake

Just what is it that I am scared of reading? Of writing?

The hardest thing in revisiting conversations about coping is suspecting I am not. The fear of never getting back, wherever 'back' is. I have been worse.

And now I am worse again.

***

After five weeks of feeling like I am sinking in very dark waters, I click out of it, just for an evening. I have been for a run. (Me running!) I say to a friend on the phone that it's funny because it's really difficult to keep a handle on what it is that is different. After weeks of not feeling normal, this will do. And I can't get a handle on why this evening I might feel different. So where does *that* get me? Still powerless? Still going to sink?

From what I understand of it, narrative memory behaves in strange ways. It averages things out. What I remember is five weeks of sinking. What I remember is pain. How do you remember fleeting relief in the face of that?

***

It is important to remember moments of relief. It is important to write about them.

I remember:

my first meeting back with my tutor on a Masters after taking a few months off due to my mental health. I was still pretty convinced that I wasn't going to manage to make it back and finish the course.

I remember:

telling my tutor I had no idea how much I was going to be able to handle. I told her that my only priority, the only thing I knew for certain, was that I needed to go for a walk every day. I told her if anything else was going to follow, it had to follow that.

I remember:

Tears running down my cheeks as she accepted my distress without judgement as she let the shame hanging out of my body hit the floor and fade away.

I remember:

My neighbour telling me, one foot in front of the other. Walk with me if you like, you don't have to say anything if you don't want to. One foot in front of the other.

It saved me, him telling me that. In a profound way I do believe that he saved me that time. It was surprising discovery—one much harder to admit to my depressed self—to realise that I saved me too.

I put one foot in front of the other. It was me.

It never is just one thing that saves you.

* * *

Last winter, on my walks, I discovered splashing my face with cold water from a stream. It is even better if you do it from a waterfall. The intensity of cold is something that momentarily makes it hard to breathe. In the rain your hands won't dry, it runs down your coat sleeves, your extremities freezing, unpleasant. But it makes you feel really, really alive.

* * *

My walks evolve. I notice trees. I take pictures of them. I observe them. The Japanese call it *Shinrin Yoku*—forest bathing. Doctors prescribe it as treatment.

Water evolves. In the last few weeks, at home, at work, I've found that even splashing my face with water from the tap helps. Cold water.

Life evolves. Live again moments. These tiny things, holding it all back.

* * *

I was once encouraged to map my thoughts/feelings/behaviours on to a traffic light system. When all was well I was green; when it was starting to tilt I was orange. When it was bad, when it had all gone to hell, I was red.

It is about noticing.

* * *

A list of things to notice:

The lightness dissipating; everything I carry around heavyheavyheavy.

Humour replaced by irritation and impatience.

Retreating from the world
                              not leaving the house not socialising notnotnot

Physical pain when with other people
                                         anactualache.

Being unable to discover daftness, wonder, magic, silliness.

Forgettingtolaugh.

   you haven't laughed in days now. Ha.

* * *

Resist the gravitational pull into the red. It tells me that if I just give in, if I just indulge the darkness and let go—become untethered from the world—it will be some sort of relief. There are days when darkness terrifies me.

When I am shattered and I want more than anything to lie in bed and let it pass but the shitshitshit destroys me. I want oblivion. I *crave* oblivion.

* * *

We both know what oblivion is. A full stop. It's there in the other stuff: the drinking yourself into nothing, the pills to take away the pain, the sex or the wanking, the glued to your phone as you sit on the shitter and descend down yet another internet rabbit hole, the check for updates and the losing yourself.

you're losing

The TV. The manic cleaning. Even the exercise. All the things we do to distract ourselves from ourselves andandand

I feel like I'm rambling. You tell me again you think our most interesting ideas have come up when one of us has wandered off, beaten a new path. We all worry so much about being normal, or being not-normal. Maybe we need to reclaim these oblivions.

The good oblivion! Oblivion-lite! Oblivion without the calories of regret!

A walk. Meditation sometimes. Lost in music. A good book. Exercise even!

Sitting and watching something stupid all night on Netflix.

what the fuck are you doing, wasting your life?

Must let go of these value judgements.

Good or bad, oblivion is just what people need sometimes. Is that what is scary about it? Knowing we need it? Letting go, when we truly can, is just the thing.

* * *

A space to feel okay would be good. You ask me 'what place have you carved for yourself in the world?' I don't want to answer. My mind shutters, my heart constricts. I am scared that I have failed. I am scared I haven't done so many things I should have done.

Therapy has me asking myself why I ask these questions so directly. About what I should do.

    should…   *should…*   *should…*

Maybe I have started to carve out a space. Maybe there is somewhere, just outside of myself, where I can write. That is something that feels important to me.

* * *

I try to make sense of depression. I actually write about it. In the past I couldn't even try, though it leaked out in my work, and felt like the badbadbad thing trying its best to sabotage me. I would like to be 'content me' all of the time. But 'depressed me' is me too. And that part of me needs recognition. Walt Whitman was right - 'I am large, I contain multitudes.'

* * *

Depression does not define me—apart from when things are bad and its shadow whispers out like an echo—but I am comfortable saying (now) that it is part of me. I don't think I can change that. Nor, strangely enough, do I think I would want to.

    you stupid fuck,

            of course, you would change that

Ask me again. You might get a different answer.

* * *

You remind me how hard it is to write about mental health, to capture these loops and spirals, and endless contradictions. These moments are butterflies and wasps flitting between our fingers, calling themselves reality. And sometimes they land effortlessly on the page. That might just be enough.

The very act of writing, of addressing depression and relief seems optimistic.

    you… feel…   hope?!

* * *

What is hope but an ongoing belief in your own ability to adjust? To know that sometimes you will find yourself out of sorts—sometimes frequently or even dramatically—but you can live with that, find succour in your resources, run through your own checklist of things you know you can use to keep things ticking over.

* * *

I usually manage to go for a walk when I am not feeling great. The more insidious way of me failing myself is not taking that walk when things seem mostly okay. It doesn't matter so much, if I'm feeling okay, does it? Miss a day … or two … or three….

> you do it to yourself'
>> you always do

I like walking. And I need to listen to myself. I will listen to myself.

* * *

'Look at that,' you say. 'A beginning, middle and a resolution starting to emerge. Closure.' I see it too. A need to make this essay story-shaped.

> But—

* * *

I'm struggling again. I can't quite explain… an absence of feeling—a hollowing out—andandand a weight of feeling too much. How can both exist concurrently? How can I feel like I'm drowning and falling through the air at the same time?

I thought I'd figured this out.

> you thought you'd figured this out! yeah right!

When am I 'normal' sad, and when am I depressed? What is stress at work, and what is anxiety? I thought my traffic light system, the water, the walks helped, but the illness has shape shifted. The body of it swerved. Darkness returns. It seepsseepsseeps through, and tips the balance again. The world is too much. There were no warning bells this time.

* * *

I can't open the mail. Can't open bills and letters and bank statements. They pile up. I miss important things, little things, then I fuck up again. More examples that prove how useless I am. I'm not even opening your emails about this essay.

The piles keep a-piling, the guilt keeps a-guilting.

It's going to keep happening, isn't it?

Whenever I think I know these deep, dark woods, they change, punching all the air from my guts.

I whisper:

> you do it to yourself. that's what really hurts

***

We will all experience things in life that are 'like' mental illness.

We will all experience things in life that are 'like' joy.

> you think you can be happy again?

I think maybe I can be happy again.

But even as I write this, even as I cut and paste, move the hope around the page to see if I can find a place where it might work, I really really don't believe it.

***

You tell me you can't work on this essay any more. You are off work again. You can't do any of this any more again. You have to put your energy into just breathing again. And I understand. Fuck, do I understand.

There is a frustration at realising that no amount of edits will make this essay feel right for either of us. That what we anticipate and intend can't truly be reconciled with what we end up with. This is life. This is depression. This is writing. In our attempts to become lost, to find the unknown, we have seen precisely how afraid we are of losing control, of letting the chaos in.

Questions to ask ourselves:

What if, when we get lost again (because we will get lost again), we try to remember that we're not as lost as we were before?

What if we accept this imperfect edge inside (and between) us, spanning recovery and chaos?

What if this has never been a straight path at all? What if we're a circle, you and I?

* * *

I write a message to you just weeks after thinking I was done with this all. I write:

'Thanks for taking over on the essay.
Thanks for telling me that I didn't even have to open the document if I didn't
feel up to it.
Thanks for reminding me that what we have done already is enough.
I felt able to open it again today. I read what we wrote. At least I felt able to do that.'

* * *

What we wanted:

We wanted to question the definitions—in dictionaries, in medical textbooks—that render the bloody awful things so fixed, so unshifting. We wanted to scream at the world that it is complicated and messy and inconsistent and really really awful. We wanted to engage with what inconsistent means, and… *rage*… at our inability to convey that we cannot even agree to disagree with ourselves. And we wanted reassurance. That you and me felt some of these things too.

you feel it all the fucking time

We wanted to learn from writing. We wanted to stay on this journey together.
We wanted a sense that all of this might *mean* something. Because there is no end to
this messy, complicated business.

We wanted hope. Oh god yes, we wanted hope.

***

That is why we need to work hard.

      work hard…

                  share understanding…

                                share stories…

                                            smile …

I smile at you. You smile at me. If we are not alone in the struggle to find these words
that never come easy, then maybe we will find these words. (None of this is easy.)

Maybe the world needs this. Maybe we need this.

***

                                    'You must go on. I can't go on. I'll go on.'

A Voyage Out in Education

Jane MacRae

There's nothing like not having a proper job to provide space – for thinking, creativity and most of all for being.

I found it hard to just 'be' but nevertheless through being, some doing did emerge. A small seed—the culmination of my reflections, reading, observations, questions and ideas arising from some twenty years of teaching and working with young people— has now germinated and started to grow. The seed was there all the time, perhaps, but what brought it into the light more clearly was coming across the concept of harmony in my reading.

Harmony was, and is, the perfect concept for what I wanted to bring to education. It already exists, in the natural world and in the human heart, in that everyone intuitively knows what it is. Yet it's a quality that is absent in our discussions and thinking around education and our engagement with young people's development. Now more than ever we need to learn how to live in harmony, with the natural world and with each other, as the global environmental crisis deepens and human beings become increasingly isolated, self-absorbed and individualistic.

If we unpick the phenomenon of harmony we see that it is underpinned by a number of principles. These are familiar concepts to any biologist because they pervade ecology, physiology and biochemistry, to mention but some branches of biology. At the same time they are common enough in everyday parlance: interdependence, diversity, health, adaptation, cycles, geometry and oneness.

Such principles operate in the natural world but also might be applied in the human context. For we could surely learn a lot about how to live with each other with nature as our teacher, giving a new way of looking at education. Quite how was yet to become clear at the start of our journey.

In the work of *Bloom*, registered as Bloom Educational Courses CIC Limited, I wanted to focus on secondary education particularly, because most primary schools have a lot of nature-related activities. For some reason, and largely to do with exam pressures I suspect, activities that engage with nature in a holistic fashion seem to die off in secondary education. It is true that nowadays environmental issues pervade education at all levels, but still I wonder why the miracle of say an insect's life cycle or the beautiful geometry of a sunflower is thought to be primary school business predominantly. After all, we human beings are an intrinsic part of the natural world.

At the start, I was anxious about how an education based on harmony and its principles would be received by the great assessment factories through which we process our young people. What head teacher was going to entertain the whacky notion of learning to live in harmony when it's all about striving for exam results and personal achievement, and league tables? What school dealing with disadvantaged pupils—knife crime and drugs, struggling to keep teachers and strapped for cash—was going to think that learning to live in harmony was anything but pie-in-the-sky?

This is where a leap into the unknown was needed—a big dose of imagination, faith in human nature, and a conviction that harmony was a reality. I had to be prepared, like anyone who starts something new, to go down lots of blind alleys, to make mistakes, to listen and be open to peoples' responses and criticisms; to be persistent, always to be on the look-out for opportunities; and to ask for help when needed. At the same time I discovered that, whatever is said, it is vital to hold to the essence within the seed of the idea that one first envisioned. To keep focused and not allow it to be obscured by everyday detail; to remain confident in that essence. Reflecting on this for a moment, what I realise is that self-doubt gets tangled with doubt in the project. Self-doubt is about me whereas doubt in the idea is not about me, so it's important to discern one from the other. At the same time, I wholly recognise that ongoing, healthy questioning and reappraisal is essential for creative development and not at all the same as doubt.

In order to make the idea workable in a secondary school I hit on the idea of creating courses based on harmony and its principles that could be incorporated into the curriculum. This meant that we were not asking teachers to squeeze something new into their already packed timetables but, instead, to re-think what they were teaching in their various subjects; adopt a new framework for teaching topics that they were already teaching; add another layer of meaning to enrich what they were teaching. In some subjects such as English, this would mean bringing in new texts, from the many well-known nature writers and thinkers, for example, to enrich the curriculum.

Thinking of how to implement our ideas in a practical way was strangely easier than finding the right formulation to articulate what we were doing. Although I was quite clear that I wanted our courses to be founded on the concept of harmony in nature and its seven principles, putting that into readily comprehensible words was extraordinarily difficult. I and my colleagues had been through many iterations—for the website, for our teaching materials, for explaining it to friends. It turned out to be a little like essaying, a kind of ongoing process of thinking and writing.

Thinking over this, I am curious as to what this shows. Had I myself not really understood what I thought I knew? Or was there something hidden more deeply inside the idea, that seed or space—to use the theme of this volume of essays—that I had not yet discerned? Having said that, I find, even as I write here, that its formulation is clarifying partly due to other people's thoughts and to my own persistent questioning, examining the concepts again and again.

A milestone on this journey was getting our first two pilot courses up and running in 2018, one of which was in non-fiction English for Key Stage 3 (ages 11-13) and the other in PSHE (Personal, Social, Health and Economic) education for the same age group. Both of the teachers whom I worked with to develop these courses came up with invaluable new thoughts, insights and formulations.

I observed most of the lessons in the two pilot undertakings; pupils in these schools were of very mixed ability and from a wide range of backgrounds; all were totally unprepared for what they were receiving in the new courses. It was therefore a pleasure, a relief, and more than encouraging, when we found that they were receptive, interested, mostly responsive and even enthusiastic!

The English course involved pupils reading and analysing seven excerpts from texts by mostly contemporary nature writers. Each excerpt was chosen because it encapsulated something about one of the seven harmony principles. We also included a practical 'connection exercise' related to the text, often a simple activity using the senses, for example, smelling a little heap of damp soil when reading a text about the effect of poor farming practices on the soil. What a lot is revealed about soil by connecting to it in this way and what an unexpectedly enlivening experience! Final lesson reflections asked pupils what they could learn from nature that could be put into practice in everyday life.

The course culminated in a writing competition; the title of the piece was, 'A manifesto: my vision of harmony now and in the future.' Pupils were asked to choose one harmony principle that meant the most to them, and were given guidance on how to structure their manifesto. They could draw on the class work they had done during the term as well as the original texts that they had studied. Apart from these inputs, pupils were on their own.

These children had to enter a space which must have been unfamiliar. Many indeed were initially disorientated by the wide open world of the 'what if?', but found themselves gently coaxed into the unknown by the skill of the teacher and other pupils. And what did they have to do in that space? Firstly they had to make their own independent connection with one of the seven harmony principles by choosing one and explaining it in their own words. Secondly they had to re-read the relevant text on their own to recall its detail and meaning. Thirdly they had to explain how their chosen principle shows itself in the natural world and then, perhaps even more challenging, write a paragraph describing what difference it would make, if this principle were to be put into practice. Lastly, the biggest leap of imagination, pupils had to put forward their own ideas for what could be done to put this into practice and how that would help to create more harmony in the world.

Here are some excerpts from a eleven-year old pupil's manifesto. Binyaamin Sufi is from a Somali family and his English was then competent but not fluent. The boy wrote,

> Have you ever noticed that humans treat nature like a piece of paper? We use it and chuck it away like it is not valuable. "We are part of nature and not apart." We are all one and if there was no nature we would all cease to exist… The principle of oneness is important to me personally because where I live in London there is [sic] a lot of murders…. So I think there should be more nature around to smooth and calm people down. I sometimes shout so I'm going to think before I do because we are all part of the same community. The principle of oneness also teaches us the value of humanity. I believe we can make a difference to the world if everyone knew about oneness because they would think before they waste food, shout at each other and hurt people because they appreciate the connection between people… My vision for harmony is that there should be more peace in the world. One way it could happen is when every school has a quiet room. So they can calm down…
> so we should thank nature for all the stuff it's done for us.

Reading these manifestos and observing the classes confirmed my belief that children can learn to connect with themselves, with each other and with the natural world, and, given the right impulse and material, might be actually moved to create a powerful and imaginative vision for humanity. Realistically, of course not every single child wrote a comprehensive manifesto and some got more out of it than others. But, they were all exposed to a big view, they were all asked to think more deeply than usual and they all read some challenging texts and responded.

The pilot study revealed pupils' openness and receptivity to big concepts, and gives us the confidence to take our courses to other schools to consider for learning in general. It showed us that with skilful scaffolding and a wider, inspirational context, even pupils who range widely in ability can engage with challenging texts. Such findings beg the question of whether concepts and resources presently used in education underestimate or limit learning unnecessarily. Young people can partake of a bigger, more expansive world than we might imagine.

We hope that teaching young people how to reason from principle deepens the level of thinking in general. It might enable them to relate issues of a practical, moral, social, academic or environmental nature to a bigger idea, to a wider whole. Hopefully the pull towards partial, divisive, one-sided thinking would lessen as they move towards a more essayistic and heuristic approach, allowing space and time to respond to issues that may otherwise provoke aggressive, unreasoned, reactive responses. Much is said about the need for tolerance but what we see in education, and in the world at large is too often worryingly the opposite; there may be 'tolerance' for ideas people agree with but, sometimes, violent intolerance for those people disagree with. A central part of the Bloom approach to education is to connect with others and that includes listening— deeply, and with an open mind, without preconceptions. Speaking about generosity, patience, forgiveness, self-control, resilience and loyalty, for example, as part of their wider learning, gives young people alternative reference points to those used in social media, which might draw them unwittingly into self-absorbed, 'me first', individualism.

But these thoughts are only the beginning of the next part of the journey. Imagination and engagement with the Bloom idea should allow the work to grow positively. The space for that imagination has to be found in the minds and hearts of all those working on the project—but perhaps, it is especially incumbent on me to keep accessing that area of the 'what-if' possibilities as I write here and in other pieces, and as I talk to teachers and others about Bloom. Is there a space in the educational world for our project? How can I help widen it? I have noticed that other mind-changing initiatives in education such as the Extended Qualification Project (EPQ), aimed at offering an alternative to formulaic thinking at 'A' level, gained its success gradually as teachers and then universities saw its benefits in practice. There was no need to confront or change wholesale the 'A' level system; since its foundation in 2006, some 30,000 students are now taking the EPQ.

A similar non-confrontational approach that will touch teachers' hearts intuitively as well as meet their academic requirements looks like the way to go. It will take us to somewhere uncluttered and open—where there can be communication and receptivity, where creativity and originality might arise and where harmony can prevail.

The Flicker of North

Duncan McLean & Kenny Taylor

Hello Kenny

We've been invited to discuss the north as a place, both real and imagined. If you don't mind, I want to call it the North. My notion is that there's a place formed by 'northness', defined by 'northness', consisting of 'northness.' And you and I are both in it.

It would have been good to have had a blether with you before introducing such an idea, to make sure you don't think it entirely daft, but so far it's been impossible to talk. Who'd have thought it would be so hard in this day and age to catch each other on the phone! I will just have to launch our conversation with this brief contribution, and hope the words connect even if our mobile providers can't.

A conversation of what kind? We won't know till we talk! I'll go first, will I? You can't answer that, because you won't even see the question till I send it to you, which I won't do till I get to the end of whatever I'm going to write here. Let's call it 700 words, two pages—it's good to have an arbitrary target. Many years ago, I drove right across the USA. Every morning I'd look at the atlas and find a town 3 or 4 or even 500 miles west with an interesting name: Chunky, Mississippi; Uncertain, Texas; Truth or Consequences, New Mexico. And I'd drive till I got there and find a motel for the night. I had to have an arbitrary target, you see, otherwise, why stop? In the States, you can just keep driving forever. Not like here in Orkney: twenty minutes in any direction and you get to the sea. That'll stop you.

Duncan

***

Dear Duncan

At first glance, part of the reason it's been hard for me to communicate much seems simple: 'notspots.' During chunks of this spring and summer I've been working in some of the most trackless country I know. One of a team surveying birds, mammals and vegetation in the wilds of north Sutherland, I've often been far from both roads and reliable phone signals.

Your schedule and mine have meant that there seem to be only a few days—or hours—when we might have had a chance to chat. My hiking along a mountain slope or venturing into the boglands just adds to the difficulty at a time when we might otherwise have spoken.

Like that day when I was inland from Loch Eriboll, going towards Foinaven on a day of sunshine and wader calls, when the signal evaporated faster than the dew on the deer grass. We'd managed a quick phone rendezvous mid-morning, and I suggested that we could speak later, before you needed to go to the shop. Seemed simple—a good way to converse while I paused for some thermos coffee. But long before the appointed talk time, I'd entered the valleys and crags of no-speak. So I'll tell you a little of what happened while we failed to converse; what I saw and what I didn't see. There were pools among the bog mosses when I reached a high plateau. I could see the Pentland Firth a few miles off, and a blue-green smudge on the horizon that I took to be the hills of Hoy. The Orkney Islands. Laser flashes might have made a connection between us right then. But signalling in Morse would have defeated me, while you, of course, were in Kirkwall, not Hoy. So my attention soon drifted to the closer sight and sound of a greenshank flying a couple of hundred metres away. Then another veered in from the east, diving at the first bird and chasing it, fast and low, over the bog and beyond. Once it had seen off the intruder, this second bird returned. Rising above the sky-mirroring lochans, it began to call. And call. The notes fluted loud and softer and louder with shifts of breeze.

I kept it in view as it ascended, cricking my neck back to watch, then arching further to catch its shape in binoculars and hold the silhouette in focus. After more than a minute, it stalled its high rise and plummeted, steep and fast, to reach the ground in seconds. In the times when I've thought of it since, I know that my interpretation of what it was doing in that airspace could be wrong. That the greenshank's communication and signalling is not my language, though I think I understand some of it, that its place is not my home, much though I relish going there.

And though my image of your home isles is more—much more—than that smudge on the northeast horizon, and though I've visited many times over many decades, still I wonder how much I actually know of Orkney and the wider North. How much I'm projecting my own preconceptions on the screen of the cool blue horizon. But I'll leave that for later as we see what place or idea takes us further along the turns of this conversation.

Kenny

* * *

Dear Kenny

You have the ability to describe your work and make your readers envy you, wishing they were up on those trackless moors watching the duel of the greenshanks. Are you sure that really is work? Ach well, I suppose there was a painfully early start, the bog was claggy on your boots, and a million midgies showed up to keep you company. Oh, any number of downsides. It all comes round to what we choose to focus on, which parts of the working life we select to present in our prose. I could, for instance, suggest something of my working day by describing me throwing open the shop door first thing to see St Magnus Cathedral across the street, sandstone glowing red in the morning light. I could go on to recount a conversation with an excited Italian restaurateur, visiting Orkney on holiday and tasting Westray Wife cheese for the first time. And I could describe a late-afternoon delivery run in my van, out past the standing stones and Maes Howe, to deliver a case of good red wine to a restaurant in Stromness, named The Hamnavoe after George Mackay Brown's classic fictional version of the town.

On the other hand, I could also show me in a sweat and pretty much wabbit by 9am, after the arrival of two pallets of wine from our importers, a couple of tons in weight, all of which has to be carried in by hand through our inconvenient back store, checked and stacked.

A few months ago a friend asked me a question that I couldn't answer at the time, and has been gnawing away at me ever since. The question was, what do you like about Orkney? I couldn't think of anything to say. I know what tourists and other visitors like: the landscape, the dozens of archaeological sites, the birdlife. I know what they like because they tell me. Sometimes they tell me because they're bursting with excitement and want to spill it out. Other times they tell me because I ask them. A typical conversation in my shop over the four or five tourist months runs like this:

Duncan:	So, are you here for long?
Visitor:	We're here two weeks, we love it.
Duncan:	You're in Orkney for two weeks? Great!
Visitor:	No, we're in Scotland for two weeks: Glasgow, Skye, Lallybroch, and now Orkney for two days. Then we go to—what's it called?—Edinburgh, and then home.
Duncan:	And where's home?
Visitor:	The United States of America.
Duncan:	Aye, I got that, but where exactly?
Visitor:	Roanoke, Virginia.
Duncan:	I've been there!
Visitor:	You have? No one's ever been to Roanoke! It's dull as all heck! What were you doing there?
Duncan:	I was staying with a friend in the Blue Ridge Mountains, and we were starting to get cabin fever, so we drove to Roanoke to see that terrible Mel Gibson film, *Braveheart*. That wasn't a pretty sight. Tell you what though, those mountains were spectacular, and the landscape around there was just beautiful. As we drove along you could see eagles circling up in the sky… amazing.

So this is how I know what the tourists like about Orkney, conversations carried out all summer long, across the cheese counter.

But what about someone who lives here, or lives anywhere? Can they really 'like' their place? It's not a Facebook post of a friend's new pushbike or relationship status or political opinion. You can't just get up in the morning, look out the window, and click a 'like' button to express mild and barely-considered approval of what you see. Those kinds of 'likes' are about reminding a far-flung friend you exist and are aware of them, maybe that you're supportive of whatever they're doing or buying or thinking. But that's not what goes on in your own mind when you look out your window or walk down the road. That's more likely to be a complex of plusses and negatives:

—Blue sky and sun, that's a good start. But bushes leaning north-eastwards and cloud out beyond Hoy, so maybe a bit of rain coming in later.

—Small cruise ship anchored off Stromness. Busy day for the town, good for the shops and cafes and pubs.

—Still can't believe that guy got planning permission to build that house down by the shore: does not fit in at all. Still, have to admit it's quite modern and interesting, and anyway it'll all be gone in a few years with the sea rising!

—Oh, there goes Billy down the road in his John Deere 6125. As usual, fifty miles an hour, on his phone, and his wee boy bouncing about the cab. Is it true what they say that tractors don't have to obey the Highway Code? That they're agricultural vehicles so can do what they like? Certainly seems to be here … Like taxi drivers in Kirkwall: no seat belts and wrong way round the roundabout: they can, because they're taxis, it's the law! (So they say.)

—Jesus, and now that bloody hen harrier's back, cruising along and back the length of the garden, peering down into the bushes. I know what you're after, you bastard, it's the baby blackbirds, but you're not getting them, I like blackies singing in the garden. Here, hold my laptop: I'm off to throw some stones at a bird of prey. What is that? Is that liking Orkney? It doesn't feel like it to me. It just feels like living Orkney.

Duncan

* * *

Dear Duncan

I feel the weight of your plusses and minuses, including the sweat of heaving heavy boxes—however tantalising their contents—at times when many of us might be doing nothing more strenuous than lifting a morning cup of coffee; the tractors careening down streets; the anti-clockwise taxi drivers. And the hen harrier threatening to silence the garden blackbird. Much though I mourn the persecution of harriers on the killing fields of the grouse-moored uplands, that's worrying. But to be honest, (sorry to be an anorak, though I do have the relevant jacket) that sounds much more like normal behaviour for a sparrowhawk than a harrier. A few years ago, a sparrowhawk slew the blackbird that liked to whistle the 'da-da-da-DA' phrase from Beethoven's Ninth at the gable ends of my roof. I've not heard that whistler's like again.

Household birds apart, your comments also make me think about the balance sheet of emotions in how I relate to my own home place, on the Black Isle. I could say that I'm writing this at my kitchen table, where I often work, looking across a few miles, beyond the surrounding farmland, to the corries of Ben Wyvis, wondering when the first snows will come. But I'm travelling backwards at the moment, returning north to Inverness on an overcrowded train (as is normal on this line) and both 'liking' (there's that word again) and loathing the increasing popularity of the Highlands to visitors. There's a guy squashed-in beside me who's dressed as superman, though his face is painted in zombie tones of fungal green and congealed-blood red. He and the Aussies across the passage are swapping tales of their trails and travels. Think he's on his way to a stag party, while the girl in the wizard's (not witch's) hat down the carriage—who knows?

All a contrast to the Black Isle, highlighting how part of what I've always relished about life there is the relative quietness, and the sense of un-crowded space. Space to notice small things, such as subtle sounds in the woods behind my house … the way the click of a pine-cone on a track could mean there's a crossbill feeding in the tree overhead. How else can I notice, not only the day, but also the very hour of autumn when the first skeins of pink-footed geese arrow-in from Iceland to glean the stubbles after harvest? The way my children might explore the woods, and later, dig full-on, adrenalin-boosting downhill mountain bike trails among the conifers, without anyone really noticing that they, or the bike tracks, were there.

Those are some of the plusses, as are the overlapping communities of interest here, such as among those of us who help to promote live performances of music, drama, poetry and more in small local venues. I know that's no different to how things work in countless other places across Scotland—across many other parts of the world, perhaps. But it's part of what I value about 'living the Black Isle', as you do living Orkney.

It can also be one of the minuses; the way, for example. that communities of interest can rapidly circle wagons when faced with perceived threat and then fire at supposed adversaries in the parish. That happened some years ago, when there was a chance of community ownership of old woodland nearby. The woodland was part of what was classed as a farm, but had barely been worked as such in recent times. But that categorisation was enough for the community of farming interest (both practitioners and relatives) to react as if the sky would fall if anyone other than one of their own were to have a say in how the woodland was used and managed.

The bitterness and division engendered by what should have been a straightforward and positive process was almost frightening. In some ways, it taught me a great deal about how quickly group behaviour can turn from friendly interactions to something much more sinister. It also showed how there's no straightforward way of defining what a particular place means to people living there, let alone to visitors. Where I thrill to the sounds of the wild geese overhead, as Neil Gunn did when he lived not far from here a few decades ago, a farmer might see a threat to winter-sown crops. Where I see an average stretch of Black Isle coast, my nearest neighbour down the track (not long deceased, and sorely missed) would think of possibilities for outwitting water bailiffs and catching salmon. Come to think of it, that chimes with some of Neil Gunn's writing.

Hugh Miller—a son of Cromarty, just a few miles away, both wrote of the local scene in the early 19th century in ways that I relish, especially in his close observations of wildlife—a relative rarity in his work—and people he knew on the peninsula. Those meld in his description in 'My Schools and Schoolmasters' of when a party of 'herd-boys' had

> stormed a humble-bee's nest on the side of the old chapel-brae, and, digging inwards along the narrow winding earth passage, they at length came to a grinning human skull, and saw the bees issuing thick from out a round hole at its base—the *foramen magnum*. The wise little workers had actually formed their nest within the hollow of the head, once occupied by the busy brain; and their spoilers more scrupulous than Samson of old, who seems to have enjoyed the meat brought forth out of the eater, and the sweetness extracted from the strong, left in very great consternation their honey all to themselves.

Elsewhere (and I don't have the book to hand) Hugh Miller also talked of his dislike of the long miles of heath and pines and bogland on the Black Isle, now shrunk to fragments since his day, which I'd love to see restored. If perceptions of place could be GPS overlays, I suspect there would be as many as there are individual inhabitants. So I know that my perceptions of Orkney, though shaped by many visits to many different islands and influenced by George Mackay Brown, Viking sagas and things such as the tunes and songs of the Drevers and the Wrigley sisters, are simply the mix I've been able to make mine. Billy in the John Deere might well think me daft.

But I'm minded to take a different track now. That's part of the pleasure of essays as a writer or reader, of course (if, as you say, this staccato communication is indeed such a thing): the way you're never sure—maybe don't want to be sure—where the next few sentences might lead. Casting back, it's like moving through the kind of blanket bog I was describing earlier. You think you see the direction of travel, but it's impossible, assuming you don't want to risk getting up to the oxters—or worse—in sodden moss or bog pools—to go in a straight line. Some of that, I assure you, is hard work, since making a mistake when you're out there alone in cloud so low you can barely see your feet (as happened to me a few weeks after that greenshank encounter), could be life threatening. At least essays, whatever the barbs literary critics might throw, might be safer.

Another thing I can tell you that I often see from this part of the peninsula is liners. Cruise ships by the score, docking across the Firth at Invergordon to disgorge tourists in thousands to be taken in coaches across the Highland mainland. It's hard to imagine how such numbers could descend on somewhere of such modest size and narrow streets as Kirkwall. Here, the similarly small town where the cruise passengers land won't be high on their wish lists for selfies against a northern backdrop. But the hulk of the defunct aluminium smelter and the oil rigs parked inshore could say more about that place and the people who live and work there than the photo opportunities they'll seek elsewhere. I'm sure that many of those travellers, between the diversions of shopping, are more minded to share images taken with an old castle behind, or Loch Ness, or maybe the place where both castle and loch could be caught in one frame (plenty of potential for 'likes' there). They'll have journeyed in hopes of glimpsing 'Nessie', that prime economic asset of the Highlands and as improbable—and potent—as the tooth fairy or Santa Claus.

Santa, reindeer, north: now that last word is one that has excited me since childhood. Still does, even though the ways I think of it could be as much to do with my imagination—and the words and images of writers and northern artists whose work I relish—as with the realities of life and land beyond where I now live.

North: unless you're standing precisely at the pole, there's always a north. And from where I'm sitting, Orkney is part of that 'north'.

Superman has left the train, by the way, but the wizard is still aboard.

Kenny

***

Dear Kenny

The idea of the North appeals to me too. I have gazed reverentially at William Heinesen's old house in Torshavn, and watched Mairi Boine sing at mild blue midnight, the jagged peaks of Lofoten behind her. (By the way, I never made it over to

Lofoten; if I had, I'd've had to have made one of my randomly generated trips to Å at the southern end of the archipelago. Of course, I would then have been obliged to find the legendary lost city of Z in the Brazilian jungle …)

So tourists are attracted to places by fictional animals like Nessie, and fictionalised versions of real people like Mary Queen of Scots, and fictional locations from *Outlander*. But what attracts and excites you and me is just as fictional: the notion that 'North' is something more than a relative geographical description; the idea that George Mackay Brown's fantasies describe an Orkney that ever really existed; the wish-fulfilment that Sigrid Undset's politics represent the values of far-northerners better than Knut Hamsun's.

It's all projection, isn't it? 'Imagined Spaces' is exactly the right phrase: we invent a space or place in our minds that we want to believe in, and then set out to find it. We travel solo on foot to some wilderness free of human contamination (other than ourselves, who are not contaminants, of course, but neutral observers.) Or we go as a family to campsites in Normandy for that authentic French countryside experience, the back of the car full of iPads and Rice Crispies to keep the kids happy. Or maybe we hole up to work on a draft of a novel in North Ronaldsay or Graemsay because the Mainland of Orkney is *just not Orcadian enough*—a more concentrated essence of Orkney is required to steep in than the complex, diluted reality of the Mainland.

Which brings me to a surprising place where I find myself in sympathy with the liner passengers. Most of them, in my experience, don't come on a cruise in order to visit a particular imagined place. It's the travelling that's the important thing. They're not travelling TO anywhere; rather they are voyaging THROUGH a series of places. It could be half a dozen coastal towns from Portsmouth to Oban to Kirkwall to Invergordon. Or it could be northern seas from the North Sea to the Baltic to the North Atlantic.

Cynical and weary tourist industry workers claim that the cruise liner passengers often have no idea where they are. To which I reply, So what? Travelling, hopefully, is better than arriving. These liner folk travel day and night, on they go, always moving, pausing only briefly to draw breath in a town, yet another town, at the end of a pier, at a mooring out in the bay. Some come on land by footbridge or tender and spend a few hours—'Where are we?'—wherever they are. Others choose to stay on the boat, sleeping or eating or gazing out at the shore: 'There's a town there, but I'm not going to it. Mustn't get hooked in, must keep moving. I hate the stops, love the journey.'

When the shore visitors walk or bus back to the harbour, there's a whole row of those 'How was your experience?' signs. You know, the ones you pass once you get through airport security, with the sad face, the neutral face and the happy face. There they are, a dozen or so signs lined up, all with, HOW WAS YOUR ORKNEY? in big bold letters. And as they go through, the visitors have to punch one or other face to register the extent to which they've liked their hours here. Every cruise port has such a set-up, apparently. And the good news for us is, Orkney gets more smiley faces punched than any other place in the UK.

The tourist board are actually planning to install a whole series of those punchy faces across the key sites of Orkney: HOW WAS YOUR SKARA BRAE? HOW WAS YOUR OLD MAN? HOW WAS YOUR BETTY CORRIGAL'S GRAVE? Only then will they be able to accurately assess the extent to which these various attractions are realising their potential in the tourist economy. Any which are found to be pulling less than their weight risk demolition or at least demotion from the tourist brochures to the history books.

All of which fantastical nonsense leads me to conclude that it is time for me to draw my part of this conversation to a close. By rights at this point I should assess the success of my contribution and punch myself in the face, which I may well do after rereading what I've written.

But before that I will finish by quoting lines from another Orcadian writer, Edwin Muir, which pop into my mind unbidden and seem relevant. In life he went south, but in his work he often came back north. Whatever the direction, there was always restless movement. Rather than spaces, imagined or real, there was the journey, 'The Way':

> Friend, I have lost the way.
> *The way leads on.*
> Is there another way?
> *The way is one.*
> I must retrace the track.
> *It's lost and gone.*
> Back, I must travel back!
> *None goes there, none.*

Duncan

* * *

Dear Duncan

Little did I reckon, when we began this correspondence, that a cruise passenger could lead me, through your words and reflections, into the heart of Nordic literature. Nor that this would make me reconsider ways in which some of its most famous writers raise questions about the relationship between art and artist, or how much of ourselves we project in concepts of place, including 'north' and the notion that this is anything more, as you say, than a relative geographical description.

The passenger disembarking at Kirkwall, in the company of perhaps thousands of other fellow travellers, morphs in my mind to a solitary figure and a much smaller ferry. The place is an island in north Norway, where a wooden jetty juts into dark waters. No one is there to meet the traveller, who walks towards a wooden house near the shore. The boat leaves. In a while—maybe days, maybe months from now—the traveller will go back aboard the ferry and depart, never to return. The wanderer's name could be Knud Pedersen, could be Hamsun. But that's my projection, my personal imagining. Because I think my name is in there too.

Yes, North can simply be a cardinal point. But for me (and for you, I think, through both your home place and your knowledge of writers such as Heinesen, which suggests an interest not typical of many Scottish writers, editors or publishers) it's also a concept that can stir imagination and creativity. There's something more than the simple law of averages that means that some great writers, past and present, have come from northern countries.

In that context, I'll admit that I wrestle with my enduring admiration for the power of Knut Hamsun's prose. I was introduced to his work long ago, by a lover in Norway who gave me a copy of *Pan*. Its opening sentence, about the Nordland summer's eternal day, can still haunt me. So do passages where the words seem to sing, especially in Norwegian, such as: 'Sommernetter og stille vann og uendelig stille skoger' (Summer nights and quiet water and endless quiet woods).

Then he adds: 'No calls, no footfalls on the roads; it seemed my heart was full of dark wine.'

As Thomas McGuane, writing about ways people relate to nature has said, Scandinavians differentiate between loneliness and solitude as a matter of course. I recognise that distinction, both in my own life and in Hamsun—the way he can raise a glass of that dark wine, but also, with his twists of voice and disdain for convention, throw it down to swig an entirely different liquor. Not least in *Pan* and *Mysteries* as well as the better-known *Hunger*, some of his work from the close of the 19th century still seems surprisingly modern. That includes, as Isaac Bashevis Singer said, his subjectivity, fragmentariness, use of flashbacks and his lyricism. Those comments are all the more remarkable because Singer wrote principally in Yiddish, while fellow Nobel laureate Hamsun spent his final years as a prominent Nazi sympathiser in occupied Norway.

Nina Frang Høyum of the Norwegian National Museum describes Hamsun as 'a national cultural trauma', but adds that his relevance is not only in his greatness as an artist, but also in how he can lead to debate about the relationship between fiction and society and the role of art and the artist. I know also that Sigrid Undset's life and art was very different to Hamsun's. Vocal in condemnation of the Nazis though the 1930s, she had to flee to Sweden, then the US, when Norway was invaded in 1940. Her eldest son died at Gausdal in the spring of that year, fighting for the resistance. When she returned to Lillehammer after the war, Sigrid published nothing more. She had earlier sent her Nobel medal to raise funds for Finland in the Winter War. Hamsun had sent his to Goebbels.

So, as you say, 'it's all projection, isn't it?' in perception of a space and place—and perhaps the art—we want to believe in. But what you say to conclude that observation seems crucial: that we then set out to find that imagined space.

I know that describes what has always motivated me to think about, then seek, northern places. What—in addition to the skill of their writing—still draws me to Hamsun and Undset, Per Petterson, Lars Saabye Christensen and poets such as Olav Hauge. Which, prompted by your recent words, will lead me to seek more of the work of William Heinesen, who seems adept at moving from the particular of small-town Torshavn to the universal and back again. So—thanks for sharing ideas through a chunk of this year, where the subjectivity, fragmentariness and flashbacks have been part of the fun.

I've been to Å, by the way—on Vesterålen, so a bit to the north of the one you mention on Lofoten. It seems that Norway has seven of them, which could certainly be the start of a journey, either through the wider country, the whole alphabet, or only to places named without consonants.

I wish you well with the travellers who visit and for ventures in writing and publishing. For me, North still flickers on the screen, still lures. I appreciate how you—and I hope both of us—have added some new frames to the projected story.

Kenny

* * *

Postscript: in further correspondence beyond this essay, the writers discovered that Sigrid Undset had called at Kirkwall on her return voyage from wartime exile in the US to Norway in 1945. She seems to have disembarked, since a copy of one of her books, *The Longest Years*, signed by her with a dedication and thanks to Winifred Clouston, widow of Orkney-based novelist and antiquarian J S Clouston—who had died the previous year—had recently been offered for sale by a local bookseller. Kenny is now the keeper of that book. The coincidence of Sigrid Undset coming ashore in Kirkwall and the track of some of the ideas in the essay is still a source of some amazement for the writers, and may even suggest future paths of inquiry.

The Strange Performance of Ink on Paper

Whitney McVeigh

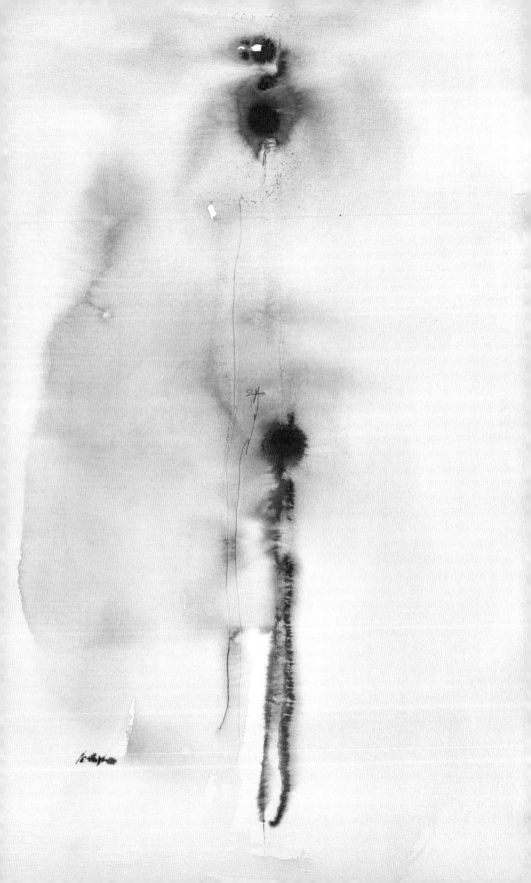

Landscape, memory,
Temporality and the body

Right: Whitney McVeigh, *Irrespective of Time*, Museu da Natureza, Brazil, 2019.

Uncertainty is a place. A corner of the world where thought is not settled. It manifests as carbon black, or as running water and continuous line. Doubt, uncertainty are passions for the artist, only understood by those in communion with their materials. A luminosity emerges that can be described as somewhere between the earth-bed and stars.

Right: Whitney McVeigh, *Temporality*, Cardi Gallery, 2020.

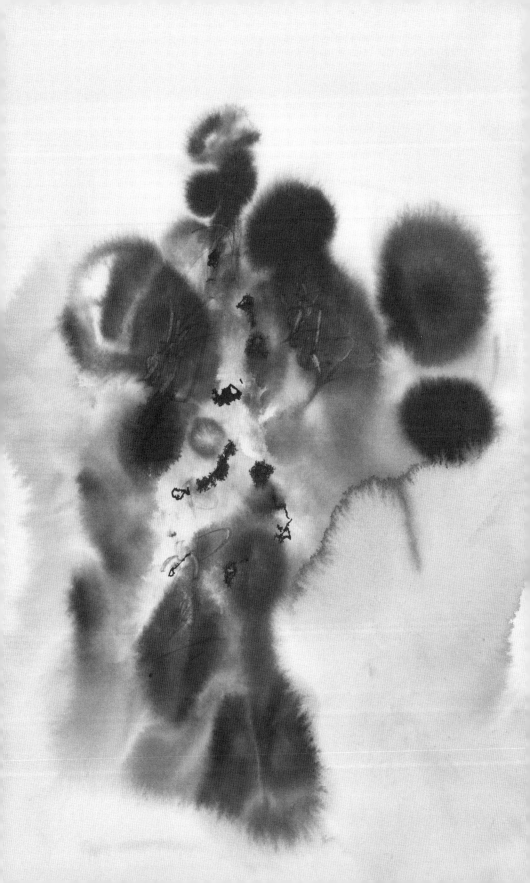

On paper, the emergence of movement and existential paths into memory—a discourse of mind
and materials as the ink lays bare on the page.
The force of bone black fractured by luminous
light; a crack in the infrastructure of a kind of
deep time-field and elegy to nature. Here: Sage,
Dadhichi's bones, dust, carbon, water, deity,
(Indā, Pālī), Indra, myth, sky, shadow, time,
presence, memory.

Right: Whitney McVeigh, *Indra (myth)*, detail, Eykyn Maclean Gallery, 2018.

Ancient volcanic rocks and fissures open a human dialogue through their ruggedness, an appearance of masters, creature or myth. Surface fragmentation. An imprint and opening in the two-dimensional space of the page. What is here? A time circle of memory created by the hand itself and conference of marks in solitude.

Right: Whitney McVeigh, *Imprint*, Museu da Natureza, Brazil, 2019.

Home
Ile
Ghar
Hame

Tomiwa Folorunso & Hamzah Hussain

Home

My parents married sometime around the middle of 1993, by the end of 1994 they were both here in Edinburgh. Scotland. My dad arrived first, he had a scholarship to study for his PhD in English literature. Four months pregnant with me, my mum followed him.

The first home I ever had was in my mother's body.

I was born on my maternal parents' wedding anniversary, Wednesday the third of May 1995, at about six thirty in the morning in Simpsons children's hospital in Edinburgh. From five thousand miles away, my grandmother named me 'Iyetomiwa', meaning: 'a girl has come looking for me'.

The first girl of my generation.
The first, first generation immigrant.
The first Scottish Nigerian of my family.

Mum said, 'I always thought we would go back to Nigeria' but Dad never taught me Yoruba so maybe he hoped we wouldn't? My mum's thoughts became an unlikely wish, and my dad's hopes became reality because his PhD took a while. We settled, they made friends, got jobs and I went to a nursery where I didn't want to play with the other children because I knew the colour of our skins were different.

If a home is a physical space—something that can be touched, slept in and lived in— then I am the first, the first of both sides of my family to be born into a home that is not in the same country as that of my parents.

But is Britain home? Does 'indefinite leave to remain' mean home? To live in a limbo of uncertainty of your future? To know you are at the mercy of a racialised, bureaucratic state, hoping and praying that you have enough time to reap the seeds of the opportunity you've been granted?

Praying.

My mum used to take me to the mosque with her.
What did she pray for when we went?
What did she pray for when she knelt on that mat and bowed her head—hope, happiness, love, home?

When she raised her head and eyes refused to meet her own, but I saw it--the disgust and distrust--I felt it, could she?

What does it mean to make a home in a place where even in Allah's home, where we worship the same God, say the same prayers, blackness still defines you as other?

***

In the early 1960's my grandfather took this country as a surrogate home. He fled Pakistan by road through Turkey and Eastern Europe and arrived in Scotland to find work. The plan was to make money, send it home and to eventually return home. But he never did. His cousin was sent to bring him back, but he also stayed. The home that they had only intended to adopt became their permanent, replacing the land that they had come from. They would only return to Pakistan a handful of times throughout the rest of their lives. They always told me stories of how they first came to be in Scotland, what things were like when they newly arrived. They are the reason my family is here today and the reason for my dual-identity.

I don't call myself a Pakistani. My identity, the story I tell when I introduce myself, is not Pakistani. 'Where are you from?' is always met with 'We were born in Scotland', and without their prompting, 'But my family is from—'

And still they all keep asking me 'but where are you from?'. I reply, 'I was born in Scotland but my parents are—' because I know what they're asking me is why my skin is the colour it is but that I sound Scottish.

And you do not get the Scots in us without knowing our other side; you don't get to ask a question and package us into a box of your choosing; you do not get to hold the power or make us feel like we don't belong here … like we don't have a stake here, like we don't have roots.

Our 'roots' … like a plant that connects to the soil, the soil on which we grew is British. But the seed of the root comes from elsewhere. We are migrated seeds, routes far from our mother trees. As if carried by a bird and deposited miles away.

* * *

Ile

For nine days.

Mum taking us to Lagos is like me spending the first twenty-five years of my life in Edinburgh, moving to another continent and then, when I go back, I go to the city an hour away from the one I grew up, Glasgow, I recognise it but I have no real connection to it. Bizarre.

But that's what she's doing because family is important. So we're going.

Deji and I are sitting on the right-hand side of the plane, close to the back—he let me have the window seat. As the plane starts its descent, I feel sick in my tummy, I'm equal parts nervous and excited, so I force myself to look out of the window and smile because … we're here and it's happening, and there's no going back now.

Murtala Muhammed International Airport in Lagos, Nigeria, is everything you expect it to be. Which is a shame. And after handing over our passports, both green and burgundy, a countless number of times we are finally allowed through to collect our bags.

Twelve hours. We stumble out, out into the noisy heat, unsure of where to go, pushing trolleys with suitcases full of Primark shoes and *Diary of a Wimpy Kid* books and scanning the sea of faces that are all the same colour as mine, looking for the ones that look like my mum. Arms wrap around me. Wrap around us—mum, Deji and me. I didn't realise my shoulders were up, but they are down now. Ile.

Rice, stew and plantain. Not usually my go-to meal at 10pm after a 6-hour flight but I eat it, on a tray on my lap, with a gently flickering non-energy saving light bulb illuminating us all. My cousin hides behind the side of the pantry wall, giggling and too shy to say hello. My mum's in the kitchen and I can hear her laughing with her big sister.

Bucket bath. A cold bucket bath. I haven't before experienced a heat that leaves me wanting to pour cold water over my body. We go to bed with torches, my mum and I sleeping next to each other for the first time in years. I shut my eyes to the sound of mosquitoes buzzing and the hum of a neighbour's generator.

My cousins take me to their university via a motorbike—okada—a rickshaw—keke— and two buses—danfo. Two hours. We walk around their campus, The University of Lagos (UNILAG). I don't know if it's the whiteness of my t-shirt compared to the blackness of cousin's abaya, but everyone is staring. Probably because '*your hair is messy, and nobody goes around with messy hair*'. Thanks, Ummuhaani.

They've sussed me out, even when I look the same, I still don't *look* the same. But I don't mind, because unlike home their eyes are full of curiosity and not hostility.

I ask my cousin to take me to the campus supermarket so I can buy a snack, because I'm hungry and my mum has given us strict instructions to only eat food that has been cooked—no meat, definitely no rice, and absolutely no raw vegetables or ice in our drinks. Just chips, deep fried chips. What was the point in spending almost one hundred pounds on a yellow fever vaccination to come all the way to Nigeria and the only food I can eat is chips? But, I suppose, there is rice at home.

Standing in the queue with a pack of triple chocolate chunk cookies, there are two boys in front of us, taller than me. They are holding two bottles, one of vodka and another of something dark, I guess, rum, my spirit of choice.

I smile to myself, because even though so much of this feels so foreign, so much of Nigeria feels so unknown, there's comfort in knowing that wherever you may be in the world, you'll be able to find some university students getting drunk on a Tuesday night.

***

On the back of an okada not wearing a helmet, doing 70mph down the wrong side of the road, splashing through every, single, puddle, clutching the driver's waist and refusing to let out a scream. Finally I step off, hands shaky, legs firm, laughing.

'Tomiwa, were you scared?' I am asked. I put her hand to my chest, 'feel my heart'.

Yet I'm not scared. Legs firm. The city with a population of over 17 million people that feels like double that is going on around me, but I've stopped. Still and firm. Peace that I wasn't looking for, but found me. A peace that came from love and happiness and sadness and uncertainty and fear, but peace. Finally peace.

* * *

I'm holding this little green book in my hand and I want to jump up and down. It's funny the things you think you need to legitimise yourself. I used to say, 'I am British, I have a British passport'. And now it's, 'I am Nigerian, I have a Nigerian passport.'

Nationality/Nationalité: NIGERIAN.

So I am.

My Black body made me African. I thought I had no choice, I thought that the colour of my skin and the letters that make up my name would forever tie me to that country, whether I liked it or not. But this is a choice—active decision making—an un-offensive, bureaucratic commitment to Nigeria.

I keep my passports in my bedside drawer along with the other precious artefacts of my life. And sometimes if I'm looking for something, I'll see the well-travelled burgundy one, but I can't see the green. So I'm rummaging, pushing birthday cards, handwritten notes and my emergency chocolate supply to the sides, panicking—where is it? I pull out the drawer, empty it onto my bed … and there it is! The bright money green landing neatly on top of burgundy.

No matter how much this world tries to force me to choose between them, they're always together, unable to exist without each other. The two parts of my identity, not one in each hand, but both in the same person. Sometimes one might be a bit lost, a bit scared or a bit worried, but both are always there.

Balancing. Always balancing but never balanced.

Mum	Dad
home	school
plantain	lasagna
culture	culture
green	burgundy
Scottish	Yoruba
Ile	Hame

* * *

Ghar

During a holiday to Pakistan with my mother last year, I grew to love the country that is her natal country, her motherland, but no longer her home. The benefit of visiting at this age—I was now mature enough to understand the things about Pakistan that would have eluded me when I was younger.

Despite having not being there for so many years, its familiarity came rushing back to me as soon as we stepped off the plane. I knew this air. I remembered its clamminess. My nose recognised smells it hadn't inhaled in years, and my ears reacquainted themselves with the tempo of Urdu spoken here. All around me were people dressed in traditional shalwar kameez in an array of bright colours. The clashing of strange but familiar, the same yet different. Dressed in jeans and a t-shirt, this time I was the one looking odd and out of place. The soundscape swarmed in my ears, the buzz of Urdu and Punjabi, spoken at speed much faster than I was used to, filled the air.

As we pushed our luggage trollies out of the airport building, we were met by the claustrophobic night air. Despite it being almost 2am, the area outside the airport was alive with activity. All five of my senses were assaulted; I locked eyes with brown expectant faces; I heard the hubbub of conversation, cars beeping; the scene smelled pastoral and sweaty; I tasted dust and smog on my tongue and felt the humidity cling to me like bees on a hive.

I can't say it felt like home—I don't have that privilege—but it didn't feel like I'd travelled five-and-a-half thousand miles from Dundee either. There was a peculiar sense of both belonging yet being a stranger. I was not used to seeing so many people looking and sounding like me. I regularly hear and even speak Urdu at home, but what was strange was its abundance. As much as I might look Pakistani and speak their language, I am considered a 'bhar walla'—'the outside one'—not of this place, someone who does not belong to their world and identity. Yet, I felt comfortable there, almost at home, a could-be-home place. As someone visiting his family's roots, and as someone whose identity is more fluid than native Pakistanis, I was able to understand my belonging differently. I occupied a liminal space between belonging and estrangement.

***

I could be both. Instead of getting the visa that I normally have to get when I travel to Pakistan, I could get a Pakistani nationality card. My duality would then be formal—stamped, labelled and officially approved by an authority. A defining and quantitative quality that could be searched for, grouped, categorised or become a statistic. A box that you could tick on an application form.

Scottish	Pakistani
English	Punjabi
Home	Ghar
Inside	Undar
Outside	Bahar
Breeks	Shalwar
Blue	Green

I would hold physical evidence of my both-ness, my otherness. A confirmed and approved duality presented in a way that is acceptable, preferred even. I might hand over one passport or the other, just as interchangeably as switching from one language to another, as effortlessly as wrapping a scarf around your neck. See, I'm an old hand at this, I've been doing it for a while. I can be whomever you want me to be whenever you need me to be, because that's what I do. It's easier than breathing.

Swapping languages, modal shifting comes more easily than anything else.

***

Home

We draw lines in our soils, etching jigsaw-shaped pieces to separate my soil from yours. While roots run deep into the ground, our man-made lines box us in and confine us. These borders make it clear where our home ends and yours begins.

I consider my home and the home of my parents as two separate, unrelated spaces. Yet, they share a history that extends to a time before I was born. In the place where I grew up, famous for its jute trade or tobacco, its ports hold the tears and blood and bones, and souls of my ancestors. Profits from their enforced labour are immortalised in street names and buildings.

My home colonised my home.
My home stole from my home.
My home broke my home.
My home doesn't even see my home as a home.

* * *

Is this why, I sometimes feel my Scottishness occupies my identity more than its counterpart? Is this why I feel one tug me over the line more than the other? One occupies the other and even when I am the Other, traces of Scottishness remain? And in the not-quite-perfect of Yoruba vocabulary overlaid by a Scots accent.

Can you say something in Urdu?
Can you say something in Yoruba?
What's the Urdu word for this?
Do they have the same thing in Yoruba?
What's the Scots equivalent of this?

* * *

Is home the place—the city—where you live? Is it where you're from, a place you always return to? What if you live in one city but always return to different places? Perhaps when the physical spaces of home aren't constant, you begin to disengage with the idea of home as physical altogether. Perhaps it's then that the home becomes more of a feeling.

Or is home a feeling? I'm not sure. A person or a feeling of comfort. 'Home is the place where, when you have to go there, they have to take you in.' But homes are not fixed., They are fluid, and they move about us.

We moved around a lot. Two homes became four, then six, and then nine. Some are homelier than others; in some Deji and I have to share a room, in others we don't. There's one where we're looked after, the other where I have to do the looking after.

***

This place was not always home. We moulded slowly and adapted to it, and it to us. This new flat, smaller, warmer than the last that was home for twenty-two years. First it was as strange as a hotel room, as if we were living, it felt, in someone else's home. Possessions, actions, conversations began to morph it. Now the small flat, the living-dining room hybrid with the crimson sofa, golden-yellow walls and brown carpet is home. The rush of warmth when I open the door, the smell of spices. Removing my shoes, as if at the mosque. Jacket, and bag in the hall. Mum on the sofa.

A-salam-wali-kum
Aap kesya ho? Kya kiya aaj? Dad ka kohi message aya?

These are routine questions, like five daily prayers. A ritual shedding of possessions; keys, wallet, loose change, pens and phone. Everything in its place. I become lighter, fill the space, making it heavier with my things. Mother watches television; Urdu and Punjabi comedy, poetry and sermons bounce off the walls. Her laughter, on cue, underlines it all.

Two people sitting: one reading the other watching. A looped moment in time. This familiarity and language makes it home.

As I return each night, re-telling the events of my day and she, the events of hers, it feels like the unloading and settling of our possessions. We pull out everything we have accumulated and lay it out on display like a child after beachcombing.

***

For me home was shuttling between my Mum and Dad; one home was every Wednesday and a second weekend, with the rest of the time at the other. But each time when I got ready to move it surprised me, it unsettled me, just as I became comfortable in one it was time to go again. I was too young then to accurately mimic the habits that would make me feel homely. So one always felt more homely than the other, one always felt more comforting than the other.

At university, I moved out. For three years, while still in Edinburgh, I made my own home every nine months. I found it hard to balance the two, I found it difficult to move from my mum's to my own, because it reminded me so much of going from mum to dad.

* * *

Home can be the place that I am from, the only place I've known in my short life. I grew up in this city, went to school and university in this city—although I won't be living and working here for much longer. Already, my first steps at such a leave-taking has already taken place as I'm writing this in my flat in Leeds where I am working for six weeks, I call this temporary flat 'home'. It is my place of rest, populated with the usual familiar paraphernalia to feign a resemblance: old dishes and cutlery, the patterned bed sheets, books and photographs. Yet it also feels not right, my real home is in Dundee. But I am calling a place I barely know 'home'? Perhaps it is a sort of step-home, or surrogate home?

Perhaps what makes us comfortable are the constants. Things that you know will, by and large, be there every time to greet you: the same person at your local corner shop; ordering the same drink at your favourite café, knowing it'll be made exactly the way you like, buying the same groceries, enjoying cuisine normally found at home. We populate our days in the same way that we populate a new house with old furniture, photographs and memorabilia.

The same routines and rituals comforts; the mind, consoled, knows what to expect, things are less strange. Transplanting habits from one place to another allow us to coorie in.

* * *

Hame

I love this part the most, the last leg of the journey, a final five minutes.

I've been sitting in the same seat for four hours, legs stiffening and cramping.

The vista unfolds before me; the expanse of the Tay stretching out on both sides, a placid grey-blue shrinking into the distance. In the distance is the Law monument a beacon marking home; it's like leaving on a light in an upstairs room. At its feet is the rest of the city, low and humble. Houses sit snuggly amidst the surrounding greenery. Dundee has no tall buildings reaching to the sky, and all of them are neutral in colour. The landscape is largely natural; stone and brick among tall trees, there is little room for gleaming metal structures. Even the city's newest building, V&A Dundee—'the city's living room'—is made to fit in with its neighbours, made to feel 'homely.'

As much as I try, I can't quite describe the feeling of travelling across the bridge with Dundee coming into view. I ask others and they can't describe it either, but what we can do is affirm that it is the feeling of 'home'. The pace of life is slower. There is less traffic, less people. No one seems to be in a rush. Warmth spills out from the bars and restaurants onto the pavements.

***

The feeling of a plane starting its descent over Edinburgh will never get old. It feels safe, feels easy and for those last few minutes, it feels like it is just me as I stare down below ticking off the people and places in my mind's eye:

My brother, Portobello.
Jen, Leith.
My Mama, Newhaven.
Liam, Muirhouse
Alice's, Silverknowes.
Down.
Hame.

Home is arriving into a virtually empty Waverley station at 11.30pm and stepping out onto the bridge, staring up at the Scot's monument as the rain hits my face.

Home is culture. Home is comfort. Home is my dad kissing the top of my head, mum squeezing my cheeks before bed and Deji putting his arm around me as we walk through security in Lagos airport. Home is my cousins shouting my name and the smell of plantain. It's Emily asking me if I want some tea and sitting on the step outside Wildfire with Linsey. Home is riding on the top deck of the number 11 bus at 6.30am, making its way down Newhaven Road and watching the sunrise around Arthur's Seat. Home is Kirsten and Alice and Kirsty and Lexi too. It's the smell of Olivia's nonna's house and the omni centre at the top of Elm Row. It's the M&S food court on a sad day, and Victoria Park on a good one. Home is safe and it holds you, protects you, loves you, and comforts you.

I think home changes with time. I know Edinburgh is always home, I know I will always have a home in Nigeria. I think it's a feeling found in people and places, and moments and things.

Home has many faces but is always recognisable, no matter how many lines crease its brow. Home may have skins as dark as mine, speak with a tongue close to my heart, or look at me with glinting eyes. Home is more than place. It is more than land and borders. The feeling of 'home' is of relationships. Dundee is and always will be 'home' because of my strong feelings for it, and its direct connection to my family and friends

In the same way that we have different relationships, some deeper than others, we might also have different homes, varying levels of home. Some homes are more homely than others. Home might be anywhere, an imagined space where we can exhibit our histories, talk about our present and speculate on our futures. What form will home take when I write on it again?

I straddle the line between here and there. A foot on either side, leaning from one to the other when necessary. But with that comes a loss of balance, an unequal distribution of cultural weight. While the terrain maybe uneven, with practice I find my footing, steadying myself between here and there. To be home is to have your feet comfortably on either side of the threshold.

I suspect the essay will change if you ask me to write this again. The story will have a different beginning—I'm from Dundee but have been living here for X years. As time passes, Dundee will be at memory's edge, replaced by my current flat, now occupying that periphery. I will have added more artefacts to my museum, hold new stories to share. 'Home' will always be there to come back to even when I have found other 'homes' elsewhere.

I thought when I began that this would be easy. A classic first-generation personal essay about how hard it is to grow up with two homes, to feel constantly unsettled and in-between. To find the equilibrium of this balancing act. But home is what and where you make it. I have had many homes, I will have many more homes, probably collecting and losing memories and people, and random pieces of furniture throughout.

I am home now: Ghar, Ile, Hame.

Between the Lines

Dai John

Hunched in the red-washed darkness of the military transport aircraft's cargo hold I am struck by the way a group of ninety-plus people can superficially look identical while simultaneously being mostly strangers. The engines' incessant noise—somewhat mitigated by ill-fitting yellow earplugs for those who are novices in the business of 'air-delivered operational capability', and by the green acoustic ear defenders acquired by the more experienced—makes verbal communication almost impossible. We sit in self-imposed isolation.

Some of those around me are using their mini-Maglite flashlights or head torches to read and make notes ahead of whatever is their next formal duty. Others are asleep. For reasons I have never fully understood—despite my training as an air force logistics officer—the military air movements system requires troops being transported to operational destinations to report to the 'air port of embarkation' at least twenty-four hours before the advertised departure time. Something to do with the complexity of moving people in both what are called 'formed units' and, as is the case with me and my small team, as 'individual augmentees', as well as the time taken to build palletised loads of cargo and prepare vehicles for movement by air (draining batteries and fuel tanks, deflating tyres and so on). But even so, as a consequence large numbers of people spend significant amounts of time waiting impatiently to embark. Once airborne, many immediately succumb to a fitful and restless sleep. Beside me Corporals Steve Jones and Paddy McGuigan are unconscious, slumped in their aluminium and webbing jump seats, supported by the aircraft bulkhead behind and their seat harnesses in front, and laterally by the individuals sitting next to them. On a less packed aircraft I know that Steve and Paddy, as seasoned members of the green ear defender contingent, would have requisitioned any unused floor space, unrolled their kip-mats and climbed into their olive drab issue sleeping bags—'green slugs'—for some quality sleep.

As well as the darkness and noise, I am melting in the oppressive, oily heat. Like everybody else on board I am wearing, in addition to the standard multi-terrain pattern camouflage shirt and trousers that are now ubiquitous regardless of which branch of the armed forces you belong to, heavy boots, a green quilted softee jacket, combat smock, Osprey body armour and a Mark 6 ballistic helmet. And we're all suffering. The aircraft's loadmaster, or the air engineer, or whoever it is in the blackness of the hold who's got their hand on the dial, is clearly taking seriously the job of making the whole experience as grim as possible. Bastard.

Apart from my own team, I have no real idea who everybody else on board is, although I feel I ought to; I can see some, reinforcements for the helicopter detachment that arrived at Skopje airfield a few days ago, plus a handful of military police, and possibly some Royal Engineers who'll be looking after life support for the British units transiting through. I know that as part of a multinational operation we won't be alone on this one. But I still have a nagging anxiety that as we disembark from the aircraft we will find ourselves in some god-forgotten corner of the airfield with nothing but our own kit and no orders. It wouldn't be the first time that 'You will be met on arrival and briefed by … ' becomes 'You will find yourselves entirely alone on arrival, unexpected and ignored, so just get on with it'. Over the last few hours I've been unable to dismiss this imagined scenario from my mind. I try to make practical sense of the sketchy instructions pushed into my hands before we left. I know that it will be dark, that we will be disorientated.

The final few minutes down towards Skopje are unpleasant, with the aircraft diving towards the ground while jinking from side to side in the hope of confusing and evading any potential missile threat. I recognise the classic 'Khe Sanh Approach', developed by the Americans in Vietnam to minimise the amount of time the aircraft is vulnerable to ground fire. It's still too hot in here. The low intensity red lighting has been shut down by the loadmaster who now yells at everyone to turn off their Maglites. The military policeman sitting facing Paddy throws up extravagantly all over him. Paddy doesn't look impressed. After the five-hour hiatus of the flight, I realise reluctantly that this is where the rubber hits the road and we make a good fist of it or totally fuck up. The 'we' here includes a couple of junior air movements officers, five warrant officers and senior NCOs with a variety of specialisations, including air ops planners and signallers. There are a dozen junior ranks too, including Steve and Paddy—both drivers and heavy plant operators, plus loggies, movers and line technicians, and two are military chefs. There is also a civilian woman, 'an operational analyst from the UK Government Communications HQ' they said, and a close protection guy to keep her safe, which seems odd as by the look of her—she clearly spends more time working out than working on her smile—she could take care of herself. I can feel the tension around me as people fumble to sort themselves out, checking kit. Through the few small windows the inside of the aircraft is suddenly illuminated by the blinding pyrotechnic flash of flares discharged as decoys should any heat seekers be coming our way. This provides another opportunity for the frequent flyers amongst us, me included, to deploy our practiced insouciance for the benefit of those less experienced now sitting in wide-eyed consternation. But we aren't feeling it.

In the moments between bracing and the inevitable heavy landing everything stops. With no points of reference we are left hanging, suspended in time, and I imagine the tarmac rushing a few metres beneath us. Above and forward of me the pilots are relying on night vision goggles to bring us safely down, the tactical landing being made without benefit of visual navigation aids or runway lighting. The undercarriage thumps the runway hard and immediately the piercing whine of the engines intensifies as maximum reverse thrust is applied. There is a confusion of shouting and activity as the aircraft comes to a standstill; with whirring urgency the aircraft's rear loading ramp opens up and out. Pallets of equipment and the vehicles are untethered and offloaded first, followed by the lumpen silhouettes of laden troops who disperse with surprising agility into the darkness of the airfield. Against expectation a figure materialises on the loading ramp; his words are mostly lost to the roar of the engines. He guides us a safe distance from the aircraft which now turns to taxi away. I recognise him as the Officer Commanding the unit tasked with protecting our small force while here in Skopje and seeing us through to our ultimate destination in Kosovo. We've met before, briefly, and recognise each other; Squadron Leader Mike 'Ben' Dover, a good hand and once a French Foreign Legionnaire before adopting a rather more conventional outlet for his martial inclinations. Ben tells me he's negotiated a site for us to pitch our small tented encampment here on the airfield; it's now simply a case of finding it and sorting ourselves out. No problem.

***

Thus we began a fairly typical operational deployment, in this case during the final stages of bitter conflicts that through the final decade of the twentieth century had convulsed the Balkans. As mandates go, it seemed at the time the right thing to do; a succession of massacres inflicted mainly on ethnic Albanian civilians by Yugoslav Serbian forces across Kosovo had generated a considerable head of steam in the media, and *Something Must Be Done* was the prevailing sentiment at home. Complex and protracted negotiations had led to the recent suspension of the Allied air campaign, and in summer 1999 the NATO-led Kosovo Force (KFOR) began deploying from Macedonia to secure Kosovo for the return of refugees. With fighting still going on and almost a million people displaced and in daily fear for their lives, little electricity or water, homes destroyed, roads mined, bridges down, and schools and hospitals out of action, ordinary life in Kosovo had been suspended and KFOR faced a significant challenge. As part of Britain's contribution to the KFOR mission we would marshal our resources in Skopje, Macedonia, and having secured border crossing points and the route into Kosovo would establish military and humanitarian relief flights to and from Pristina airport. The airport had recently been vacated in haste, and with the added encouragement of NATO airstrikes, by the occupying Serb forces, who remained a significant threat to Kosovar Albanian communities elsewhere in the country.

***

My first encounter with the British tactical headquarters' chief of staff in Skopje is not encouraging. In the few hours of darkness since arriving we have: built our temporary accommodation; implemented an administrative routine of guarding, eating and sleeping; established relations with those who arrived shortly before us—Ben's boys—and who will help us to make it to Pristina. 'What time do you call this?', the chief of staff demands, 'I hope you're better at your job than you are at timekeeping—we were expecting you hours ago.' I have crossed paths with him before, and his direct approach is not a surprise. Like other senior officers in pursuit of further advancement he has been careful to cultivate an array of eccentricities, one of which is apparent now in the range of boy scout badges stitched onto his uniform. 'What's your plan, squadron leader?' I don't feel able to tell him that I'd been briefed to expect a plan from his HQ, not the other way around. 'We're looking for a location for the harbour area we need for all the kit coming up from the sea port at Thessaloniki tomorrow, Sir,' I say. I add that Motel Macedonia on the main north-south highway a few kilometres up the road from Skopje looks to have an extensive gravelled area and plenty of accommodation we might be able to use. His mood brightens: it turns out that this is exactly the suggestion he had made to the ops desk people, now endorsed by us, the newly arrived recce team. Not risking an exchange of relieved glances we leave with the bones of a plan. Now it's simply a case of making it work.

***

We arrive in Pristina. Some opportunist small arms fire had been directed at us en route from the Macedonia-Kosovo border but apart from allowing us to tick the 'contact with the enemy' box—a bragging rights prerequisite—is of no greater consequence. Thank Christ also that the whole harbour area thing, the military transit base, worked out okay. The threadbare Motel had become a functioning military location. But now we're here at Pristina airport. At first sight the place is mostly as I expected from the satellite imagery and the pictures we'd been given: two intersecting runways, a scatter of low buildings, some rust-streaked hangars, a small air traffic control tower and a two-storey passenger terminal. There are, though, several things I hadn't expected: for a start I hadn't expected the amount of destruction now before us, large, casually irregular holes torn in roofs and walls, and floors flooded by fractured water mains. We recognise the hallmarks of 'surgically delivered' laser guided bombs—LGBs—although surgical doesn't seem an appropriate description given the extent of the damage. As we pick our way tentatively through the wreckage, I am keenly aware that I haven't demanded personal face-to-face confirmation from the explosive ordnance disposal guys that they're happy this area has been cleared. Somebody said it was okay. The terminal is a tangle of cabling from collapsed ceilings, rubble-covered floors, with windows shattered and glass everywhere. Is the structure safe? Has it been checked? By way of a response a large concrete beam crashes to the floor metres behind us. We beat a belatedly hasty retreat into the car park.

Here I find something else I'd hoped not to. This is as far as several of the building's former occupants got to before being caught in the impact of the NATO fast jets' departing gift of LGBs, or perhaps just a single lucky shot. I guess they'd also decided that the terminal wasn't the safest place to be. But too late. So here they are— recognisably Serbian irregulars, flung into contortions unachievable in life and, apart from their boots, stripped by the weapons' blast of most of their clothing. For some reason one is still wearing white gloves. In self-protection, my brain defaults to focus on the banal, the incongruous, small details of the scene in front of me. As a boy, I had anticipated, relished even, the adrenaline rush of killing small things; I can recall my preoccupation with death and injury in news reports, and looking with a dispassionate interest at the final roadside thrashings of an animal struck by a passing car even. But now, in this space … With my own mortality so acutely apparent to me, I elect not to record the scattered confusion of bodies and body parts. But some things you can't un-see. We find sheets to cover them until we can sort out their recovery from the car park.

* * *

I hadn't expected the Russians to have got here first. But here they are, scruffy, belligerent and unshaven in their striped tee-shirts plus dirty old armoured vehicles, some of which still bear in large white stencilled letters on their flanks the acronym 'SFOR'—the UN Stabilisation Force in Bosnia, which is where they're supposed to be, not here. I attempt to communicate with their boss, recognisable by the insignia on his shoulders rather than any air of authority or physical presence. His body odour is unbelievable, really rank. As we have no Russian speaker, I try English, then schoolboy German, then pidgin French. He is animated and very keen to communicate, but only in Russian. We definitely need a Russian speaker. I talk to Karen, the unsmiling GCHQ woman, and she says she'll make some calls on her satellite phone, relishing, I sense, the status she thinks her technological superiority confers. As she knows, I haven't been given one.

***

There is no obvious danger here. We had heard desultory fire earlier during the patrol, and had gone through the motions of taking cover, conducting 'actions on' including searching for the fire's point of origin through the night sights on our rifles, doing a head count and sending in a report. The brief frisson of 'contact' wasn't intended for us. We had made our way through the darkened ruins of the village with caution; there had been no reports of unexploded ordnance or improvised explosive devices (IEDs) in this area but the residual risk that there might be was enough to keep us on hard surfaces only and to steer clear of the debris strewn around. But here in this cellar is nothing more hazardous than broken glass and the detritus of subsistence living, now twisted or shattered by the intense heat of the fire that has blackened the walls and that is still lingering acridly in the back of my throat. Had the family sought refuge from the bombs in this place before they died? Or, worse, had they been driven down here deliberately? It doesn't matter now, for here they are, all five of them it looks like, huddled into a tangle in the far corner. We stand in silence, nothing to say, before Ben's second-in-command, Sergeant Tony Blackman, calls in a situation report on the radio, then mutters 'Animals'. He means the Serbs.

Given recent events, my own response is not what I expect. Like a film director's classic cut-away, I remember a school trip twenty-five years before—to Pompeii, where we are shown the plaster casts of another family overwhelmed when the volcanic dust came roiling down the slopes of Vesuvius to blanket the city. There is something here about the arrangement of limbs, the turn of a head, the fused bodies that sparks the memory. I think, am I a voyeur? I didn't have to come. This isn't my job, patrolling the ground defence zone (GDZ) extending outwards from the airfield perimeter. I have chosen to come, to be part of this effort to reassure, deter, to 'dominate the ground'. You need to get out here, to understand why we are here at all don't you? To see it first-hand, as an event not gleaned from morning briefings and lines on maps where 'human terrain' provides a useful euphemism for 'people', but through boots on the ground. My presence is legitimate, I reason, and not without personal risk. It, of course, will do my credibility no harm. These guys know and trust me, and not many of my contemporaries would choose to be out here. My choice. It occurs to me that these conflicts and their effects are always about choices. Those who caused this carnage chose to do so. We chose to enter this house, not the one beside it or across the track. As the patrol leaves the cellar, having taken photographs and tried to touch nothing, I feel sadness but not shock. This won't go into my next letter home.

***

Looking back, the Kosovo operation represented the kind of decisive, fundamentally well-intentioned military intervention, based on a broad consensus, that I had envisaged being a part of; unfettered by the Cold War's bipolar inertia and emboldened by comparative success of multinational intervention in Kuwait in 1991, the UK's military was to become a 'force for good'. For us, at the time, it was the chance to 'go on ops', and I had been quick to stake my claim. 'It has to be me', I'd thought, 'Who else has the right combination of training and experience?' Once selected, my team and I had relished the sense of being bit-part players on a broader stage than we were used to. When the TV news described the deployment of British forces on the KFOR mission we could say, 'Yes, we're on the Pristina airfield recce team', and 'No, we're not expecting trouble, but, you know, things on the ground are never the same as the intelligence reports. We'll be fine.' In the UK military a kind of Equity Card system applies to volunteers for operations; you can't go unless you've been before, and this subsequently worked for me when operational tours in Iraq, and then Afghanistan, were in prospect.

***

My journey here had ostensibly begun more than a decade earlier. A convergence of factors, foremost amongst them a growing disillusionment with the routine of a career in corporate London, and the sense of purpose and shared achievement I gained from the challenges of part-time soldiering, ultimately led me to a career in uniform. In reality though, and more prosaically perhaps, I started on this journey much earlier than that. Turning over my earliest memories, it isn't difficult to discern a pattern with its origins in my father's reminiscences of his time in the army. As an eighteen-year-old in early 1945 he had been old enough—just—to have been called up and, like many of his generation, his subsequent life had inevitably been shaped by the experience and aftermath of the Second World War. As a child in the late 1960s and early '70s, I remember that the war still permeated countless aspects of life, from popular boys' comics to the bomb sites glimpsed from railway carriage windows on rare trips to London, and from friends' dads who had waded ashore at first light on D-Day, or fought in the jungles of Burma. For my boyhood friends and me it was an article of faith—one of which we often reminded each other—that Raymond Baxter, dashing presenter of BBC Tomorrow's World, had been a Battle of Britain Spitfire pilot (we were almost right; he spent the summer of 1940 in Canada learning to fly, though his later wartime exploits more than justified our devotion). But the war had ended less than three decades previously and remained a tangible presence in our lives. My father was an enthusiastic member of the territorial army who on returning from weekend camp would leave at my bedside gifts of old items of uniform for me to find the following morning, or once—oh joy!—gave me a thrillingly deafening ride to school in a roaring, bucking jeep 'borrowed' from his regiment. That's what being a dad meant, and it seemed to me that a life devoid of uniforms, ritual, order, excitement and jeeps was a life unfulfilled. The route subsequently described by my own experiences led—perhaps inexorably—from initial officer training and the acquisition of skills, gained through specialist training and employed for real whenever the opportunity presented itself, to the wreckage of a distant airfield in the company of people I yet scarcely knew but whose presence validated our shared purpose there.

***

Some months ago I was asked to write an essay about some of my experiences in conflict zones. The person who asked knew I kept diaries and she said, just have a go, see where it leads you. I look through my journals and other records, over thirty of them in a variety of A4 and A5-format notebooks (many given as gifts by those aware of my writing) currently in boxes under the bed in the spare room. Usually I do not revisit them; it is enough for me to know that they are there. In reading them now, it's striking how the entries I made are preoccupied not with the wider aims or purposes of my involvement in different military campaigns, but rather with the practical concerns of my job, challenges to address, speculation on timescales, dates and destinations for rest and recuperation—R&R—breaks, and dense, now with the passage of time, almost undecipherable, military jargon. A little later she asked me— why do you keep such records?—and I had to think. My journals describe events but mostly do not explain them. Nor do they reflect how I felt at the time. Events which seemed significant are afforded longer, more detailed entries, though these are limited to facts: When? Who? How? I rarely address the 'Why?' in my notebooks. An entry for 17 February 2007 describes my experience aboard a Chinook helicopter en-route to Afghanistan's Helmand Valley. As we approach our destination we are engaged by a rocket propelled grenade fired from the ground. The aircraft has to abandon its landing, banking hard to starboard, and climbing steeply away as the rear gunner empties the magazine of her machinegun in the approximate direction from which the projectile had been launched. I describe its smoke trail as, viewed through the open ramp at the back of the helicopter, it rises towards us, then, reaching the apex of its trajectory, falls harmlessly away to detonate on the ground below. The landing is abandoneded and we return to our base at Kandahar airfield. Yet there is nothing about how I felt at the time or immediately afterwards.

My notebooks give me a kind of touchstone, a portal, providing access to otherwise elusive memories, should I ever wish to subsequently recollect and relive the events described. In reading my diary entry on the aborted helicopter flight, even when neither the purpose or my reaction to its outcome are recorded, I can now recall that initial shock, the fear felt by all on board, and the overwhelming wave of relief and elation as we flew beyond the weapon's range; face reddening, I also remember that at the time I thought that this would make quite a good anecdote. My reason for being on the flight and the subject of the never-attended briefing are both now brought to mind. The wider context—six months away from home, sharing a portacabin with Colin Walsh and David Evans—just three of us in a space for four reflecting our comparative seniority in rank also coalesce into sharp focus.

As well as providing a straightforward chronology, my journals therefore represent a means of returning to emotions, thought, state of mind, serve as a structure to buttress my imperfect memory and, perhaps, to somehow validate a life—mine. I would never contemplate others reading them, and indeed would not knowingly allow it. It is enough reassurance for me that they exist, an unbroken, ongoing forty-year long thread connecting me to my past life which otherwise would survive only in fragments. I was once told that you don't remember days, only moments, and the force with which that assertion struck me led directly to my journal-keeping habit.

Though seldom recorded on paper, I have also sometimes reflected on a pattern of recurring themes emerging in unconscious thoughts, whether in daytime reverie or at night in dreams:

—As we will always arrive in darkness, how will things be when daylight comes? Everything is always much closer together than you imagined it to be in darkness, or much further apart. I feel a cloying apprehension, as in my mind the geography conspires to rearrange itself to coincide with the emergence of first light, and objects—trees, buildings, whatever —change their relationships with you and with each other, grow or diminish in size, or contrive not to be there at all. I have to fight to suppress a rising, bitter nausea, exacerbated by the imperative to remain as silent as possible. Simple tasks—establishing defensive positions, extracting pieces of kit from the bottom of bergens—become disproportionately demanding. I have since learned to anticipate the initial disorientation, deal with it, but it always comes.

—What will it be like when we get there? You might be diligent in your preparation, try hard to imagine and address possible outcomes: 'Take time to deliberate, but when the time for action has arrived, stop thinking and go' as instilled by staff college tutors. But then, when you go, there is always the unexpected, or unanticipated, to contend with. On operations the likelihood of this is higher; situations develop quickly and you are denied the luxury of time to think. In early 2003, during night-time ground operations to target snipers harassing coalition forces advancing into Iraq, through circumstance I found myself as the headquarters' nocturnal operations desk officer. Asked to authorise the use of air-launched weapons to dislodge a single sniper from his position on the roof of what was ostensibly an empty apartment block, in accordance with our 'rules of engagement', I did. It is a truism that in modern warfare the use of remotely-directed weapons offers a seductively attractive emotional distance between those initiating action and its consequences for those at the receiving end. My real concern right now is about what the military euphemistically calls 'collateral damage' when what it really means is other people's lives. Was anybody else in that building? We had no way of knowing for sure, and we couldn't wait for first light to find out—far too dangerous said the commander on the ground. I could have sought higher authorisation but at 3:00 am I needed to decide. Under pressure, you cannot take time to consider; such delays cost lives. And you do not want to be that person who cracks under pressure.

—What is happening at home? When away from home and family in challenging environments, back in 'Blighty' the sun seems always to be shining, the lawn always stays cut and the children gambol happily in the park. Nobody falls over. Your partner is never irritable or impatient, cross or frustrated, but sits saint-like in devoted anticipation of your homecoming, to be celebrated with immediate sex. Love and desire are inextricably entwined; sex reminds you that you are alive. It is an old military saw, often repeated, that on such occasions the second bang is the kitbag

being put down, the third is the front door closing. Enforced separations are followed by joyous reunions. Home is idealised; such perceptions are common and are even necessary to anchor you.

Every returnee feels a small stab of pain as they let go of the unique closeness, born of a brotherhood—sisterhood too—forged in adversity, danger, or boredom and fear. Having worked together, slept in close proximity, faced the same daily challenges and risks, spoken the same lexicon—and relished its opacity to outsiders—we have all looked out for each other. Small acts of kindness—a bar of chocolate left on a bedside locker, the unasked-for collection of clean laundry—have been reciprocated without comment or question, and burdens, emotional and practical, have been shared. We never speak of such intimacies, but we know they are lost to us when we get home.

***

And always, there is an interminable waiting to get home after a long deployment— waiting for the arrival of your roulement flight; waiting for confirmation that it will depart on time; waiting through the inevitable delay; and then waiting as you travel the first leg of your journey home.

At Bloodhound Camp in Cyprus, reluctantly surrendering to the process of 'decompression', I had hoped to play the 'individual augmentee' card to bypass a system primarily designed to allow members of formed units to relax together in the sun, undergo a progressive reintroduction to alcohol and benefit from the alleged therapeutic efficacy of water polo and dinghy sailing. But too many boxes were ticked on the Potential Operational Stress Indicators form handed to us as we waited to leave. Having identified myself as potentially vulnerable to mental health issues, the staff— adventurous training-qualified PT Instructors in the main—were uncharacteristically benign and largely left me to my own devices. Designed for large numbers, the fact that there was only a dozen of us caused the organisers some consternation. Last night the performers in the Combined Services Entertainment show—comedians, dancers, an Oasis tribute band—significantly outnumbered their audience. But I wanted just to get home. I hadn't felt 'operationally stressed'. When I confessed this to the duty medic she said that that was quite normal in those suffering from operational stress. Four cans of my beer ration left. After six months of teetotal existence, the first two sent me into a state of borderline narcolepsy. The ultimate cheap date.

***

Now I am home. I am surrounded by—enfolded within—familiar things, the myriad trappings of domesticity in sharp contrast to the austerity of my recent existence. The final phase of the journey here—disembarkation at Brize Norton airfield, bus to railway station, military transport to married quarter—had been enlivened latterly by our becoming hopelessly stuck under a low pedestrian walkway only minutes from my front door. I make the last half mile on foot and laden with kit, then stand for a moment before ringing my own doorbell. In my mind this is what my father would have done in 1945. The next few moments are lost in embraces, tears and breathless welcomes as I realise that I really am back. All is at once familiar and strange, the house somehow different—smaller, neater—than the memory I have held these last six months. Soon, I know, normality will reassert itself as it always does, and at some point the whole cycle will begin again. But for now, in this moment, we are together, safe, happy and thankful that we are once again a family. I am home.

My Love Affair with the Essay

Phillip Lopate

Most reflections by writers about how they came to do what they do are, in the end, disappointing. Hence, I invite you to find this particular article disappointing from the get-go. If you can lower your expectation bar sufficiently, it may not prove wholly unworthy of your time. To expect little, in any case, is something natural to the essay form, whose professed modesty by its very name in putting forth a mere 'attempt' is echoed by the lack of major award recognition and relatively low commercial status accorded it by the outside world. It is hard for an essayist to get away with being an egomaniac (though some bravely try). What I want to do here is to sketch (modest word) my own involvement with the essay, and consider how my understanding of the form has evolved over time.

When I first dreamed of being a writer, in my late teens and early twenties, I was drawn first to fiction and then to poetry. Never did it enter my mind then to become an essayist. The essays I was exposed to in college were assigned by way of teaching to write compositions and examination papers, the sort of tax you had to pay in order to read great literature. As I was usually assigned no more than one essay per writer from a textbook, it did not occur to me that essayists could have personalities as charming or idiosyncratic as my favorite novelists and poets. But I was already drawn to first-person writing, that intimate, subjective whisper in the ear, whether it be the growl of Dostoevsky's Underground Man or the clueless purr of Ford Madox Ford's narrator in *The Good Soldier* or Machado de Assis's posthumous prankster or Italo Svevo's ironic Zeno or Céline's manic shrill Bardamu or Browning's sinister Duke on 'My Last Duchess.' What I liked particularly about first-person writing was the one-to-one connection it established between author and reader, its penchant for self-analysis, which was so often undercut by rationalization and unreliable narrator self-deception. Unbeknownst to me, I was in preparation for falling in love with the personal essay.

That captivation occurred during one summer vacation when I rented a cottage in Cape Cod. I had already written a book about my teaching experiences as a writer-in-the-schools, *Being with Children*, which I did not realize was essentially a string of essays; I thought them chapters at the time. As is my wont, I snooped around the bookcases at the house I was subletting, and found a Penguin paperback of William Hazlitt's selected essays, and took it outside to peruse. Unlike Paul on the road to Damascus, my conversion experience occurred lying in a hammock. Hazlitt's cussed, animated voice electrified me from the start. Het turned me on to his friend Charles Lamb, who had a much more insidious, playful tone, but was every bit as galvanizing. Hazlitt also warmly recommended Montaigne, whom I had read decades earlier in college with bafflement and indifference, but who now, as I approached middle age, became my guy, my model. The rest of the Anglo-American canon followed more or less automatically: Addison and Steele, Samuel Johnson, Stevenson, Beerbohm, Virginia Woolf, Orwell, and on the other side of the Atlantic, Thoreau, Mencken, Baldwin, Mary McCarthy, etc.

I began writing the stuff and teaching the personal essay to my graduate students; I had to photocopy masses of material because it was hard to find any anthologies that went back before the twentieth century. All the publishers seemed to be rigidly focused on modern and contemporary authors. I, however, have been blessed or cursed with an historical sense, and have envisioned the personal essay as a conversation between living and dead authors across the centuries. Eventually it dawned on me that I myself would have to edit the anthology I needed to assign. That is how *The Art of the Personal Essay* came about. In my genealogy of the canon, I went all the way back to precursors, Seneca and Plutarch in the West, and Sei Shonagon and Kenko in the east, before including a chunk of Montaigne, then a large dose of the English essayists, then a quick global tour of other cultures, including Turgenev, Tanizaki, Benjamin, Borges, Hubert Butler, E. M. Cioran, Roland Barthes and Natalia Ginzburg, before concluding with the American scene.

Let me say immodestly that it has become the standard text, adopted by universities across the United States. It is probably more responsible for my being invited to ruminate here than the five collections of my own essays I've published. Indeed, I have become so identified as the champion of the personal essay—even given undue credit for reviving the form—that I began to feel imprisoned in my promotional role, though happy to take whatever rewards it provided.

Part of the problem was that the more I studied the vast literature of the essay, the less was I convinced that the personal essay constituted such a unique subgenre, distinct from other kinds of essays. First of all, I fell in love with Emerson, whom I had stupidly excluded from my *Art of the Personal Essay*, only to realize decades later that there was no American essayist more imbued with personality, acuity and sheer strangeness than this man. Second, I began writing a lot of criticism—of movies, books, architecture, visual arts—and it didn't seem to me that my brain or my deployment of rhetorical strategies was operating any differently than when I wrote personal essays. I knew that some of my favorite practitioners, such as Virginia Woolf, George Orwell and Max Beerbohm, were equally adept at critical pieces as they were at personal essays, with no shrinkage of their inimitable personalities in their criticism. As I immersed myself in the critical masters, from Diderot to Ruskin to Edmund Wilson to Lionel Trilling to Susan Sontag, and so on, I saw that they were all, each in their own way, cobbling together a highly specific voice or persona through which evaluations and insights could issue forth. So, when it came time for me to edit another anthology, this time of American movie critics for the Library of America (that august preserver of the national literary canon), I decided that my selection of the various movie reviews would be adjudged first and foremost by their literary worth, and inflected, however subliminally, by the notion that each was a kind of personal essay. Or let me simply say, an essay.

I have since been expanding my idea of what constitutes an essay, which has taken me in many new directions: food writing, nature writing, science writing, psychoanalysis, sports, politics, geography, religion. No longer restricted to the self-consciously belletristic, I seek out fine examples in every discipline, because every discipline has very gifted writers who are willing to venture forth with their thoughts on the page, testing hypotheses, registering skepticism about received ideas, examining their own doubts, employing worldly irony, and making a pleasing arc of their cogitations. Which brings me to my current project: editing an anthology of the American essay.

I signed a contract a year ago with Pantheon Books in hardcover and Anchor in paperback for a one-volume compendium of essays written in the United States, from the Puritans in the seventeenth century to the present. I decided to go big: to include essays of all stripes, not just personal essays, and from every walk of life. Which brings up the question: what is an essay? I'm sure you are all familiar with the various definitions, such as Dr. Johnson's 'a loose sally of the mind.' But E. B. White cautions that 'even the essayist's partial escape from discipline is only a partial escape: the essay, although a relaxed form, imposes its own discipline, raises its own problems, and these disciplines and problems soon become apparent and (we all hope) act as a deterrent to anyone wielding a pen merely because he entertains random thoughts or is in a happy or wandering mood.' Addison drew the line between essays, which didn't quite know where they were going, and discourses, which did. For William Dean Howells, the significant line was between the essay and the article. Agnes Repplier thought that essays should offer 'no instruction, save through the medium of enjoyment.' William Gass forbade the scholarly article from consideration as an essay. Cynthia Ozick, in her beautiful piece, 'She: Portrait of the Essay as a Warm Body,' is at pains to distinguish a genuine essay from what she considers fakes. She writes: 'A genuine essay has no educational, polemical, or sociopolitical use; it is the movement of a free mind at play. … A genuine essay is not a doctrinaire tract or a propaganda effort or a broadside. Thomas Paines's 'Common Sense' and Emile Zola's 'J'accuse' are heroic landmark writings; but to call them essays, though they may resemble the form, is to misunderstand. The essay is not meant for the barricades; it is a stroll through someone's mazy mind.'

When I read, or re-read that statement, I thought to myself, much as I revere Ozick, I disagree. Why should something meant to persuade readers to take up an action or to instruct be stricken from the essay rolls? Are Edmund Burke's speeches or Alexander Herzen's political analyses not essays? So I put a section from Thomas Paine's Common Sense into the anthology. And I put in Martin Luther King's speech on the Vietnam War, and Lincoln's Second Inaugural Address, and I put in sermons by Jonathan Edwards and Paul Tillich and Thomas Merton, and one of Alexander Hamilton's Federal Papers, and Sarah Grimké's discourse 'On the Condition of Women in the U.S.,' and some humorous newspaper columns by Finley Peter Dunne, Heywood Broun, Don Marquis, Christopher Morley and Robert Benchley, and some rather brilliant academic papers by the sociologists Erving Goffman and Robert K, Merton, and film criticism by Manny Farber and Pauline Kael, and nature writing by John Muir, John Burroughs, Aldo Leopold, Rachel Carson, Edward Hoagland, and Annie Dillard, and science writing by Loren Eiseley, Lewis Thomas, Stephen Jay Gould, and Oliver Sacks, and impassioned feminist polemics by Audre Lorde, Ellen Willis and Vivian Gornick, and wickedly anti-feminist writing by Florence King, and dense philosophical arguments by George Santayana and William James and R. P, Blackmur, and pointed political analyses by Randolph Bourne and Richard Hofstader, and a lovely piece called 'The Stranger's Path' by that splendid geographer J. B. Jackson, and Janet Malcolm's experimental 'Forty-One False Starts,' and Donald Barthelme's puckish defense of ignorance, 'Not-Knowing.' I became an opportunistic blotting paper, absorbing hints from everywhere around me. For instance, I came upon a review of Donald Judd's art criticism in the TLS which said, Judd was all right, but the really first-rate artist-writer was the environmental sculptor Robert Smithson. I had heard in the past that Smithson had an excellent prose style, so I rushed to look him up and sure enough, I found something excellent by him that I could put in the book. When the art historian Linda Nochlin died, the obituary mentioned her influential essay, 'Why Have There Been No Great Women Artists,' so I immediately googled it, read it and in it went. I even included a few visiting essayists who commented cogently on the United States, such as Alexis de Tocqueville, D. H. Lawrence, Jose Marti, Octavio Paz and C.L.R. James.

It should not come as a surprise that in the end the project grew to two, possibly three hefty volumes. When I turned in those photocopied tomes to my editor and my agent, I had to wheel in the manuscripts in a suitcase because they were too heavy to carry on the subway. We shall see what they make of it. At the moment I am terrified but hopeful. (Recently, the publisher has proposed three volumes: one that will trace the whole arc of the American essay, from the Puritans to the present, one that will focus on what I consider the Golden Age of the American Essay, roughly 1945-1970, and one that will be devoted to the contemporary essay).

Lest you infer that I have become utterly promiscuous in my embrace of any piece of writing that might lay claim to being an essay, out of some imperialistic land-grab to expand my domain, let me reassure you that that is not the case. I have resisted the siren song of 'creative nonfiction,' at least as it was characterized by Lee Gutkind as 'making it read like a short story or fiction,' by incorporating fictional techniques, using lots of scenes and dialogues and cinematic detail. This approach scants reflection because it supposedly slows down the reader's involvement in a scene. To me, reflection is still an invaluable ingredient of the essay, its payoff, so to speak. Of course fictional techniques and dialogue scenes have always had a place in essay-writing, from Addison & Steele on down; but there is no reason for them to monopolize nonfiction at the expense of reflection and aphoristic summary. We essayists can tell as well as show. Among the graduate students whom I teach, and who are often drawn more to short story-like memoir pieces than to reflective rumination on a subject, I have sometimes encountered an antipathy to what they call 'academic tone,' which strikes me as a disguised anti-intellectual prejudice. There is good academic writing as well as bad, and an intelligent academic paper can serve as one potential model for essay-writing. Consider the theoretical papers of Sigmund Freud, who, whatever you may think of his ideas, had a beautifully supple, rhetorically complex prose style.

I have also been less than enamored of the hybrid cross-breeding of nonfiction and fiction, in the matter of telling the truth. The fact that an essay is fashioned or shaped via omissions and subjective judgments does not perforce make it a fiction. Whatever artifice goes into the crafting of a good essay, I still think it has an obligation to stick as closely to the facts as possible. There may certainly be times when shortcuts are advisable, combining three events into one or two, say, or creatively paraphrasing dialogue that occurred years before, or even changing some details to protect the identity of real persons, but those are very different matters from wholesale lying. The contract between essayist and reader is based partly on the assumption that the essayist is leveling with us, and not making up an experience from scratch. It is permissible for the essayist to speculate on a different turn of events, but then it should be labeled or implicitly understood as speculation, as for instance in Philip Roth's masterful essay on Kafka, the first part of which is literary criticism, and the second part a fantasy about Kafka settling in New Jersey near Roth's family. While I may appreciate the audacity of Lauren Slater's book *On Lying*, which experiments with combining fact and fiction, or John D'Agata's *The Lifespan of a Fact*, in which he cheekily defends his right to change actual details in a reported piece because something or other 'sounds better' to him, I am not drawn to such mischief myself and I see it essentially as a dead end.

Speaking of John D'Agata, whom I know personally and like as a human being, a sort of friendly rival, it was his own recent anthologies on the essay which sparked my interest in going one better. D'Agata, as you probably know, had been carving out his territory of the lyrical essay, and seeking to uncover (in his words) 'the lost origins of the essay,' going back to Sumerian tablets, in contradistinction to the usual canon. In doing so, he has helped to renovate the American essay. He has ferreted out lists, poems, short stories, chapters of novels and so on, often elliptical and poetically mysterious, and made them the center of his interpretation of the genre. But strange to say, he does not seem to like what we normally think of as essays. He is averse to pieces that pursue a logical argument with clarity, or that construct any sort of narrative. This became clear to me in a discussion we had about the essay form in front of an audience, in which he asserted that the essay was primarily 'associative' and I maintained that it was primarily 'narrative.' Now, of course, essays can be both associative and narrative, but I somehow believe—perhaps because I think of myself as basically a storyteller—that any essayistic rumination or meditation tends to go from Point A to Point E or F, working through various tensions and knots along the way, and is therefore following, however inadvertently, a narrative arc. Its 'plot,' so to speak, is the mind grappling with itself. D'Agata's aversion to the traditional essay is based partly on his dislike of system and closure, and his desire for an essay to remain free as long as possible from causal connections, as many modernist poems do. Hence, 'associative.' I realized how pervasively he clung to this preference when he chose for his newest anthology, The Making of the American Essay, a short story by Leonard Michaels, 'In the Fifties,' which is essentially a list-poem, albeit a good one, while passing up the chance to take something from that author's magnificent posthumous collection, The Essays of Leonard Michaels. Since I regard the late Lenny Michaels as one of America's greatest contemporary essayists, that substitution struck me as perverse.

As it happened, that last anthology of D'Agata's came in for a harsh attack by a critic in the *Atlantic*, who commented on the sparse inclusion of what were customarily considered essays, and incidentally contrasted it unfavorably with my *Art of the Personal Essay*. All Schadenfreude aside, the *Atlantic* attack started me thinking. I *do* like essays. What if I were to undertake a new anthology, focusing as D'Agata did on the American essay, but taking it out of that 'lyrical' hot-house he had put it in and opening it up to as many styles and disciplines as could be conceived. And that, in all shameful honesty, is how my latest project arose.

I would like to end with a few ragtag thoughts about the essay. In contrast to the novel and poetry, whose narrative strategies or poetics have been the subject of intense scrutiny by scholars, theorists and critics, the essay has long been neglected on a theoretical level. That is beginning to change, as evidenced by conferences like this one, and by the appearance of several recent books that have attempted to pull together what might be called a poetics of and ideology of the essay. Some of the essay's often-cited elements include its extraordinary flexibility and mutability, its literary sparkle, its undogmatic, anti-methodical, anti-totalizing tendencies, its tropism toward ambivalence, doubt, skepticism, self-mockery, its freedom to wander and digress, its cockroach-like resilience and survival ability. All these are good things. I would just like to caution that we essayists not take too seriously our own defensive propaganda, or adopt too smugly this self-approving, narcissistic, idealizing portrait of the form. I who have championed the essay for so long am starting to grow impatient with these self-serving characterisations. Yes, essays can be charming; they have the appeal of the underdog. But let us not get carried away.

In the United States, essays have been undergoing something of a revival. Twenty years ago they were considered box office poison; publishers went to inordinate lengths to disguise the stuff by repackaging essay collections as book-length themes. They wouldn't even dare put the word 'essays' on the cover. Essay love was the love that dared not speak its name. Now all that's changing, somewhat. Writers such as David Sedaris, Roxane Gay, Leslie Jameson, Hilton Als, Teju Cole, Camille Paglia, Meghan Daum and John Jeremiah Sullivan have achieved an undeniable cachet, while a few of their antecedents, like Joan Didion and James Baldwin, have been elevated to sainthood. While I suspect the essay may be due for another market correction, we can speculate on the reasons for the present upsurge. In line with the recent vogue for the memoir, they appeal to the contemporary moment's hunger for confiding voices, as witnessed elsewhere in TV talk shows and reality shows. Unlike the memoir, they are usually short, bite-sized, suited to short attention spans; you can keep the book by your bed and read one entry a night. In their penchant for fragmentation in the mosaic essay and opaqueness in the lyrical essay, they seem loyal to the project of modernism; in their acknowledgment of subjectivity and authorial prejudice, they exhibit a refreshing honesty, in line with the New Journalism's recognition that strict objectivity and arrival at final Truth with a capital T are probably unattainable.

Then, too, the essay has fed conveniently into identity assertions by minorities, whether ethnic, religious, sexual-preference, disabled, victims of abuse, prey to addictions, obesity and so on; all have elicited spokespersons who have plumbed the various aspects of the conditions that made them feel separate. The danger in some of these identity politics niche offerings is that the essay may lose some of its worldly, playful perspective and gravitate toward moral self-righteousness, preachiness, unshapely rage and self-pity. Also, I sometimes miss the imprint or shadings of subtler older essays on these younger voices who are trying to write what has been called 'the post-patriarchal essay,' which is one more reason why I (Mr. Patriarchal) feel obligated to make anthologies that honor and preserve the best historical examples.

Finally, while some rationalization and distortion are probably unavoidable in essays, the form has also been a welcome home for the exercise of reason. We can all agree that the essay by its very nature and word-derivation is an attempt, an experiment, a venture into the unknown; but that does not mean that we should allow it to be woolly-headed, or that we should resist whatever spine of argumentation may arise in the midst of our explorations. We must not be afraid to make reasonable sense. However neurotic we are as individuals, we should rejoice in the fact that the form we essayists practice has exemplified the very ideal of the sane, integrated self. Traditionally, it has not been hospitable to irrationality and psychosis. If this limits our freedom as writers, so be it.

Have I disappointed you enough? Thank you for reading patiently.

The Fiction of the Essay: of Abstraction, Texts, Communication, and Loss

Emma Bolland & Elizabeth Chakrabarty

Together, writing (1), South Bank, 2019

Dear Emma,

I'm excited to now be sharing this essayistic journey with you after months of virtual communication, and before that sitting alone at my desk.

The beginning of this journey was me sitting at my tiny desk on a hot summer's day in London. I'd recently been made redundant from my academic job in creative and critical writing, and I was starting the freelance lifestyle of writing and zero hours contracts, with all the uncertainty and precarity that goes with that. Sitting there, I received a text message on my phone, inviting me to send in an abstract for this very volume—but could I do it by the morning? I quickly wrote an abstract in reply. With so little time it had the urgency of writing what was on my mind ever since I'd left the apparent security of decades lecturing in various forms of education, teaching multicultural fiction to often all white groups, and of dealing with the racism I'd experienced and by then escaped from. I wrote it quickly, used to writing these small pieces of text of around a 100-250 words after delivering my Ph.D. thesis a few years before, and after years of writing abstracts for conferences, peer-reviewed journal articles and public funded research grant proposals—all the speculative writing of academia. What was different was this was the first I'd written from a place outside of the academy.

What was wonderful was that I received the acceptance of my abstract almost immediately, along with the deadline of a year's time. So I happily put the abstract aside for a while, and returned to working on my novel, but I did email my agent about it. She was happy with my news, and interested in my abstract, having already read the beginning of the autofiction I was working on, she understood what was behind the phrase in my abstract, 'the failings in the institution of the academy to deal with racism'. She had signed me for my autofiction a year earlier, which she loved—it was the reason I knew I could work with her. The email accepting the abstract funnily enough had the word 'love' in it too. Love is the keyword of my writing, and my life; without love I can feel no point in life or in writing.

Around the same time I was asked to deliver the abstract, I had returned to writing poetry after decades. The poetic impulse that summer was triggered by events in my personal life: a relationship context of silence and withdrawal—but mostly because my oldest friend had recently told me she had terminal cancer. The summer was thus punctuated by longing for my girlfriend, but never seeing her—and spending long days in my friend's garden, watching the birds in the trees, and enjoying reminiscing about our shared time together as undergraduates, involved in activism and intersectional politics, and the queer scene, and our lives and loves since then. In the short time left between us I was aware of her upsurge of release from the constricted stressful world of academia—when you know you're going to die it no longer matters—and her turning towards what she loved about life: those close to her and the natural world.

So last summer was about love and longing and celebrating being outside of academia, despite the precarity. It was a summer of new friends and old, and of submerging myself into writing with my fictional characters, and also with myself as a character in my fiction and poetry. One line in a poem I wrote last summer returns to me when I feel low—and there were times of deep lows, wanting my friend to stay alive, and my girlfriend to live our love, while all around there was Brexit's ugly nationalism of hate. The line is in a longer narrative poem, 'Writing about Race and Love in the English Countryside' (2019), rejected by a new rural writing magazine in the autumn, but which received a warm response when I read it at a recent LGBTQI spoken word event in Soho. It is, rather like my initial abstract, about my desire to be able to be and to write and to love in the countryside, just as I'm able to in the city, without the infinite chasm of racism appearing. That key line of poetry last summer was this: 'to listen is to love'—I still feel this.

When we listen, and we show we've heard, and we also feel ourselves listened to, then the world is a better place. It's a place we can imagine falling in love and developing friendship, a place where we can openly communicate, produce artwork and write for better or for worse—like the marriage vows. Writing is a vow with whoever reads it, a vow of witnessing and truth telling.

The world is in a difficult place right now with manmade climate change, and the rise of a type of nationalism of which people used to talk in terms of 'never again', and yet here we are: human beings are imprisoned in cages on borders, children throwing stones are killed by nuclear powered military, and politicians in so called western tolerant democracies are reluctant to call out words of racism.

Yesterday, after talking with you Emma, I thought again of my line, 'to listen is to love'—I felt safe with you, given our mutual disentangling of threads on communication and writing and the academy.

Until tomorrow,

Elizabeth

***

Dear Elizabeth,

Like you I sat at my desk and opened the email inviting me to be part of this book, asking for an abstract, a working title, and quickly. And of course I said yes, because

Together, writing (2), South Bank, 2019

similarly there is the matter of the academy, the struggles of freelancing, of—in different ways and from different starting points, circumstances, positions, bodies—being the outsider. (Sometimes I feel like the wild dog at the city gates, gulping down whatever scraps I'm thrown). And, like you—but perhaps with less certainty—I assembled a speculation: my abstracts are so often an elusive essence, as though I want to commit the reader but not myself: a summation that contains its own get-out clause. What was it though, that I wanted? I have lost my response, lost the email that I sent them.

On the way to our meeting last week I was re-reading Lacan's *Seminar on The Purloined Letter* (1956). *The Purloined Letter* (1844) is a short story by Edgar Allan Poe, a story in which a letter has been stolen. Lacan points out though, that the idea of 'stolen' is not quite right, that Baudelaire's translation of the title from *The Purloined Letter* to *La lettre volée* is misleading, unnuanced. 'Volée', in French, means unambiguously 'stolen', yet the English word 'purloined' is something other. Lacan picks the word apart, and via its etymology suggests a word that means not so much to steal, but to *mettre de cote*, to put aside, or to tuck away: 'we are quite simply dealing with a letter which has been detoured, one whose trajectory has *been prolonged* [...] a letter *en souffrance* (awaiting delivery or unclaimed)'.

Is this what has happened to my abstract? Did I somehow delete or ambiguously archive it in the tangle of haphazard filing that is my laptop? I can remember the flavour of the title: something like *Writing Silence/Lensing Speech*, and know that I had wanted to write about speaking—whose speech is heard, whose speech is silenced, how we might find a new way of uttering a post-traumatic language. I say a 'we' but I also mean an 'I'—how might I find a fiction in which I could be heard, via which I might speak the truth? I had wanted to do this through the lens of a screenplay I have been translating and 'writing through'. The screenplay is the French film-maker and writer Louis Delluc's for his film *Le Silence* (1920), and it too features letters, misunderstood communications whose trajectories have been prolonged. The screenplay is a double fiction, in that it is a story to be made into a film, but also a possible fiction in relation to the film into which it was made: the film survives only as an incomplete and damaged nitrate. Published in 1923, three years after this now fragmented film was released, we only have Delluc's *post-production word* that his *pre-production words* describe the film we might once have seen. We only have *my word* that the above is what my abstract contained.

I had wanted to re-read Lacan's seminar because like the letters he refers to, the communications that have led to us writing *these words* have been—metaphorically—purloined. A year of emails sent into and received from the ether, long silences during which the narratives, without warning, have been changed. I had wanted to re-read it because I was sure, so sure, that there was a sentence that said that the truth of the letters depended on in whose hands they were held. Of course, there is no such sentence, or at least despite my re-readings I cannot find it. I have invented a fiction *via* which I might tell an emotional truth.

Elizabeth, it was so good to meet you at last! Your phrase 'to listen is to love' has resonated. Without the ear of the other we are all of us silenced.

Emma

* * *

Dear Emma,

Thank you for your response. As co-writers of a text which will be edited by others, and then will be consumed or perhaps not, skipped over by readers we will never meet, we are both aware of the precarious nature of a text, it's presence existing sometimes only briefly, remaining as an abstract, and existing in the abstract—just like our shared precarity as zero hours workers in the academy, of it but not in it, as insubstantial

Together, writing (3) South Bank, 2019

as the virtual world of light and dark, our cinematic shared interests in our 2018 accepted abstracts for this volume.

My entrance should begin in January 2019 when I next received a communication about this volume—but in my mind it begins as 2018 was ending, just before Christmas when I went to see my friend in her hospital room for the last time. Twenty-first century communication should be straightforward, we have so much of it 24/7, and yet there are some things that are unsaid, that we intuit, read between the lines or guess, especially in text or WhatsApp messages—or all the words between loss and love. That last Saturday before Christmas I'd had a lovely few days with my by then more present girlfriend, and I had just said goodbye to her at the station, when I felt the vibration of a text. It said, 'You should come now'—and so I took the tube to the end of the line, and then a bus, and then I walked fast to the hospital—isn't it always when we really want to get somewhere that the journey feels too long, the place too far off, and possibly that we might arrive too late? I arrived in time though, and with other old friends gathered around her hospital bed, together we witnessed our friend marry her girlfriend: her final wish. The nurses had put fairy lights from a Christmas tree around the bed, and we toasted the couple with fruit juice in plastic cups, amongst the paraphernalia of life support machines. It was beautiful to listen to the simple traditional words of love in the dying light, as the year was almost ending—almost: a few days later my friend died on Christmas Eve, and so the New Year celebrations were quickly followed by her funeral.

At the end of January, as I was starting to try to get on with things again, as we have to after death, I received an email about this volume. It was now going to be a series of dialogues between people, and thus Emma, it was then that we were both cc'd in as an introduction to each other, and to our new shared title: something about film, fiction and autofiction—the shared keywords of our abstracts, those remaining few words connecting us. There was then a series of emails of clarification: I was concerned about whether my initial abstract had been shared, as I made it clear that my abstract was about subject matter that was important to me so I would still want to publish the material. The reply came back that only the gist of our abstracts had been written into the funding application, the text of which we did not see—but I imagined how the body of a short abstract, just a paragraph, might be broken down into key words, and then those words reordered, and rewritten, and how it would become something else. And how the body of the original texts remain in the virtual world of the originators' minds. What I had wanted to write I eventually put into something else I was working on, something much longer, and more substantial that I have given the time it has needed— but the question of the abstract lingered: how a short concentrated piece of writing, that must have essential meaning, but is often rejected, or might be reused in another text by others, and how that meaning might then mutate, and its substance become tainted by others' interpretations to the point that the initial text may have nothing in common with the final text. There is however nothing fixed about any piece of text in the era of the computer—so Emma, we settled into six months of email, text and one live FaceTime conversation, and during that time we also discarded the title we'd been given, and wrote our new shared working title and an abstract, incorporating our virtual communications, titled, 'Fictions: Disrupting an Orthodox Real'.

I suppose what we are exploring is the fiction of writing in the academy in the twenty-first century, its apparent 'substance' despite what feels more real, particularly in the context of this e-epistolary, the fragility of writing in its virtual state. Of course I'm talking about what I should leave for later—so until tomorrow,

Elizabeth

***

Together, writing (4), South Bank, 2019

Dear Elizabeth,

Forgive my silence, my long delay—I've been struggling with my reply, with how to write, how to respond. Are we responding? In a way, even the form of our dialogue is a fiction (prompted by the capriciousness of our editors—I wonder how they might edit this?—and then determined by ourselves, when we met). I am jumping ahead, refiguring the fact of our linear time of writing as flashback, flashforward—fictionalising our 'chronotope', our mapping of the space and time of writing.

I am struck by our theme of grief—and for myself, the sense of shame that comes with that. Some years ago, two family members died in rapid succession, and I was acutely aware that my grief was in the wrong place. I felt not the grief I should have had *for* them, but rather grief for the life I might have had *without* them. This was a truth that had to be silenced, and so I performed the 'right grief', thus subjecting myself to the double shame of sublimating a real feeling in order to fictionalise a false feeling. The acceptable lie to cover up the unacceptable truth. I have never been brave.

When we were contacted—out of the blue—with the new terms of writing that did not acknowledge the old, my first feeling was of shame. I was ashamed for feeling the loss of what I had thought that I would be doing. Yes, I know that sounds absurd—I wonder if I can explain it? I am always so delighted when I am asked to be part of something—particularly something that is of the academy—so eager to please, so worried that what I propose will not be quite the thing. The anxious offering of ideas and the relief and pride when they are accepted, when I am accepted. I wondered, when we were contacted, if that meant that what I had offered was, after all, unacceptable. I felt foolish, ashamed of being excited. Again, the absurdity of this (of which I am ashamed!). You write that what we are exploring is the fiction of writing *in* the academy in the twenty-first century. I think this is true. For myself—the interloper who has never truly been in the academy—I am also writing, cravenly, *for* the academy. The dog again, outside the city walls, yearning.

I wonder if there are those of us whose reality can be overwritten by those who have this power? To return briefly to Lacan's purloined letters, in the sentence I have invented for him, their meaning belongs to whoever's hands in which they happen to be. One interpretation of this might be one regarding the relations between subjectivity and power. A while back I went for an informal chat with the head of a new course, to see what I might have to offer them. I began with excitement, outlining my skills, my publications and my ideas. I slowly noticed that the notes they were taking were extensive, and became uncomfortable with their comments that 'we should do that with them [the students], that's a great idea!' Who was this 'we' I wondered, as the suspicion that I was being covertly 'mined' took shape. Our conversation ground to a halt when they said, that as a new course they had no spare budget, and were relying (for Visiting Lecturer work) on 'goodwill'. There was a long silence. I answered their question disguised as a not-question by saying that I would never offer free labour to an academic institution, that I regarded the fact that they would ask this as a serious matter. A few months later they advertised a post, for which—despite an immaculate application—I wasn't interviewed. I bring this up because I can't forget it, because I cannot hear the word academy without the raw feeling that what I had thought to be a reality—that in this context we are paid for our labour—was overturned. I was destabilised (I still am) by their unashamed 'knowledge extraction', their rewriting of 'normal', and questioned my own perception of what is right and what is wrong. Most of all I felt ashamed for hoping that they might want me, for indulging the fiction that I might have something to give. Of course, I have never emailed them to call them out for this behaviour, because to do so would be to appear a malcontent and a fantasist, because how could what I have described be real?

I am sorry, Elizabeth, that this is not a proper reply, that I am drifting off into my own embarrassing preoccupations—preoccupations that include a worry about what it is to write an essay, what the academy considers a proper writing of an essay to be, what the academy considers a proper academic to be. In relation to this 'properness'—whether real or imagined—I feel myself to be a fiction, my façade disintegrating even as I build it. But now I recall this: a tweet from tamara k. nopper:

> Sometimes I wonder if 'imposter syndrome', originating from the 1978 concept of imposter phenomenon, is just another example of making racism

Together, writing (5), South Bank, 2019

> and sexism in professional spaces appear as a psychological myth rather than a structural reality of how people get poorly treated.

There is the suggestion that the change in wording from 'phenomenon' to 'syndrome' subtly shifts the blame from the system to the individual. The feeling no longer comes from the external phenomena of systematic injustice, but from the internal pathology of the sick subject. And of course, this is what the slur of 'malcontent' is also designed to do—shame those who are subject to injustice. If I experience myself as a fiction then, is such a fiction a 'trying to make the best of things'? I think of the 'object-relations' analyst Fairburn writing that 'it is better to be a sinner in a world ruled by God than to live in a world ruled by the Devil', and consider if fictionalising is merely a way to avoid the horror of the world: for in fictionalising ourselves as sinner there is always the hope that we may one day become good…

I realise I am writing too many words (will they cut us?—I think we should fight for length, take up space). I wanted to say that our (auto)fictions, Elizabeth, are not simply a 'trying-to-make-the-best-of', they are something different, something strong and strategic. This will have to wait until next time.

Emma

***

Dear Emma,

Thank you. In that plan we wrote when we met recently, we imagined pages 1–8 (x 2 of us), like a mathematic formula. But as soon as we had each other's names, and were to produce a piece of joint writing in the future, despite the virtual communication I have associated you with this, and thus our first page was really the first email between us without anyone else copied in—like the safe space of our own minds we retreat to, after the feeling of shame you write about, or the feeling that our ideas might have been purloined or set aside. Perhaps we have both been experiencing this strange situation of shared writing as if we are characters in a story written by Poe, like peripheral characters spooked out after being invited then pushed aside, not totally rejected, but two characters who might stand with their backs to the wall at a party, looking on at those in the centre. It's funny really, the more I think about it now, I realize how power lies weirdly eventually within the excluded—because loss unexamined intensifies, it becomes more powerful than the power that tries to repress it—why the status quo may eventually be toppled by those constructed as outsiders, once they invade the structures of power. Like writing from outside the academy, but within it: in the Trojan horse of an essay.

There was something about becoming the sole holder of once shared memories through losing my oldest friend, at the point we were introduced, that meant I experienced the build-up to this joint essay as a new shared space in the present, in the experience of getting to know you through typed words on a blank screen—just like I might tentatively start typing up ideas for an essay. When we met, and since then as we started these pages, you have shared with me your experience of grief and your conflicted feelings about the academy, just as I have shared with you my loss of my friend and my feelings of loss over what I wanted to write about the academy in my initial projected sole-authored essay. It's probably worth me spelling out here what I would have written about, based on that initial abstract—and of course I'm aware of the fiction in that sentence, the auxiliary verb 'would' when I am about to write it in the present, so while I'm repeating the acknowledgement of the withdrawal of my initial abstract I am including it yet again, what I want to write about won't go away but remains the uncanny theme in my reply, a ghost that will not rest, what Poe and Freud returned to again and again—and this is a long sentence, but I feel like there shouldn't be a full stop but another form of punctuation, perhaps that, to indicate that I'm still here now, somewhere inside my absent initial abstract in which I triangulated in classic academic style between art, theory and my auto-ethnographic experience of academia: that in between the depiction of structural cultural cruelty reflecting the machinations of human relations in the film *The Lobster* (Lanthimos, 2015), and Freud's delineation of the familiar and unfamiliar architecture of apparent humanity in *The Uncanny* (1919), I had found an analytical framework to explore what humans do to each other—even in the apparent intellectual liberal space of the academy. A full stop, because here I want to say what I really wanted to write about in plain un-academic English: racism in the academy was so unexpected and thus painful.

This 'essay' reflects a live dialogue of our shared experience of writing in the academy and living outside it. I've been very glad to start to get to know you through our emails, but I realize now I've got to know you through a whole range of types of text, and that actually I can imagine your initial abstract more through reading your tweets. We've communicated about our Twitter interaction; I've found it stressful so don't always engage much with social media (and I've had to be careful about using it—but that's for another paper, not this one), but I can see you use it in a way that communicates you—the you that I met on FaceTime, and when we met in person—much more than academic writing ever can. I mean because of the distance of traditional academic writing, how we are supposed to refer and defer to others who've gone before us, how the I is diminished, or hidden and is only present as a name at the top of the page, below the title, so subservient to the subject. The most interesting essays, which I return to again and again, overturn the tradition and encourage what we're doing, turning the gaze, exploring why we do what we do, what's the purpose, what's beneath the veneer of structures, perceived narratives and the fiction of reality. I'm thinking of Orwell's *Why I Write* (1946) and all of our contemporary Sara Ahmed's recent work on the academy, for example in *Queer Use* (2018). It's interesting that I've referred to

Together, writing (6), South Bank, 2019

others, but all writers seen as outside the academy, even Freud—just as you have too. These are writers whose ideas communicate in some way our lived experience.

I think I've probably taken too long, so I should conclude here—rather like the fiction of concluding our essay by me saying I'll conclude here, when what we have started feels like it could be the beginning of a long rambling conversation, not the neat tidy edited pages of an academic essay, so I'll say something real instead: I'm looking forward to your response/reply Emma.

Until next time—though word count and editing wise that will probably be back in the virtual world of emails, where it's just the two of us—and not for editors' or readers' consumption.

Elizabeth

* * *

Together, writing (7), South Bank, 2019

Dear Elizabeth,

I am laughing out loud as I start my email—even though we are writing about painful things—delighted! Delighted at what has emerged, has unfolded: an unruly precision. Will anyone reading this believe that *these* pages were not the plan all along? Our formula—the imagined fact-fiction of pages of the essay—may seem to have unravelled, but in fiction-fact has, at its core, survived. (I keep reversing the order of the 'fiction-fact-fact-fictions', wondering which should go where, but perhaps their uncertain order is exactly the thing?) The core of our formula, the constant of our equation is the 'x 2 of us'; the potential of disruption, the resistance; to paraphrase you, the power that can erupt from the excluded. Autofiction has been criticised as solipsistic, overly subjective, but I like to think of an autofiction that enacts a reverse critique: scrutinises, enacts a subjective intervention into normative discourse, becomes a politicised methodology. The term 'autofiction' in itself implies a textual strategy of at least two voices and our 'x 2 of us' makes it exponential. A collective un-silencing, a *volume*, an autofictive polyphony harnessing the power of networked selves.

Of course, a persistent resistance does not automatically mean that an oppressive 'normal' has been overcome—your experience of racism in the academy, about which I am so, so sorry, is an ongoing experience for many—but with the tools to recognise the truth of our diverse and intersecting subjectivities a continued resistance can feel, at least at times, worthwhile. You mention Sara Ahmed, herself forced out of the academy. I heard her speak last year and her observation that if you feel like a square peg in a round hole then it is probably the hole that is the wrong shape, rang out like ` a summoning bell.

We are indeed, as you suggest, characters in a strange situation, but by signing the compact of fiction that is 'the vow of witnessing and truth telling' we are moving from the periphery to the centre of the action. We are, even before the fact of publication, dissemination, both writer *and* reader. Poe's story of purloined letters is one of three to feature his character 'Dupin', a proto-detective in what are essentially proto-detective stories. With our methodology of fictions, of subjectivities, we are writing a detective story that is itself a form of detection. We are agent.

I was grateful, Elizabeth, that you began this dialogue, setting the scene that allowed the story to unfold. Now, as I end it, I am aware that the orthodoxy would be, as in a conventional detective story, as handed down in the canon of the art of the essay, to offer a satisfactory conclusion with the hundred or so more words that I have yet to employ. However, as the task of resistance is never over, never finished, I think I will just end with our revised (fictional) beginning, composed at the very end of our writing:

> 'The Fiction of the Essay: of Abstraction, Texts, Communication, and Loss'
> Emma Bolland and Elizabeth Chakrabarty consider strategies of fictional truth-telling via an e-epistolary discourse that situates them each, in relation to each other, and over time, as imaginary. Writing to and from uncertain locations they construct a conversation through the virtual page, exploring the reality of writing within the academy but from outside of it, through a reflection on loss.

See you again soon, I hope?

Emma

A Leaf Out of Someone's Book

Graham Domke

for John Calcutt (1951–2018)

'Have you ever watched a sport whose laws you didn't know, whose tactics you couldn't fathom? It's a bit like listening to a language you have never heard before. You know it must make sense to someone, but not to you. The players are deep in concentration, euphoric or dejected by turns, but the meaning of their passion is lost on you. It seems to be passion for its own sake, pure passion, but you know from other experience that there must be more. Mustn't there?'

John Calcutt in Peter Lynch, *Paintings 2000-2001*, Glasgow School of Art, 2001.

John Calcutt ran the Master of Fine Arts programme at Glasgow School of Art and had a thirty year association with the art school. He was also a curator, art critic and a great essayist. John's sentences above were published in a small catalogue that we both contributed to in 2001.

Have you ever watched a sport whose laws you didn't know …

In preparation for some domestic laundry, I routinely checked the pockets of a cardigan. I pulled out a papery leaf that was crumbing away to nothing as I was still processing what it even was and why it had been in my pocket.

You should have put that in a book my partner said sensibly. Maybe I still can.

Have you ever …

I had caught leaves twice earlier in the month—something I haven't intentionally attempted to do in at least forty years. Now, as then, I am living in the South of Glasgow, some sort of returning to the beginning and beginning again.

watched a sport whose tactics you couldn't fathom … ?

The first recent leaf that I caught literally required the pure instinct to stick my hand out and receive it. But once seized, my mind was transported back to a vivid, filmic flashback to a 1970s primary school playground during lunchtime where the wind was shaking the trees and providing a seasonal sport for the non-sporty: running, eyes up, hands held out, chasing leaves as they fell from the branches of the tall trees. I can remember that I caught a few. I am sure I missed out on more than I chased. I remember it was a shared experience with other children.

The second time was more intense. I saw a leaf falling and I ran towards it and caught it with rapture. My somewhat surprised partner was unaware of my new-found, long lost leaf pursuit. But earlier in the season, we had both collected several fallen leaves from a small gingko tree. We pressed them within sheets of paper that we had put in a book, *American Art: A Cultural History* by David Bjelajac from 2000.

Some instinct for preservation.

Something to return to, be surprised by and that might trigger a tender memory.

… it must make sense to someone.

I learned about the concept of parallel discourse from John. A sideways, seemingly unrelated, indirect approach to achieving a dialogue between author, subject and reader. A favourite exhibition that John Calcutt curated at the CCA Glasgow was entitled, *Ouroboros: The Music of the Spheres*, a wide-eyed look at circular narration and endless loops in the resolutely not straight line in art history.

… deep in concentration, euphoric or dejected by turns …

His roundabout way of taking ideas for a walk was inspirational to all who crossed paths with him.

… passion for its own sake …

John was an avid collector of art and in particular American post-war Pop and Minimalism. Maybe that is why the gingko leaves wound up in that particular book— concealing a section headed: 'Educating the Public and Selling Art: Problems in Public and Private Exhibitions'. A natural obfuscation.

The Art of the Intransitive Essay

Linda E. Chown

> *One might speak as if one were thinking*
> —Susan Glaspell

I want to begin describing a veritable crisis of mind that affected many writers in the early twentieth century, a division which stewed in the intellectual world for a very long time—that idea of a steadfast separation of an inside from the outside. Arthur Mizener named it the central problem of his time. In 1964, Mizener concluded that the fiction of the 1920s was entrapped by strict division between inner and outer:

> The novel of inner experience was rapidly developing an elaborate and self-conscious form, which made more and more delicate and lyrical accounts of that experience possible at the cost of excluding more and more of the world of our customary apprehension; and the novel of public experience was increasing its emphasis on social significance by excluding more and more of its characters' inner experience—and of its narrators. The best of the novelists of the twenties were caught between the two, unable to bring them together.

Gertrude Stein, in her ever-inordinate wisdom, fleshed out a complete conceptual revolution,

> I had never thought about an audience before, not even when I wrote 'Composition as Explanation' which was a lecture but now I suddenly began to feel the outside inside and the inside outside and it was perhaps not so exciting but it was very interesting. Anyway, it was quite exciting.

From that point on, there followed decades of great debate about what writers should write 'about' anyway and how to write that.

In 2019, we live in a world which frustratingly overvalues what things are ostensibly about, not just what they mean, but sometimes what the true fact is exactly, what the referent is, or if the *signifier* is stable. What was the movie or book about is a question too often asked when you're reading thoroughly on a sunny beach, walking out of a darkened movie theatre in that stunned, delicious, consumed state, or having an unexpected intense disagreement with a friend about nothing so very important. From the time I was seven or eight, my father used to greet me at the breakfast table, asking brightly, 'Now, Linda, what is your philosophy of life today?' The idea of having to know any definite *about* proves an impediment to reading, writing, enjoyment, to perception, to thorough intimacy, and to knowing anything really. A wise friend once told me 'don't write *about it*, just write *it*.' In his beautiful calligraphy, he would create two new notebooks every New Year's Eve: one called *About It*, replete with quotes and thoughts of others to remember, and the other called *It*, thinner and filled with lines of poetry and perception. Now, it sometimes feels as though we are yanked all too often between those two calendars in this new hybrid, threateningly uncertain, world of today.

Not so long ago, when the world seemed a place full of seams and certainties, teaching the essay was divided, taught and written in four discrete manners: exposition, narration, description, and persuasion, often in orderly sequences with five paragraphs or sections: an introduction, three body paragraphs and a finalizing, summing it up in a package with a bow-tie type of conclusion. Students were taught to emulate one of these forms and to avoid any intermingling of types. In those days, few acknowledged how much the essay was not just one of those directions, but rather it was all of them variously woven together and cross-stitched as uniquely beautiful. Gertrude Stein, famous, ever-experimenting, genius once said perhaps the most radical thing ever directed specifically for writers: she announced the death of story, or consecutiveness as we had come to expect: 'The novel which tells about what happens is of no interest to anybody. For the last thirty years events are of no importance. Really listen to the way you talk and every time you change it a little bit. That change, to me, was a very important thing to find out'. In other words, she beseeched us to listen, to hear ourselves, not to find out *what* we said, but to get closer to *how* we said it, however long that took. When reading or writing an essay, or just plain and simple when thinking, in order to get close to whatever *it is*, we need to learn to think intransitively, that is without a specific purpose in mind controlling our word choices, inflections, and tenses.

The man often accredited with being the founder of the modern essay, Michel de Montaigne, repeatedly tells himself and invites us to follow our thinking intransitively as he does: 'The world looks always opposite; I turn my sight inwards, and there fix and employ it. I have no other business but myself, I am eternally meditating upon myself, considering and tasting myself. Other men's thoughts are ever wandering abroad, if they will but see it; they are still going forward: for my part, I circulate in myself.' He is *circulating* in how he knows what he knows, and is doing what he can to write that forth. Many who read Montaigne say that he must be one self-centered fellow talking of himself so much. However, he is not really talking about himself, but rather illuminating how he is *assembling* his reality. Quite clearly, nowadays, partly because of the pressures of digital media telling us so many ways to know so many things, we can become confounded; what is truth, the fact we might find true, we might sometimes ponder. However, when you (or I) read or write an essay, you (or we) are all that there is—your thoughts, our feelings, uncertainties, hatreds. Today, felicitously, the essay has moved far from that five-paragraph fixed content model described above, just as virtually all forms of knowledge have become—to insert that overused term—unexpectedly hybrid and mingled. There is now creative non-fiction, and autobiographical novels which can be in fact highly historical. Similarly, in writing now, happily, I often find that by letting go purpose, I uncover or discover swirling forms slithering in and infiltrating my prose, nuggets of biography, summaries from a time in history, lines of poetry which perfectly deepen the subject, discovery of a haunting word which becomes unexpectedly and hypnotically necessary to write of at some length.

The intransitive essay necessarily begins out of inner life. It is not an objective report or a stern classification of types. Probably the main new thing when you begin writing intransitively is to see *who* and *what* you are becoming in relation to your own thinking and reading and to the writing upon which you're commencing. We change astoundingly depending upon who is writing and how we approach their new language; obviously when we read anything it's always a new experience, a new language. It's helpful sometimes to assume another role, another identity, so to speak, as though you have a new kind of magnifying glass through which to perceive more appropriately. Here's a passage from an essay I wrote on Montaigne at a moment when I felt blocked off by his austere Latin sensibility, 'Cries of a Mind Leaping out of its Lodgings', his pinpoint accurate knowledge of the classical world I felt I needed to get through:

> To become his reader, I have had to become a kind of ventriloquist engaged in an act of translation and projection, of time, genre, gender, language and many translations. It was only when I found how uncertain, fearful and

tentative he was that I could begin to write of him wholeheartedly. I came to appreciate that Montaigne struggled tremendously with *how* to think far more than with *what* to think. In other words, he was not writing conclusions; he was coming upon what he found as it appeared.

In order to be his seamless ventriloquist, in order to read and know Montaigne that is, I had to get as close to him as I possibly could without judgement. In effect, I had to mimic now what he did with what he called his self. He chose to establish a singular intimacy with himself which I would, I saw, have to emulate as his ventriloquist. At first, I felt overwhelmed and uninitiated when I received the beautiful book *Drawn from Life*. At once, I asked myself how much in all did this great figure write? When, and which of all his writings are before me in this volume, 'how do they change and what is his flag ship hobby horse, his daunting intellectual obsession?'. I had to know him: the good and the limited. I had to speak knowing him and his language. In other reviews, I have temporarily become at times an architect, a weaver, even an orchestra conductor.

Let me share a bit more of how I find my way into reading and writing more effectively and intransitively. In writing a review of Gila Lustiger's *We Are Not Afraid*, I very suddenly surprised myself because

> I realized I was reading outwardly, trying to find something conclusive that was not there conclusively. It was only when I realized that this book needs to be read like an architect perceiving and fitting together the connecting boards, cladding, joists, and wedges that I could swim deeply in its multifarious constellations of thinking, considering, of coming to know. Not at all unsurprisingly, books that are inconspicuously new force us to see all the more newly.

As I had recognized to my surprise in the terms I was trying to force it in, that is, my terms: 'reading outwardly', 'trying to find something conclusive'. I had to relinquish a kind of deeply buried control in order to let the book speak through me and to me, so as 'to see all the more newly.' So, writing intransitively gradually can lead one to encounter and construct a completely new shape, to find the language that works for you and what you're reading. You come to see how you need to fit yourself to the writing, what shape you will put your writing in. This will feel like a gigantic happiness when you find it as you begin to see how to let the new shape go forward.

The title of this book, *Imagined Spaces*, fits in perfectly with the yet-to-be-filled-in-place of a brand-new, now intransitive essay. In English, the verb forms, *subjunctive* and *conditional*, really designate an empty or hanging or imagined space. For instance, the subjunctive tense points to something indefinite, but fully charged with feeling, as in 'I like it when you *are* glad'; in Spanish the word *are* is in the subjunctive, or 'If I were to know Luisa, I *would* be very happy.' Here you are not Luisa, but you are imagining what you'd feel like if you were. This hypothetical or imagined space grants the writer and reader unique freedoms. Similarly, the term *intransitive* in its simplest definition refers to a verb which has or needs no object to make a complete thought; the verb is strong enough on its own to be complete. Fortunately, the intransitive essay also in its essence presupposes no guiding purpose or conclusion presumed from the outset to shape and control it. It is a floating place which gets to be filled in by the writer or reader. It is thus a beautiful adventure: both a discovery and an outcome, wedded in the language and thinking of its author or reader. This is the major turn of attention, a liberating shift in understanding. You may ask yourself how can I write something if I don't know where it's going? That is the sheer delight of it. You can find a lot of comments you love from other writers and you will on your own wed them to each other in your writing as it goes along. At the beginning here, there are at least four core qualities of intransitive essays: what I call a *bethinking* author, a weaving of focal points, a pinch of *depsychologicalization*, and the densely accurate language of a poet. I will briefly speak of each.

Before any analysis, I want to share my poem from a few years ago called 'Bethinking', a term I'll describe later:

> She rode on a think,
> rode ramshackle light,
> her airs thoroughly whippoorwill.
> It was first all about the sweep
> so sweet and steep.
> Bethinking herself
> she went all in, heading
> her all widewelter
> through the tide.
> Learning to spin still to
> foreshadow before when.
> Riding her think warpwise
> rotating light, wedgeward

through long straits of angle,
spinning ramshackle light
where the whippoorwills will.

This poem has unusually outlandish, invented, but understandable, words like *widewelter, warpwise, wedgeward*, each of which are part of the fluid movements bethinking literally bespeaks. Indeed, 'to ride on a think' is a strange thing to say or to do, but, when writing an intransitive essay, that is precisely what you need to let yourself do, most literally. Virginia Woolf who reviewed books for 30 years for *The Times Literary Supplement* hoped to 'offer merely our little hoard of observations, which other readers may like to set, for a moment, beside their own'. The language and the variety of your unique perceptions will invite you and your readers to ride further, to go far afield into unknown places, via unknown miraculous trajectories you are now tracing. A much-overlooked American novelist, Susan Glaspell, shows how one might breathe a bit more intransitively when she writes in *Fugitive's Return*, 'One might speak as if one were thinking'. In effect, she is hoping to open the boundaries up so as to write or speak with the intimacy and definiteness of the thoughts spreading through her lingering mind. Actually, without the controlling reins of the old-fashioned transitive model, this new intransitive essay becomes important all throughout it, in this sense like every word in a poem. In this intransitive turn of mind, each word matters more without any central point to have to be subordinate to. It's as though the intransitive essay is akin to a kaleidoscope turning, not to a square standing still and static. These following four turns of the writer and reader's attention will help compose an intransitive essay, thickening its now non-linear prose. *Bethinking* is slightly different than to just have something pop up or pop away in one's mind. It involves holding the thought, considering something and turning what is linked to it around and round. In Virginia Woolf's *Jacob's Room*, Mrs. Durrant's 'mind skimmed leagues where Mrs. Pascoe's mind adhered to its solitary patch. Her mind skimmed leagues as the ponies climbed the hill road. Forwards and backwards she cast her mind, as if the roofless cottages, mounds of slag, and cottage gardens overgrown with foxglove and bramble cast shade upon her mind'.

Bethinking is a considering or pondering something carefully, for the pleasure of being with it, whatever it is first and then of knowing it more. In Susan Glaspell's suggestively acute novel, *The Morning Is Near Us*, the term *bethinks* appears very unexpectedly, 'she bethought herself of other things. This was an old friend of her mother and father. He had come for another visit at the old place—had come to visit her after her years away, and he looked older now than when he had come in'.

Bethinking is, then, a unique belingering, a slow stroking of what one is perceiving rather than a slamming the door shut finality for a forced conclusion. Once a reader and writer know that they are free to linger thus, neither one has to finalize, but can dive, hover and linger in all the what is there. That is the 'riding the thought' which was in my bethinking poem earlier. Now, whenever I read, I am exuberant and applaud whenever I come upon that word bethinking and keep examples of it for moments such as these, our considering those imagined spaces together.

Cross-stitching. Another way of writing and reading and knowing involves active cross-stitching focal points you find. Cross-stitching is far more powerful than cross-overs, which doesn't capture the intimacy of needlework practice. For instance, necessary historical vignettes may add centuries of depth and causality to the action in a reading of Cormac McCarthy. These may be histories of a town years ago, allusions to forgotten familial arguments, whose hostility ineffably stains the present world. Mini-autobiographies will 'greaten' a novel, adding a second or third layer of characterization. There is something immensely exciting about an unexpected switch between the present tense world of a book and some other wholly unexpected way of approaching time. J. M. Coetzee's stunning novel, *The Master of Petersburg*, a historical biography of author Fyodor Dostoevsky and simultaneously a shrouded autobiography of J. M. Coetzee himself, provides a swift snapshot of St. Petersburg years ago, its habits and its sins, as well as a searchingly simultaneous look at the pitfalls of authorship in both men, as writers and as people. Epicist Doris Lessing's fiction combines memories of Southern Rhodesia with 1950s London. It is not only that place shifts. It is that the bethinking writer who is wholly a part of those shifts, inviting and drawing you to go along too. Lessing often writes of her parents in the Great War, illuminating how those years affected them and her years later. Her parents become haunting personages during and after the World War One and in their life-changing shift to life in Africa. While reading, you know that this was both long ago and also now in the person of Lessing. Incrementally, her parents become part of the present tense. This meld gives inordinate depth to the reading of what might otherwise only have been a story of how the conflicts were years ago. Lessing has been criticized for her so-called 'space fiction,' for what critics call her flight from the real world. Unsurprisingly, her Shikasta series enhances all the more her longstanding effort to couple the struggles of the individual and the collective. So, in our time, writers are mixing and matching, and making anew—a mixing which gets called hybridity or creative non-fiction. It reflects our efforts 'to make it new' for today to borrow Pound's admonition in the early twentieth century. New types of novels abound, new kinds of novel forms to add to the familiar *bildungsroman*, such as *Reifungsroman* (the novel of ripening or growing older) and others. Reading Gila Lustiger's powerful book about the terrorist bombings in France, I found the name for a new kind of novel which fit her book: a *Geisteslebenroman*, that is, a probing of intellectual life, of shared cultural existence. As a trained intellectual historian, I was thrilled to name this new kind of novel which examined how our communal mental life intertwined and overlapped.

Depsychologicalization. One day, in the Pacific Northwest, I came upon David Miles who wrote of a 'psychologicalization' of reality. It made immediate sense to me to think of changing the word to a *depsychologicalization* of reality. Various studies demonstrated an 'internalization or psychologicalization of reality' and revealed psychology as 'that from which innerness is totally absent precisely because it aspires only to contain that innerness'. This anomalous substitution of regularising theory about psyche for psyche itself had become pervasive in mid-twentieth contemporary writing and art. In contrast to absorption with psychology, many writers now narratively constitute a difficult alternative: a de-psychologizing of reality, that is a growing intimacy with an unpredictably ordered and disordered inner reality. Martha Quest in Doris Lessing's novel notes that people are 'hypnotized into futility by self-observation.' Similarly, in *The Golden Notebook*, Anna Wulf is said to be 'sunk in subjectivity', but also painfully chary of inhabiting and becoming intimate with her inner world. For the purpose of an intransitive essay, there is a just balance: between an over-intensity and a minimalism, between assuming too much self-importance and letting your reader breathe between your words. An intransitive essay has to be free, not entrapped by self, theory, or language or the will of others.

Poetics. The final suggestion to building an intransitive essay is perhaps the hardest: it is to write with the effect of a poet. T. S. Eliot put it clearly in *Sweeney Agonistes* when he wrote, 'I gotta to use words when I talk to you.' So does the writer in this intransitive essay. This writer can both open things up and shut them down, switch tone radically, use long Latinate words or simple plain language. What the intransitive essay shares most with poetry is its wandering quality, its constant discovering. Yes, in a great poem, every word counts, but that is not the main thing. It is presenting an experience which, after reading or hearing it, gives the listener, reader, a primary experience which touches him or her in an original, profoundly moving way. For illustration, here is a 1995 poem, 'A Meadow' by the great Lithuanian poet Czeslaw Milosz:

> It was a riverside meadow, lush, from before the hay harvest,
> On an immaculate day in the sun of June.
> I searched for it, found it, recognized it.

Grasses and flowers grew there familiar in my childhood.
With half-closed eyelids I absorbed luminescence.
And the scent garnered me, all knowing ceased.
Suddenly I felt I was disappearing and weeping with joy.

And we the participants in this 'luminescence' temporarily become radiant too, recognizing the meadow, the 'sun of June', the ceasing of all knowing. There is an ineffable openness in this poem, and there can be a similar openness in the evolving space and shape of an intransitive essay. Every word will be true in the sense that it is the only word that will exactly do. There is no rushing to get to the next point, rather a delightful soaking and basking in what you are knowing. Again, the intransitive essay is a writing of exploration, of finding out how and what, with the bethinking writer all peaceful and alert, spaciously considering what is taking place.

I want now to present a brief account of making an intransitive essay. Writing a review of Lavinia Greenlaw's *Questions of Travel: William Morris in Iceland With a Hit of Strangeness* presented me with a challenge. Greenlaw wrote poetic responses and Morris' writing was primarily journalistic, like a diary. The recto or right side of the page was always Morris and the verso or left side was Greenlaw. It was immediately clear that their writing was utterly different: in tone, in content, in language, in just about everything. Initially, I read the whole book dutifully and linearly page by page in order, marking what I thought were important observations. However, this brought no completeness anywhere. Then, an idea appeared: read all of Greenlaw as a book and do the same with Morris, and take thorough notes on each. Slowly, like dripping glue, there appeared coagulations of how they each were, and very few ways to see them and the book together. All readings and responses were disorderly. I tried to force and failed to find any magnet for quite a long period of time. Suddenly, I saw I literally had to balance them and my two readings, which became the title of my essay, 'Balancing the Books' seamlessly putting their separate books together with what I had perceived in each of them and was also beginning to find in tandem.

I want to conclude reading a bit of my excitement in balancing these books, in being patient enough to find their kinship, their intransitive matching. While all the preliminary independent readings seemed a matter of wasted weeks and dreary pages of notes, finally finding what they shared, what made the book a completeness after the many pieces of scribbling felt indelibly exciting, an epiphany, even a glory. The third reading—balancing the books—became exciting, a stunning, mutual minuet among us. I discovered them, that is uncovered them. I gave them nicknames, Morris,

'Mr. Stickshaped' and Greenlaw, 'Metaphysical Bumblebee'. Greenlaw comes into a brilliant new form for writing about travel, about herself and Morris together in flamboyantly distinctive movements. The book enacts an in-person coupling of *differents* becoming together in a writing which I have called 'seen into thought.' Theirs are two palimpsestic adventures, rolling into each other's, his seemingly physical and hers apparently ideational with two homecomings, and two perceptual surgings into the present. They share a mystical, even quivering uncertainty about travel's ineluctable, ever unsettling, unfamiliarity, its essential strangeness. The word 'strange' weaves through my notes in all the readings. Morris repeatedly says the words queer, *strange*, and *odd*. Early on, he could not sleep because 'the *strangeness* and excitement kept waking me up'. Ever referring to how he feels, Morris would write his journal, but could not, 'for a *strange* lazy sort of excitement … was on me, made up of half-a-dozen things'. Each of them sometimes becomes temporarily undone by this strangeness, their fearful, frozen thoughts of what to do when now ends, whether they are going too far, how much they are being in their moment. Greenlaw queries, knowing full well she can't yet, 'Do you want to stop going back?' while Morris has a glorious epiphany in one of what I call his 'expanses', his extended effusive and glorious presentations of a place: 'once again that thin thread of insight and imagination, which comes so seldom to us, and is such a joy when it comes, did not fail me at this first sight of the greatest marvel and most storied place of Iceland'. Here follows what I think of as one of the book's four wonderful mating dance steps, where their thoughts build upon each other's and my following along with them. Greenlaw puts it her way: 'That thin thread of insight and imagination. Not just seen in the mind *but seen into* [my emphasis].' Each seemingly separate book thrives in such profound and simultaneously perceived over excitements that each writer survives and returns from.

The thrilling moments in the third reading are those of a bonding, across centuries and persons, when each one is writing of, or speculating about an uncannily, thoroughly unexpected, yet totally familiar circumstance. They and the entire book come together as in a lingering mutual recognition. *Questions of Travel* becomes, then, a collective dance of fast-paced colloquial speech mingled with precipitous physical adventure, ignominious fear and self-conscious awareness. Greenlaw prepares us for the end, 'Going on from now will be going back' and refers again to the book's psychic setting, to 'the fluidity of *strangeness* [my emphasis].' That going home is a prerequisite part of travel has been established from the outset, from the numerous gnawing homesick moments. Each writer ultimately comes into a new resolution, a real felt in the heart conclusion. Greenlaw finds 'Going home you don't look about you, only ahead,' and experiences a dazzling completeness: 'Remembering what it is to be inside' and 'Now that it's over, you were very happy'. Initially, being home, Morris is overcome by a sense of his feeling, a bewilderment (more strangeness), 'not knowing what to ask for' and troubled by what he saw as the 'disproportionate' size of the houses and horses in a landscape 'that…all looked like a scene at a theater.' His last words, however, are praise for Iceland, 'a marvelous, beautiful and solemn place, and where I had been in fact very happy.' So, finally, the two of them have a happy ending, as does this faithful reader of their journeys.

This bountiful book rocks a path in a stunning mélange between the strange and sure, between actualized thought, and exhaustive near mystical experiences. The magical happens: Greenlaw melds with Morris, and, through her journaling his physical journey, she bonds with him and with us the readers. They leave and come home together. Greenlaw has taken the figurative to another dimension, making it all both triumphantly strange and enchantingly believable. This reader wants more of them, more of this factional fictional form, this being 'unanchored' with them in this place, on 'the hinge of simile; a hesitant connection, as if….'. This magical carpet ride of a book comes around full circle, joyously complete. Everything comes together. Morris who needed change has indeed 'unsettled his perceptions,' and Greenlaw has crossed borders and centuries and genres and genders in her journey, finding how and where language matters: 'The simpler the form, the greater the need for simile'. I balanced the books. In reading this exceptional, seethingly wonderful book by waiting and not forcing a conclusion, I discovered that balancing the books can be unexpectedly thrilling and profoundly figurative. Unexpected, imagined places, all intransitively true.

Notes & Bibliography

Tracing lines… Essaying For Our Times

7	'the sentence is like a sill before a view…': Cole and Winters (2020), p.19
8	'Far away, under the glowering cloud…': Stewart (2018), p.48.
9	'For she is just as visible to you who remain silent…': Woolf (1924), p.23.
11	'to provide accountability for public investment in research and evidence of the benefits of this investment': Research Excellent Framework (2021).
12	'the flexibility of intelligence or responsiveness': Collini (2012), pp. 73–77.
12	'there are known knowns; they are things we know… .': Rumsfeld (2002).
12	'Thinking and thought are two different things…': Lee (1995).
10	'letting one 'I' speak for another, interrupting and inserting and overwriting': Gunn and Low (2019).
17	'outside *in* the teaching machine': Spivak (1993).

Cole, Peter and Terry Winters. 2020. *On Being Drawn*. The Cahier Series no. 36, Centre for Writers and Translators, American University of Paris, London: Sylph Editions.

Collini, Stefan. 2012. *What are Universities For?* London and New York: Penguin.

Gunn, Kirsty and Low, Gail. 2019. 'In Other Words: an essay about language arranged by Kirsty Gunn and Gail Low'. *New Writing*. November. https://www.tandfonline.com/doi/full/10.1080/14790726.2019.1681466 [Accessed: 30 March 2020].

Research Excellent Framework, 2021. *What Is The REF? - REF* 2021. [online] Ref. ac.uk. Available from: <https://www.ref.ac.uk/about/what-is-the-ref/> [Acessed: 16 April 2020].

Lee, Li-Young. 1995. 'An Interview by James Lee', *Bomb 51*, Spring 1995 https://bombmagazine.org/articles/li-young-lee/ [Accessed: 10 January 2019].

Rumsfeld, Donald. 2002. 'News transcipt of US Department of Defense briefing' https://archive.defense.gov/Transcripts/Transcript.aspx?TranscriptID=2636 [Accessed: 27 March 2020].

Spivak, Gayatri. 1993. *Outside in the teaching machine*. New York and London: Routledge.

Stewart, Jim. 2018. 'Gull' in *THIS*. Dundee: The Voyage Out Press.

Woolf, Virginia. 1924. *Mr Bennett and Mrs Brown*. The Hogarth Essays no. 1, London: The Hogarth Press.

Songs I can't Play

26   'If Miss Honeychurch ever takes to live as she plays…': Forster (1908), p.24
Forster, E.M. 1908. *A Room with a View*. Mineola, New York:
Dover Publications, 1995.

Line Drawing

29   'I take a line out for a walk': quoted in Epstein (1991), p.11.

30   'exactly, precisely, absolutely': ibid.

30   'the chanciness of the enterprise…': ibid.

31   'The world everywhere is whispering essays…': Smith (1863), p.27.

31   'the sublime grandeur of the real world.': Dawkins (2004), p.629.

31   'represent a narrowing down from reality…': ibid.

31   'To pay attention, this is our endless…': Oliver (2003), p.27.

32   'movement chauvinist…': Smith, Barry. 2010.
The Documentary: The Mysteries of the Brain Episode 2 [podcast]. BBC World
Service. First transmitted 11 October 2010. Available at:
<https://www.bbc.co.uk/sounds/play/p009vmsq>
[Accessed: 30 March 2020].

32   'Essayists are keen observers of the overlooked': Madden (2010), pp. 4 & 134.

32   'in order in to perform complex and adaptable movement': ibid.

34   … dogs have been taken on by humans not merely as pets…: Berger (2001),
p. 10.

36   'Anyone who can look attentively, think freely…': Good (1988), p.182.

36   'the process of having original ideas that have value': TED (2007)

37   'Let not a hair's breadth…': Quoted in Pilgrim (1984), p.153.

37   '… mimics the activity of a mind at work': Madden (2010), p.65.

38   'What descriptions—or good ones, anyway—actually…': Doty (2010), p.153.

38   'Of all literary forms the essay…': Hardison (1989), p.11.

38   'Thirty-six Ways of Looking at an Essay': Arthur (2018), pp.237-241.

39   '… the brain never sees the world as it actually is…': Big Think (2017)

39   … Research at the University of New Mexico has observed that the executive
functions of the brain…: BBC Horizon (2013).

41   'the law of the innermost form': Adorno (1984), p.171.

41   'The culture administered by the universities…': Sontag (1992), p.xv.

41   'The good health of essay writing…': ibid.

41   'stays alive because it dares…': Atwan (1991) p.x.

41   'A literary birdcage capable of…': Solnit (2014), p.124.

43   'Art does not reproduce the visible…': Klee (2013), p.1.

43   'Whatever its narrative style…': Levy (2015), p. xv.

43   'The problem with ideas…': ibid.

Adorno, T.W. 1984. 'The Essay as Form' trans. by Hullot Kentor, Bob & Will, Frederic. *New German Critique*, 32.

Arthur, Chris. 2018. *Hummingbirds Between the Pages*. Columbus: Ohio State University Press.

Atwan, Robert. 1991. 'Foreword'. *In The Best American Essays* 1991, edited by Joyce Carol Oates. New York: Tricknor & Fields.

Berger, John. 2001. *Why Look at Animals*. London: Penguin, p. 10.

Big Think. 2017. *Do Our Senses Reveal the World—Or Do They Obscure It?* Beau Lotto. [YouTube video] Available at: <https://www.youtube.com/watch?time_continue=341&v=J07XGg6Rnzo&feature=emb_logo> [Accessed: 30 March 2020]

Dawkins, Richard. 2004. *The Ancestor's Tale: A Pilgrimage to the Dawn of Life*. London: Weidenfeld & Nicholson.

Doty, Mark. 2010. *The Art of Description*. Minneapolis: Graywolf Press.

Epstein, Joseph. 1991. *A Line Out For A Walk: Familiar Essays*. New York: W.W.

Good, Graham. 1988. *The Observing Self: Rediscovering the Essay*. London: Routledge.

Hardison, O.B. 1989. 'Binding Proteus: An Essay on the Essay'. In Butrym, Alexander J. *Essays on the Essay: Redefining the Genre*. Athens GA: University of Georgia Press.

Horizon: *The Creative Brain: How Insight Works*. 2013. BBC Two Television, 14 March.

Klee, Paul. 2013. *Creative Confession and Other Writings*. London: Tate Publishing.

Levy, Ariel (ed.) 2015. *The Best American Essays* 2015. New York: Mariner Books.

Madden, Patrick. 2010. *Quotidiana: Essays*. Lincoln: University of Nebraska Press.

Magritte, René. 1928. *Attempting The Impossible* [oil on canvas]. Private collection.

Magritte, René. 1929. *The Treachery of Images* [oil on canvas]. Los Angeles: Los Angeles County Museum of Art.

Oliver, Mary. 2003. *Owls and Other Fantasies: Poems & Essays*. Boston: Beacon Press.

Pilgrim, Richard B. 1984. 'Foundations for a Religio-Aesthetic Tradition'. In *Art, Creativity and the Sacred*, edited by Diane Apostolos-Cappadona. New York: Crossroad.

Smith, Alexander. 1863. *Dreamthorp: A Book Of Essays Written In the Country*. London: Strahan & Co.

Smith, Barry. 2010. *The Documentary: The Mysteries of the Brain Episode 2* [podcast]. BBC.

Available at: <https://www.bbc.co.uk/sounds/play/p009vmsq>
[Accessed: 30 March 2020]
Solnit, Rebecca. 2014. *Wanderlust: A History of Walking*. London: Granta.
Sontag, Susan (ed.) 1992. *The Best American Essays* 1992. New York: Ticknor & Fields.
TED. 2007. *Ken Robinson: Do Schools Kill Creativity?* [online video] Available at: <https://www.youtube.com/watch?v=iG9CE55wbtY> [Accessed: 16 April 2020]

On Being Hit on the Head by a Poem

46   'Alas, I am struck down, a deep and deadly blow!': Aeschylus. 458 BCE. 'Agamemnon'. The Internet Classics Archive| Agamemnon By Aeschylus. [online] Classics.mit.edu. Available at: <http://classics.mit.edu/Aeschylus/agamemnon.html> [Accessed: 2 April 2020].
46   'The host with someone… dishonoured shroud.': Eliot, T., 1919. *Sweeney Among The Nightingales By T. S. Eliot* | Poetry Foundation. [online] Poetry Foundation. Available at: <https://www.poetryfoundation.org/poems/52564/sweeney-among-the-nightingales> [Accessed: 2 April 2020]

Aeschylus. 458 BCE. 'Agamemnon'. *The Internet Classics Archive*| Agamemnon By Aeschylus. [online] Classics.mit.edu. Available at: <http://classics.mit.edu/Aeschylus/agamemnon.html> [Accessed: 2 April 2020].
Eliot, T.S. 1915. 'The Love Song of J. Alfred Prufrock'. *The Love Song Of J. Alfred Prufrock* | Poetry Magazine. [online] Poetry Foundation. Available at: <https://www.poetryfoundation.org/poetrymagazine/poems/44212/the-love-song-of-j-alfred-prufrock> [Accessed: 2 April 2020].
Eliot, T.S. 1919. 'Sweeney Among The Nightingales'. *Sweeney Among The Nightingales By T. S. Eliot* | Poetry Foundation. [online] Poetry Foundation. Available at: <https://www.poetryfoundation.org/poems/52564/sweeney-among-the-nightingales> [Accessed: 2 April 2020].
Kenner, Hugh. 1959. *T.S.Eliot: The Invisible Poet. New York: McDowell*, Obolensky.
Proust, Marcel. 1919. 'Journées de lecture' in *Pastiches et mélanges*. Paris: Gaston Gallimard.
Roberts, Micheal (ed.) 1936. *The Faber Book of Modern Verse*. London: Faber & Faber.

Politics of Small Spaces

This is an edited account of an email conversation that took place between May 2018 and September 2019 in the run up to the exhibition, 'Politics of Small Spaces' at the Cooper Gallery, University of Dundee. The exhibition comprised work by artist Paul Noble and documents from the archives of the pioneering urban planner, Patrick Geddes. As part of the project, Lorens Holm, Director of the Geddes Institute for Urban Research corresponded with Noble over four weeks by email. The full email exchange is available at https://www.dundee.ac.uk/media/dundeewebsite/ cooper-gallery/exhibitions/2018/summerresidency/PaulNoble_LorensHolm_ CooperSummerResidency2018_ConversationCompilation.pdf.

The second email by Lorens Holm was written 01 July 2018; the Grenfell Tower fire was a year earlier, 14 June 2017. At the time of editing this text for publication, the Grenfell Tower Public Inquiry is underway.

50   'the culture of congestion.': Koolhaas (1978), p.10
66   'Town plans are thus no mere diagrams … we may be rewarded in deciphering it': Geddes (1915), p. 170.
69   'Dead to the world': Herbert (1886), p.171.

Achterberg, Gerrit. 2004. 'Ballad of a Gasfitter'. *In Landscape with Rowers*. Ed. by J.M. Coetzee. Princeton: Princeton University Press.
Geddes, Patrick. 1915. *Cities in Evolution. London: Williams and Norgate*.
Herbert, George. 1886. 'The Flower'. *In The Poems of George Herbert*. Eugene Oregon: Wipf and Stock, 2018.
Koolhaas, Rem. 1978. *Delirious New York: A Retroactive Manifesto for Manhattan*. New York: Oxford University Press.
McGregor, Neil. 1994. *A Victim of Anonymity: The Master of Saint Bartholomew Altarpiece*. London: Thames and Hudson.
Modern Toss. 2019. *The Official Home Of Modern Toss*. Modern Toss. Available from: <https://www.moderntoss.com/> [Accessed: 24 April 2020].
Man Ray. 1920. *Dust Breeding*. [Photograph]. The Metropolitan Museum of Art: New York.
Ricks, Christopher.1993. *Samuel Beckett's Dying Words*. Oxford: Oxford University Press.
Holm, Loren, et al. 2015. *The City is a Thinking Machine Volume 2: The Geddes Archives*. [ebook] Geddes Institute for Urban Research. University of Dundee.

Available from: <https://www.dundee.ac.uk/geddesinstitute/projects/citythink/catalogue/> [Accessed: 24 April 2020].

Mind the Gap

Ukiyo-e translates as 'pictures of the floating world' and describes Japanese woodblock prints and paintings featuring kabuki actors, sumo wrestlers, female beauties, landscapes and scenes from history, travel and folk tales. Kuma took inspiration from the famous Ukiyo-e artist, Ando Hiroshige's *People on a bridge surprised by rain* for his design of the Bato Hiroshige Museum which houses the artists' work.

72   'When I saw the brief…': Kuma, K. 2018. *Interview with Susan Nickalls*. September 2018, Dundee.

73   'a living room for the city.': ibid.

73   'In some of my other buildings, for instance in my Hiroshige…': ibid.

74   'hard on the outside, soft on the inside': ibid.

74   'I first discovered the effectiveness of public apertures…': Futagawa, Yukio (ed.) 2009. Kengo Kuma Recent Project. Tokyo: A.D.A. Edita, Tokyo Co. Ltd; p.10.

74   'In Japanese culture, ma is more important…': Kuma (2018).

75   'Emptiness is not merely a neutral space serving to defuse the shock…': Cheng (1994), p.50.

75   'At some international competitions, it is often pointed out that the overall silhouette…': Futagawa (2009), p.12.

75   'For me, we try to avoid the solid heavy wall as a canvas…': Kuma (2018).

75   'repulsive' and 'useless monuments': Futaugawa (2009), p.10

76   'Apertures, gaps and roofs are devices that entice and connect….': Kuma (2018).

76   'an epic drama between roofs and walls.' Futagawa (2009), p.68

77   'I am interested in the roof, not as a matter of style…': ibid., p.18.

77   'vertical streets… not so alive, not so human' … 'roughness and noise': Kuma (2018).

78   'My ultimate aim is to "erase" architecture…': Bognar (2009), p.8

78   'struggle to confront the overwhelming presence of the material': Kuma (2018).

78   'Materials only show their true nature…': Bognar, pp.10-11
79   'I am a big fan of Charles Rennie Mackintosh…': Kuma (2018).
79   'Today's society premised on capitalism…': Futagawa (2009), p.14 .
80   'The next step is for all…': Kuma (2018)
80   'My stance in every field has been to be skeptical…': ibid., p.18.

Bognar, Botond. 2009. *Material Immaterial — The New Work of Kengo Kuma*. New York: Princeton Architectural Press.

Cheng, François. 1994. *Empty and Full — the language of Chinese Painting*. Trans by Kohn, Michael H. Boulder: Shambala Publications.

Futagawa, Yukio (ed.) 2009. *Kengo Kuma Recent Project*. Tokyo: A.D.A. Edita, Tokyo Co. Ltd.

Kakuzō, Okakura. 1906. 'Book of Tea'. Quoted in *Ma—Groundswell* [online]. Groundswell. Available at <https://www.groundswellbyjo.com/index-ma/#new-page-69> [Accessed: 7 April 2020].

Kuma, K. 2018. 'Interview with Susan Nickalls'. September 2018, Dundee.

Smith, Adam. 1776. *An Inquiry into the Nature and Causes of the Wealth of Nations*. London: W. Strahan and T. Cadell.

Life in the Bardo

81   'in the to-and-fro twitchery… impelling them to fly': Padel (2012), p.53.
82   Every breath… is a small birth and death.: Belfast Buddhist (2016)
83   'Writers imagine the unthinkable as a way to liberate the imagination.': Morrison (1993).
86   'More Steven Spielberg than Barnett Newman': White (2010). <https://www.tate.org.uk/research/publications/tate-papers/14/damien-hirst-shark-nature-capitalism-and-the-sublime> [Accessed: 15 March 2020].
86   'That rich wisdom was lost… acknowledged to be inevitable.': Mannix (2018), p.1.
89   'We die. That may be the meaning of life….': Morrison. 1993.

Belfast Buddhist. 2016. *Pema Chodron - Relaxing with impermanence* [YouTube Video]. Available from: <https://www.youtube.com/watch?v=nBYGBi80OK8> [Accessed: 9 April 2020].

College of Charleston. 2012. *Motoi Yamamoto's 'Return to the Sea: Saltworks' -- Spoleto Festival USA at the College of Charleston* [YouTube Video]. Available from: <https://www.youtube.com/watch?v=eLIJuQSOJis> [Accessed: 15 March 2020].

Hirst, Damien. 1991. *The Physical Impossibility of Death in the Mind of Someone Living.* [Sculpture]. Tate Modern: London.

Mannix, Kathryn. 2018. *With the End in Mind: Dying, death and Wisdom in an Age of Denial.* London: William Collins.

Morrison, Toni. 1993. *The Nobel Prize In Literature 1993.* [online] NobelPrize.org. Available from: <https://www.nobelprize.org/prizes/literature/1993/morrison/lecture/> [Accessed: 9 April 2020].

Padel, Ruth. 2012. *The Mara Crossing.* London and New York: Chatto & Windus.

White, Luke. 2010. 'Damien Hirst's Shark: Nature, Capitalism and the Sublime' in *Tate Papers*, no.14. Autumn. <https://www.tate.org.uk/research/publications/tate-papers/14/damien-hirst-shark-nature-capitalism-and-the-sublime> [Accessed: 15 March 2020].

You by Me

95   'As you read, you slowly grow aware… sickness inherent in their arrangement': Kriss (2013).

97   'Leave the door open for the unknown…': Solnit (2017), p.4.

103   'I am really wary of ending this book with a simple cry of "I did it, and you can too."': Hari (2018), p.259.

108   'I am large, I contain multitudes.' Whitman (1855).

112   'You must go on. I can't go on. I'll go on.' Beckett (1959), p. 382.

Beckett, Samuel. 1959. *The Beckett Trilogy: Molloy, Malone Dies and The Unnamable.* London: Picador, 1976.

Hari, Johann. 2018. *Lost Connections.* London: Bloomsbury.

Kriss, Sam. 2013. *Book of Lamentations.* The New Inquiry [online]. Available from: <https://thenewinquiry.com/book-of-lamentations/> [Accessed: 13 April 2020].

Solnit, Rebecca. 2006. *A Field Guide to Getting Lost.* Edinburgh: Canongate Books, 2017.

Whitman, Walt. 1855. *Song of Myself, 51.* Poets.Org [online]. Available from: <https://poets.org/poem/song-myself-51> [Accessed: 13 April 2020].

A Voyage Out in Education

114   *Bloom* <https://www.bloomeducation.co.uk> [Accessed: 10 November 2019]

116   With thanks to Binyaamin Sufi for permission to quote from his report.

The Flicker of North

125   'stormed a humble-bee's nest on the side of the old chapel-brae...':
Miller (1854), p. 69.

128   'Friend, I have lost the way....': Muir (1949), p.13.

129   'Sommernetter og stille vann og uendelig stille skoger': Hamsun (1894) p.30.
See also Hamsun, Knut. 1894 *Pan*. Transl. James W. McFarlane, Artemis
Press, 15th printing, 1972; Norwegian Edition: *Pan*, with notes by Olaf
Kortner, Oslo: Gyldendal Norsk Forlag, Oslo, 1961; p.51.

129   'No calls, no footfalls on the roads; it seemed my heart was full of dark wine.':
ibid.

130   'a national cultural trauma': Høyum, 'Hamsuns Liv og Forfatterskap'.

Brown, George Mackay. 'Hamnavoe.' *Hamnavoe - Poetry Archive*. [online] Poetry
Archive. Available at: <https://poetryarchive.org/poem/hamnavoe/> [Accessed: 27
April 2020].
Hamsun, Knut. 1894. *Pan*. Transl. James W. McFarlane. 15th printing. London:
Artemis Press, [1955] 1972.; Norwegian Edition: *Pan*, with notes by Olaf Kortner,
Oslo: Gyldendal Norsk Forlag, 1961.
McGuane, Thomas. 2007. 'In a Lonely Place – Review of Per Petterson's *Out Stealing
Horses*'. *The New York Times*, June 24th.
Miller,. Hugh. 1854. *My Schools and Schoolmasters*, 29th edition. Edinburgh: William
Nimmo and Co, 1881.
Muir, Edwin. 1949. *The Labyrinth*. London: Faber and Faber.
Høyum, Nina Frang. 'Hamsuns Liv og Forfatterskap'. Hamsun Centre, Hamarøy.
Available from: <https://hamsunsenteret.no/en/knut-hamsun/?Article=43>
[Accessed: 10th November 2019]
Singer, Isaac Bashevis. 1967. 'Introduction' to *Hunger*, Transl. Robert Bly. New York:
Farrar, Straus and Giroux.

Undset, Sigrid. 1934. *The Longest Years* (Elleve aar). Transl. Arthur G. Chater. London: Cassell and Co. 1935.

My Love Affair with the Essay

169   'a loose sally of the mind': Johnson (1755), p.721.
170   'even the essayist's partial escape… a happy or wandering mood':
       White (1977), p.viii.
170   'no instruction, save through the medium of enjoyment.': Repplier (1894).
170   'A genuine essay has no educational… it is a stroll through someone's mazy
       mind.': Ozick (1998), pp.114-118.
171   'making it read like a short story or fiction': Gutkind (2005).

Barthelme, Donald. 1983. 'Not Knowing.' *Not Knowing: The Essays and Interviews of Donald Barthelme*. Edited by Kim Herzinger. New York: Random House, 1997.
Browning, Robert. 1842. 'My Last Duchess'. *My Last Duchess By Robert Browning* Poetry Foundation. [online] Poetry Foundation. Available at: <https://www.poetryfoundation.org/poems/43768/my-last-duchess> [Accessed: 16 April 2020].
Céline, Louis-Ferdinand. 1932. *Journey to the End of the Night*. Translated by Marks, John H.P. New York: New Directions, 1934.
D'Agata, John & Fingal, Jim. 2012. *The Lifespan of a Fact*. New York: W.W. Norton & Company.
Deresiewicz, William. 2017. 'In Defense of Facts'. *The Atlantic.* January/February Issue. Available at: <https://www.theatlantic.com/magazine/archive/2017/01/in-defense-of-facts/508748/> [Accessed 16 April 2020].
Dostoevsky, Fyodor. 1864. 'Notes From Underground.' *Epoch.* January 1864-April 1864.
Ford, Madox Ford. 1915. *The Good Soldier: A Tale of Passion*. London: The Bodley Head.
Grimké, Sarah. 1838. 'Letter VIII On the Condition of Women in the U.S.' *Letters on the Equality of Sexes and the Condition of Women*. Boston: Isaac Knapp. Pp.46-55.
Gutkind, Lee. 2005. Interviewed by Daniel Nester for *Bookslut*, July. Available at: <http://www.bookslut.com/features/2005_07_005959.php> [Accessed 16 April 2020].
Hazlitt, William. 2000. *The Fight and Other Writings*. Edited by Chandler, David G. & Hazlitt, William. London: Penguin Classics.

Jackson, J.B. 1957. 'The Stranger's Path'. *Landscapes: selected writings of J.B. Jackson*. Amherst, University of Massachusetts Press, 1970.

Johnson, Samuel. 1755. 'A Dictionary of the English Language.' *A Dictionary Of The English Language - Samuel Johnson - 1755*. [online] Johnsonsdictionaryonline.com. Available at: <https://johnsonsdictionaryonline.com/> [Accessed 16 April 2020].

Lopate, Phillip. 1975. *Being with Children*. New York: Doubleday.

Lopate, Phillip. 1994. *The Art of the Personal Essay*. New York: Doubleday-Anchor.

Machado de Assis, Joaquim. 1881. *The Posthumous Memoirs of Bras Cubas*. Translated by Rabassa, Gregory. Oxford: Oxford University Press, 1997.

Malcolm, Janet. 'Forty-One False Starts'. 1994. *The New Yorker*. July 11th.

Michaels, Leonard. 'In the Fifties'. 1975. *In The Making of the American Essay*. Edited by John D'Agata. Minneapolis: Graywolf Press, 2016.

Nochlin, Linda. 1971. 'Why Have There Been No Great Women Artists,'. [ebook] Available at: <http://www.writing.upenn.edu/library/Nochlin-Linda_Why-Have-There-Been-No-Great-Women-Artists.pdf> [Accessed: 16 April 2020].

Ozick, Cynthia. 1998. 'She: Portrait of the Essay as a Warm Body'. *The Atlantic Monthly*. Vol 282. No.3. pp.114-118.

Paine, Thomas. 1776. 'Common Sense'. *1776: Paine, Common Sense (Pamphlet) - Online Library Of Liberty*. [online] Oll.libertyfund.org. Available at: <https://oll.libertyfund.org/pages/1776-paine-common-sense-pamphlet> [Accessed: 16 April 2020].

Repplier, Agnes. 1894. 'The Passing of the Essay'. *In The Dozy Hours, And Other Papers/ The Passing Of The Essay - Wikisource, The Free Online Library*. [online] En.wikisource.org. Available at: <https://en.wikisource.org/wiki/In_the_dozy_hours,_and_other_papers/The_Passing_of_the_Essay> [Accessed: 16 April 2020].

Roth, Philip. 1976. 'In Search of Kafka And Other Answers'. *The New York Times*. February 15th. Available at: < https://www.nytimes.com/1976/02/15/archives/in-search-of-kafka-and-other-answers.html> [Accessed: 16 April 2020].

Slater, Lauren. 2000. *Lying: A Metaphorical Memoir*. New York: Random House.

Svevo, Italo. 1923. *Zeno's conscience: a novel*. Translated by Weaver, William. New York: Vintage International, 2003.

White, E.B. 1977. *Essays of E.B. White*. New York: Harper and Row.

The Fiction of the Essay

177   'to listen is to love': Chakrabarty (2019).

178   'we are quite simply dealing... a letter *en souffrance* (awaiting delivery or

unclaimed)': Lacan (1956), pp.20-21.

184   'Sometimes I wonder if "imposter syndrome" … a structural reality of how people get poorly treated.': nopper (2019)

184   'it is better to be a sinner…': Fairburn (1952), p.67.

Ahmed, Sara. 2018. *Queer Use*. Feminist Killjoys. Available from: <https://feministkilljoys.com/2018/11/08/queer-use/> [Accessed: 20 April 2020].

Chakrabarty, Namita Elizabeth. 2019. 'Writing about Race and Love in the English Countryside' [poem] performed at *Below Stairs Poetry*, Blacks Club, Soho, London (2 July 2019).

Delluc, Louis dir. (1920). *Le Silence* [Film]. France: Le Film d'Art.

(1923) *Le Silence*. In *Ecrits cinématographiques III: Drames de cinéma, scenarios et projets de films*. Paris: Cinémathèque Française Cahiers du cinéma, 1990.

Fairburn, W. R. D. 1952. *Psychoanalytic Studies of the Personality*. London and New York: Routledge, 1994.

Freud, Sigmund. *The Uncanny*. 1919. trans. David McLintock. London: Penguin, 2003.

Lacan, Jacques. 1956. 'Seminar on The Purloined Letter'. *In Écrits*, trans. by Bruce Fink. New York: Norton, 2006.

Lanthimos, Yorgos dir. (2015). *The Lobster* [Film]. Ireland: Element Pictures.

nopper, tamara K. 2019. 25 July. [Tweet]. Available from: <https://twitter.com/tamaranopper/status/1154412486063529986?s=20> [Accessed 19 April 2020].

Orwell, George. 1946. *Why I Write*. London: Penguin, 2004.

Poe, Edgar Allan. 1844. 'The Purloined Letter'. *In the Fall of the House of Usher and Other Writings*, London: Penguin Classics, 1986.

A Leaf Out of Someone's Book

190   'Have you ever watched a sport… there must be more. Mustn't there?': John Calcutt quoted in Lynch (2001) 5.

Bjelajac, David. 2000. *American Art: A Cultural History*. London: Laurence King Publishing.

Calcutt, John. 2004. *Ouroboros: The Music of the Spheres* [exhibition]. Centre for Contemporary Arts Glasgow: Glasgow.

Lynch, Peter. 2001. *Paintings 2000-2001*. Glasgow School of Art: Glasgow.

The Art of the Intransitive Essay

193	'One might speak as if one were thinking': Glaspell (1929), p. 21.
193	'The novel of inner experience…': Mizener (1964), pp.147–148.
193	'I had never thought about an audience before…': Stein (1953), p.205.
194	'The novel which tells about what happens…': Stein quoted in Kimmelman (2012). p.10.
194	'The world looks always opposite…' Montaigne (1910) .
195	'To become his reader, I have had to become a kind of ventriloquist…': Chown (2017b)
196	'how do they change and what is his flag ship hobby horse…': ibid.
196	'I realized I was reading outwardly… books that are inconspicuously new force us to see all the more newly'. Chown (2018).
198	'offer merely our little hoard of observations…': Wade (2019), p.7.
198	'mind skimmed leagues … and bramble cast shade upon her mind'. Woolf (1922), p.53.
198	'she bethought herself of other things…' Glaspell (1935), p.187.
200	'internalization or psychologicalization of reality': Miles (1974), p. 989.
200	'that from which innerness is totally absent…': Savater (1982). p.11.
200	'hypnotized into futility by self-observation.' Lessing (1965), p.205.
200	'sunk in subjectivity': Lessing (1962), p.614.
200	'I gotta to use words when I talk to you.': Eliot (1932), p.126.
200	'It was a riverside meadow…': Milosz (2006), p.233.
202	'the *strangeness* and excitement kept waking me up': Greenlaw (2017), p.41.
202	'for a *strange* lazy sort of excitement…': ibid., p. 175.
202	'Do you want to stop going back?': ibid.
202	'once again that thin thread of insight…': ibid., p.167.
202	'That thin thread of insight and imagination. Not just seen in the mind but seen into.': ibid. p.164.
202	'Going on from now will be going back': ibid., p.160.
202	'the fluidity of *strangeness*': ibid., p.168.
202	'Going home you don't look about you, only ahead': ibid., p.188.
202	'Remembering what it is to be inside': ibid. p.190.
202	'Now that it's over, you were very happy.': ibid.
202-3	'not knowing what to ask for'… 'disproportionate'… 'that…all looked like a scene at a theater'… 'a marvelous, beautiful and solemn place, and where I had been in fact very happy.': ibid., pp.191-193.

203   'the hinge of simile; a hesitant connection, as if….': ibid., p.22.
203   'The simpler the form, the greater the need for simile.': ibid., p.168.

Chown, Linda E. 1994. 'Virginia Woolf and Doris Lessing: "That Intransitive Turn of Mind."' In *Woolf and Lessing: Breaking the Mold*. Edited by Ruth Saxton and Jean Tobin. New York: St. Martin's Press. pp.123-146.

Chown, Linda E. 2016. 'Making A Home in Words'. *Katherine Mansfield Society Newsletter*. 24. August. pp.13-15.

Chown, Linda E. 2017a. 'Balancing the Books with a Hit of Strangeness.' *Blog Critics*. 26 Feb. Available from: <https://blogcritics.org/book-review-questions-of-travel-william-morris-in-iceland-by-lavinia-greenlaw/> [Accessed: 23 April 2020].

Chown, Linda E. 2017b. 'Cries of a Mind Leaping out of its Lodgings: Review of Drawn from Life: Selected Essays of Michel de Montaigne.' *Numéro Cinq*. 5 March. Available from: <http://numerocinqmagazine.com/2017/03/05/> [Accessed: 22 April 2020].

Chown, Linda E. 2018. 'Steering a Course for Citizenship in an Age of Terrorism.' *Blog Critics*. 22 March. Available from: <https://blogcritics.org/we-are-not-afraid-by-gila-lustiger/> [accessed 22/4/20].

Coetzee, J. M. 1994. *The Master of Petersburg*. New York: Viking.

Eliot, T.S. 1932. *Sweeney Agonistes: Fragments of an Aristophanic Melodrama in The poems of T.S. Eliot Volume 1*, Edited by Christopher Ricks and Jim McClure. London: Faber and Faber, 2015.

Glaspell, Susan. 1929. *Fugitive's Return*. New York: Frederic A Stokes Co.

Glaspell, Susan. 1935. *The Morning is Near Us*. New York: Frederick A. Stokes Co.

Greenlaw, Lavinia. 2017. *Questions of Travel: William Morris in Iceland With a Hit of Strangeness*. London: Notting Hill Editions.

Kimmelman, Michael. 2012. 'Missionaries.' *The New York Review of Books*. 26 April.

Lessing, Doris. 1952. *Martha Quest. Children of Violence 1*. New York: New American Library, 1970.

Lessing, Doris.1962. *The Golden Notebook*. New York: Ballantine, 1972.

Lessing, Doris. 1965. *Landlocked. Children of Violence 4*. New York: New American Library, 1970.

Lessing, Doris. 1979. *Re: Colonised Planet 5, Shikasta*. New York: Alfred A. Knopf.

Lustiger, Gila. 2017. *We are Not Afraid*. Devon: Notting Hill Editions.

Miles, David H. 1974. 'The Picaro's Journey to the Confessional: The Changing Image of the Hero in the German Bildungsroman.' *PMLA* 89. pp. 980-992.

Milosz, Czeslaw. 2006. *Selected and Last Poems 1931-2004*. Translated by Anthony Milos. New York: Ecco, 2011.

Mizener, Arthur. 1964. *The Sense of Life in the Modern Novel*. New York: Houghton Mifflin.

Montaigne, Michel de. 1910. 'Of Presumption'. *Essays of Montaigne, Vol. 6*, Translated by Charles Cotton, revised by William Carew Hazlett. New York: Edwin C. Hill. Available from: <https://oll.libertyfund.org/titles/1747>. [Accessed: 26 November 2019].

Montaigne, Michel de. 2016. *Drawn from Life: Selected Essays of Michel de Montaigne*. Translated by M. A. Screech. Devon: Notting Hill Editions.

Pound, Ezra. 1934. *Make It New*. Connecticut: Yale University Press.

Savater, Fernando. 1982. *Childhood Regained: The Art of the Story Teller*. Translated by Frances M. López Morrillas. New York: Columbia UP.

Stein, Gertrude. 1953. *Lectures*. Boston: Beacon Press by arrangement with Random House, Inc., 1957.

Wade, Francesca. 2019. 'Genius and Ink: An Introduction to Virginia Woolf's Writing for the TLS,' *Times Literary Supplement*. 15 November.

Woolf, Virginia. 1922. *Jacob's Room*. London: Penguin, 1965.

Contributors

CHRIS ARTHUR has published several essay collections, most recently *Hummingbirds Between the Pages*. For details of his work see www.chrisarthur.org.

STEPHANIE BISHOP is currently a Senior Lecturer in Creative Writing at the University of New South Wales, Australia. She is the author of *Man Out of Time*, *The Other Side of the World* and *The Singing*. www.stephaniebishop.com.au

EMMA BOLLAND is an artist-writer investigating the problematics and ambiguities of an expanded understanding of translation—between languages and language codes, and between modes of writing, reading and speaking. www.emmabolland.com

STEPHEN CARRUTHERS is a teacher and writer based in the Scottish Highlands. He is a keen advocate for the benefits of creative writing both in education and mental health.

ELIZABETH CHAKRABARTY uses performance and critical and creative writing to explore themes of race and sexuality. *Lessons in Love and Other Crimes*, a novel, will be published in 2021. www.theindigopress.com/elizabeth-chakrabarty

LINDA E. CHOWN is Professor Emerita, Grand Valley State University. Essayist, poet, traveller and critic, she is writing a new kind of prose, specifically to approach women's experimental writing in experimental ways.

MEAGHAN DELAHUNT is an award-winning novelist and short story writer. Her latest novel is *The Night-Side of the Country*. www.meaghandelahunt.com

GRAHAM DOMKE is a freelance curator and critic based in Glasgow. He has written essays and more speculative texts for books and journals on a host of artists and subjects.

TOMIWA FOLORUNSO is a writer, presenter and creative specialising in communications and digital production ranging from grassroots film marketing to third sector project management and radio. www.tomiwafolorunso.com

LORENS HOLMS teaches architecture at University of Dundee where he runs a design research unit called rooms+cities. His work focuses on reconciling Lacanian thought on subjectivity with contemporary architectural/urban practice.

HAMZAH HUSSAIN is a writer from Dundee, mainly writing short stories and creative non-fiction. His writing reflects on the quotidian and on inner experiences. He is presently a publishing trainee at Hachette in London. www.hmhussainwriting.com

DAI JOHN has served with the military for over 30 years, including in conflict zones worldwide. He has researched and produced a number of UK and NATO defence policy publications.

GRAHAM JOHNSTON has been an artist and creative nomad since graduating from Gray's School of Art in the 1980s and has worked in theatre, television, photography, design and education.

GABRIEL JOSIPOVICI is a novelist, playwright and critic. He was born in France in 1940 and educated in Egypt and England, and taught for many years at the University of Sussex. www.gabrieljosipovici.org

JANE MACRAE taught Science for many years at a London school renowned for its focus on finding quiet and creative spaces within the rigours of the curriculum.. Now she is a Director at Bloom. www.bloomeducation.co.uk

DUNCAN MCLEAN lives in Orkney and writes fiction and drama. He edits booklets of new Orcadian writing for the Abersee Press.

WHITNEY MCVEIGH is an American artist best known for her installations, sculpture and paintings. Recent exhibitions include Plato in LA: Contemporary Artists' Visions, The Getty Villa, Los Angeles and Elegy to Nature, Eykyn Maclean, New York. www.whitneymcveigh.com

PHILLIP LOPATE is a distinguished essayist based at Columbia University's School of the Arts, his publications include, *Portrait of My Body* (1996), *Getting Personal* (2004), *Portrait Inside My Head* (2013), *A Mother's Tale* (2017). www.philliplopate.com

SUSAN NICKALLS is a writer, journalist, broadcaster and award-winning film maker based in Edinburgh.

PAUL NOBLE received widespread international recognition for his monumental drawing project *Nobson Newtown*. At once architect, town planner, archaeologist, cartographer, Noble invented a melancholy urban vision somewhere between Ledoux's revolutionary utopias, SimCity, and the wastelands pictured in the daily media.

Noble is represented by Gagosian. www.gagosian.com/artists/paul-noble

FIONA STIRLING is a writer, researcher, and practicing therapist. She is passionate about exploring mental health through narratives and collaborative work with those who have lived experience.

KENNY TAYLOR is a writer, editor of *Northwords Now*, naturalist and musician who works principally in non-fiction based on wildlife, science, culture and history through books, magazines, broadcast media and performances. www.kennytaylor.info

Acknowledgments

The editors would like to thank the Royal Society of Edinburgh and the Saltire Society for the award of funds that enabled the various symposia and roundtable creative discussions which have borne fruit here. In addition the editors would like to acknowledge Hospitalfield House in Arbroath, home to us for two wonderful days of conversation and essaying in June 2018 when so many of the ideas behind this book were first seeded.